W9-BWG-697

SEW

STEP BY STEP

SEW

STEP BY STEP

HOW TO USE YOUR SEWING MACHINE TO MAKE, MEND, AND CUSTOMIZE

ALISON SMITH

CONTENTS

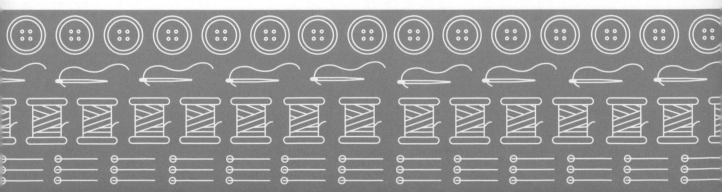

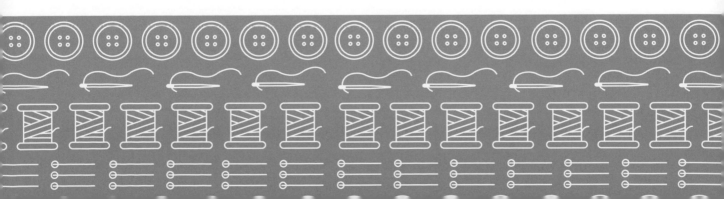

INTRODUCTION

If you are new to sewing and eager to master the key techniques, *Sew Step by Step* is the book for you. These clearly laid out pages cover all the basics (plus a bit more) to help you make and restyle simple soft furnishings, clothes, and accessories.

Starting with equipment and notions and moving on through fabrics to the many techniques, *Sew Step by Step* demonstrates all the basic stitches, shows you how to master seams, hems, and edges; teaches you easy ways to add shape to clothing, with gathers, darts, and waistlines; and how to finish your work with pockets and fastenings.

I hope this book will encourage you to enjoy this satisfying hobby and inspire you to create beautiful things—for yourself or for your family and friends.

Happy sewing!

Alison Smith

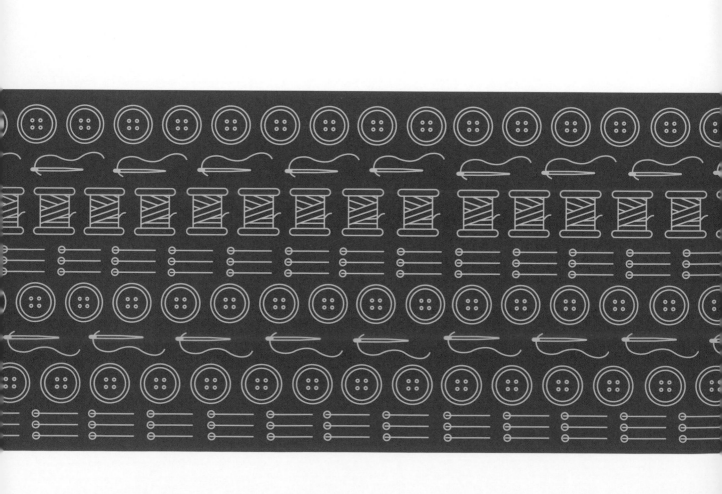

SEWING EQUIPMENT

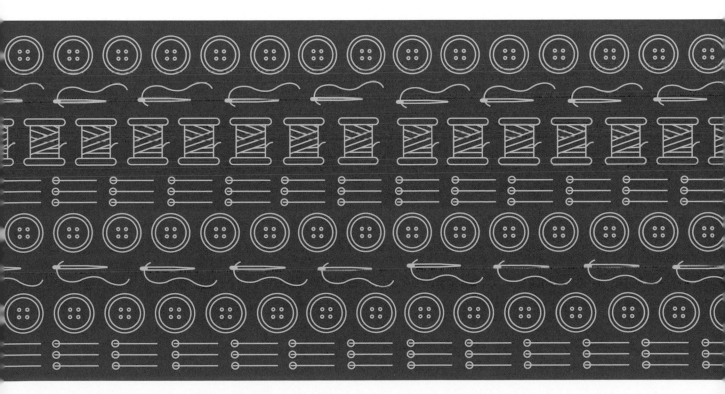

BASIC SEWING KIT

A well-equipped sewing kit will include all of the items shown below and many more, depending on the type of sewing that you do regularly. It is important that a suitable container is used to keep your tools together, so that they will be readily at hand, and to keep them organized.

Cutting shears
Required for cutting fabric. When buying, select a pair that feels comfortable in your hand and that is not too heavy. **See p.13.**

Seam ripper
To remove any stitches that have been sewn in the wrong place. Various sizes of seam rippers are available. Keep the cover on when not in use to protect the sharp point. **See p.12**.

Embroidery scissors
Small pair of scissors with very sharp points to clip threads close to the fabric. **See p.12.**

Pins
Needed by every sewer to hold the fabric together prior to sewing it permanently. There are different types of pins for different types of work. **See p.23.**

Safety pins
In a variety of sizes and useful for emergency repairs, as well as threading elastics. **See p.23**.

Thimble
This is useful to protect the end of your finger when hand sewing. Thimbles are available in various shapes and sizes. **See p.16.**

Tape measure
Essential not only to take body measurements, but also to help measure fabric, seams, and so on. Choose one that gives both inches and centimeters. A tape made of plastic is best, as it will not stretch. **See p.14.**

Zipper
It is always a good idea to keep a couple of zippers in your sewing kit. Black, cream, and navy are the most useful colors. **See pp.133–139.**

Threads

A selection of threads for hand sewing and machine/serger sewing in a variety of colors. Some threads are made of polyester, while others are cotton or rayon. **See pp.20–21.**

Needles

A good selection of different types of needles for sewing by hand. This will enable you to tackle any hand sewing project. **See p.22.**

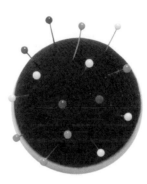

Pincushion

To keep your needles and pins safe and clean. Choose one that has a fabric cover and is firm. **See p.23.**

Notions

All the odds and ends a sewer needs, including everything from buttons and snaps to trims and elastic. A selection of buttons and snaps in your basic kit is useful for a quick repair. **See pp.18–19.**

Buttonhole cutter

An exceedingly sharp knife that gives a clean cut through machine buttonholes. Place a cutting mat underneath when using this tool, or you might damage the blade. **See p.12.**

Sewing gauge

A handy tool for small measurements. The slide can be set to measure hem depths, buttonhole diameters, and much more. **See p.14.**

OTHER USEFUL SEWING KIT ITEMS

CUTTING TOOLS 12–13
Bent-handled shears
Paper scissors
Pinking shears
Snips
Trimming scissors

MEASURING TOOLS 14
Other tape measures

MARKING AIDS 15
Chalk pencil
Chalk cartridge pencil
Tailor's chalk
Tracing wheel and carbon paper
Water/air-soluble pen

USEFUL EXTRAS 16
14-in-1 measure
Beeswax
Collar point turner
Emergency sewing kit
Glue pen
Liquid sealant
Loop turner
Tweezers

PRESSING AIDS 17
Iron
Ironing board
Pressing cloth
Pressing mitten
Tailor's ham

NEEDLE THREADERS 22

CUTTING TOOLS

There are many types of cutting tools, but one rule applies to all: buy good-quality products that can be resharpened. Cutting shears should fit the span of your hand so that you can comfortably open the whole of the blade with one action, which is very important for clean and accurate cutting lines. A seam ripper is essential for removing misplaced stitches or for unpicking seams for mending.

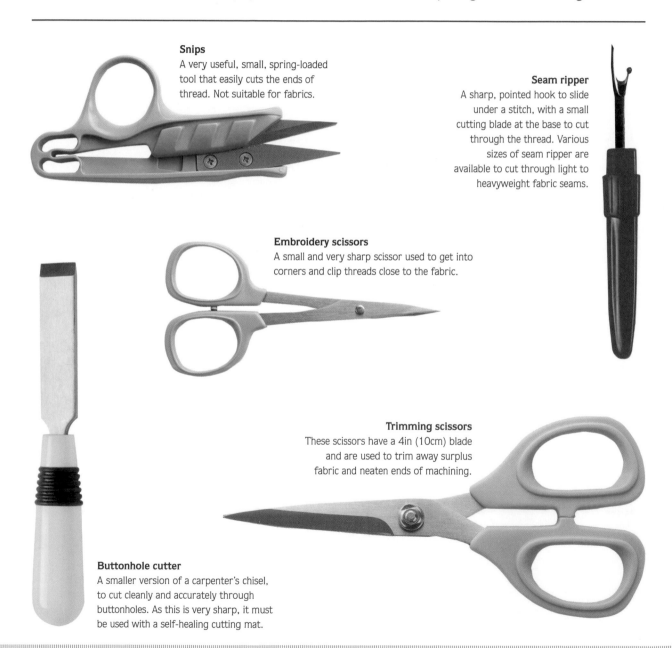

Snips
A very useful, small, spring-loaded tool that easily cuts the ends of thread. Not suitable for fabrics.

Seam ripper
A sharp, pointed hook to slide under a stitch, with a small cutting blade at the base to cut through the thread. Various sizes of seam ripper are available to cut through light to heavyweight fabric seams.

Embroidery scissors
A small and very sharp scissor used to get into corners and clip threads close to the fabric.

Trimming scissors
These scissors have a 4in (10cm) blade and are used to trim away surplus fabric and neaten ends of machining.

Buttonhole cutter
A smaller version of a carpenter's chisel, to cut cleanly and accurately through buttonholes. As this is very sharp, it must be used with a self-healing cutting mat.

Bent-handled shears
This type of shear has a blade that can sit flat against the table when cutting out due to the angle between the blade and handle. Popular for cutting long, straight edges.

Pinking shears
Similar in size to cutting shears, but with a blade that cuts with a zigzag pattern. Used for neatening seams and decorative edges.

Cutting shears
The most popular type of shear, used for cutting large pieces of fabric. The length of the blade can vary from 8–12in (20–30cm).

Paper scissors
Use these to cut around pattern pieces—cutting paper will dull blades of fabric scissors and shears.

MEASURING TOOLS AND MARKING AIDS

A huge range of tools enables a sewer to measure accurately. Choosing the correct tool for the task at hand is important so that your measurements are precise. The next step is to mark your work using the appropriate marking technique or tool.

⋊ MEASURING TOOLS

There are many tools available to help you measure everything from the width of a seam or hem, to body dimensions, to the area of a window. One of the most basic yet invaluable measuring tools is the tape measure. Be sure to keep yours in good condition—once it stretches or gets snipped on the edges, it will no longer be accurate and should be replaced.

Metal tape for windows
A metal tape that can be secured when extended is used to measure windows and soft furnishings.

Tape measure
Available in various colors and widths. Try to choose one that is the same width as standard seam allowance (⅝in/1.5cm), because it will prove very useful.

Retractable tape
Very useful to take with you when shopping, as you never know when you may need to measure something!

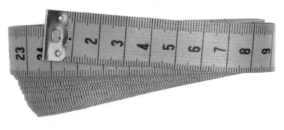

Extra-long tape
This is usually twice the length of a normal tape measure, at 10ft (300cm) long. Use it when making home goods. It's also useful to help measure the length of bridal trains.

Sewing gauge
A small, handy tool about 6in (15cm) long, marked in inches and centimeters, with a sliding tab. Use as an accurate measure for small measurements such as hems.

◤ MARKING AIDS

Marking certain parts of your work is essential to make sure that things like pockets and darts are placed correctly and seamlines are straight as drawn on the pattern. With some marking tools, such as pens and a tracing wheel and carbon paper, it is always a good idea to test on a scrap of fabric first to make sure that the mark made will not be permanent.

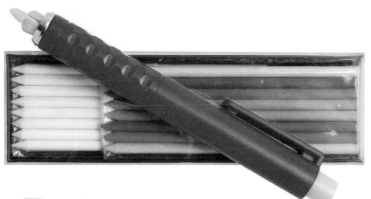

Tailor's chalk
Also known as French chalk, this solid piece of chalk in either a square or triangular shape is available in a large variety of colors. The chalk easily brushes off fabric.

Chalk cartridge pencil
Chalk leads of different colors can be inserted into this pencil, making it a very versatile marking tool. The leads can be sharpened.

Chalk pencil
Available in blue, pink, and white. As it can be sharpened like a normal pencil, it will draw accurate lines on fabric.

Tracing wheel and carbon paper
These two items are used together to transfer markings from a paper pattern or a design onto fabric. Not suitable for all types of fabric though, as marks may not be able to be removed easily.

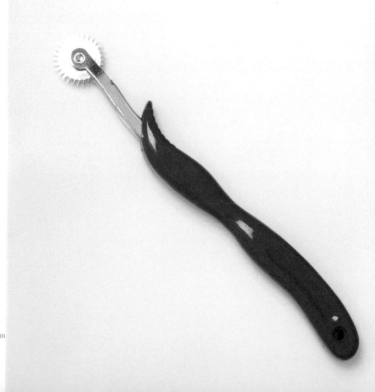

Water/air-soluble pen
This resembles a felt marker. Marks made can be removed from the fabric with either a spray of water or by leaving to air-dry. Be careful—if you press over the marks, they may become permanent.

USEFUL EXTRAS

There are many more accessories that can be purchased to help with your sewing, and knowing which products to choose and for which job can be daunting. The tools shown here can be useful aids, although it depends on the type of sewing that you do—dressmaking, craft work, making soft furnishings, or running repairs—as to whether you would need all of them in your sewing kit.

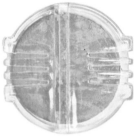

Beeswax
When hand sewing, this will prevent the thread from tangling and will strengthen it. First draw the thread through the wax, then press the wax into the thread by running your fingers along it.

Collar point turner
This is excellent for pushing out those hard-to-reach corners in collars and cuffs.

14-in-1 measure
A strange-looking tool that has 14 different measurements on it. Use to turn hems or edges accurately. Available in both inches and centimeters.

Bias tape maker
Available in ½, ¾, and 1 in (12, 18, and 25mm) widths, this tool evenly folds the edges of a fabric strip, which can then be pressed to make binding.

Thimble
An essential item for many sewers to protect the middle finger from the end of the needle. Choose a thimble that fits your finger comfortably, as there are many varieties to choose from.

Tweezers
These can be used for removing stubborn basting stitches that have become caught in the machine stitching. An essential aid to threading the serger.

Liquid sealant
Used to seal the cut edge of ribbons and trims to prevent fraying. Also useful to seal the ends of serger stitching.

Glue pen
Similar to a glue stick for paper, this will hold fabric or trims temporarily in place until they can be secured with stitches. It will not damage the fabric or make the sewing needle sticky.

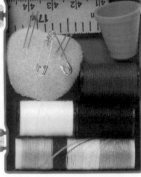

Emergency sewing kit
All the absolute essentials to fix loose buttons or dropped hems while away from your sewing machine. Take it with you when traveling.

Loop turner
A thin metal rod with a latch at the end. Use to turn narrow fabric tubes or to thread ribbons through a slotted lace.

PRESSING AIDS

Successful sewing relies on successful pressing. Without the correct pressing equipment, sewing can look too "homemade," whereas if correctly pressed, any sewn item will have a neat, professional finish.

Pressing mitten
Slips onto your hand to enable more control over where you are pressing.

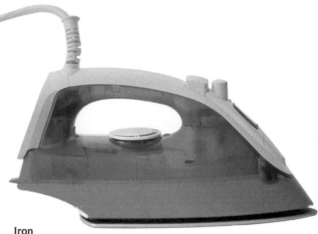

Iron
A good-quality steam iron is a wonderful asset. Choose a reasonably heavy iron that has steam and a shot of steam facility.

Pressing cloth
Choose a cloth made from silk organza or muslin, as you can see through it. The cloth will stop the iron from marking fabric and prevent burning delicate fabrics.

Ironing board
Essential to iron on. Make sure the board is height-adjustable.

Tailor's ham
A ham-shaped pressing cushion that is used to press darts and the shape into curves of collars and shoulders, and in making tailored garments.

NOTIONS

The term notions covers all the bits and pieces that sewers tend to need—for example, fasteners such as buttons, snaps, hooks and eyes, and Velcro™. But notions also includes elastic, ribbons, trims of all types, and boning.

▶ BUTTONS

Buttons can be made from almost anything—shell, bone, coconut, nylon, plastic, brass, silver, and so on. They can be any shape, from geometric, to abstract, to animal shapes. A button may have a shank or have holes on the surface to enable it to be attached to fabric.

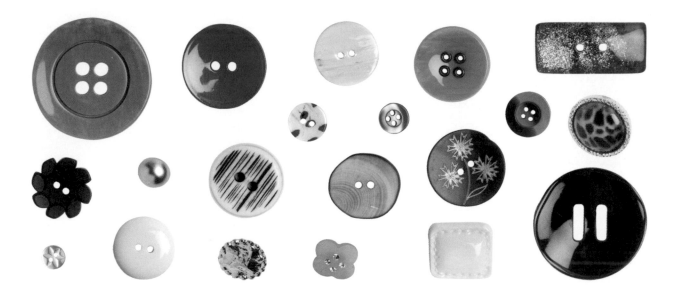

▶ OTHER FASTENERS

Hooks and eyes (below left), snaps (below center), and Velcro™ (below right) all come in a wide variety of forms, differing in size, shape, and color. Some hooks and eyes are designed to be seen, while snaps and Velcro™ are intended to be hidden fasteners.

TRIMS, DECORATIONS, FRINGES, AND BRAIDS

Decorative finishing touches—fringes, strips of sequins, braids, feathers, pearls, bows, flowers, and beads—can dress up a garment, embellish a bag, or personalize soft furnishings. Some are designed to be inserted into seams, while others are surface-mounted.

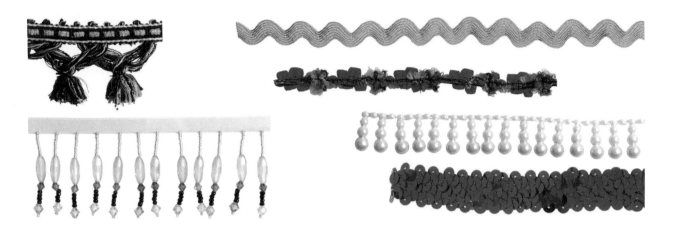

RIBBONS

From the narrowest strips to wide widths, ribbons are made from a variety of yarns, such as nylon, polyester, and cotton. They can be printed or plain and may feature metallic threads or wired edges.

ELASTIC

Elastic is available in many forms, from very narrow, round cord to wide strips (below left). It may have buttonhole slots in it (below right) or even have a decorative edge.

BONING

You can buy various types of boning in varying widths. Polyester boning (bottom left), used in boned bodices, can be sewn through, while nylon boning (bottom right), also used in boned bodices, has to be inserted into a casing. Specialty metal boning (below left and right), which may be either straight or spiral, is for corsets and bridal wear.

THREADS

There are so many threads available that knowing which ones to choose can be confusing. There are specialty threads designed for special tasks, such as machine embroidery or quilting. Threads also vary in fiber content, from pure cotton, to rayon, to polyester. Some threads are very fine, while others are thick and coarse. Failure to choose the correct thread can spoil your project and lead to problems with the stitch quality of the sewing machine.

Cotton thread
A 100 percent cotton thread. Smooth and firm, this is designed to be used with cotton fabrics and is much favored by quilters.

Metallic thread
A rayon and metal thread for decorative machining and machine embroidery. This thread usually requires a specialty sewing-machine needle.

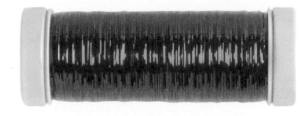

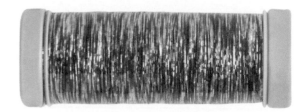

Elastic thread
A thin, round elastic thread normally used on the bobbin of the sewing machine for stretch effects, such as shirring.

Embroidery thread
Often made from a rayon yarn for shine. This is a finer thread designed for machine embroidery. Available on much larger reels for economy.

Polyester all-purpose thread
A cotton-coated polyester thread that has a very slight "give," making it suitable to sew all types of fabrics and garments, as well as home goods. The most popular type of thread.

Button thread
A thicker polyester thread used for decorative top-stitching and buttonholes. Also for hand sewing buttons on thicker fabrics and some soft furnishings.

NEEDLES AND PINS

Using the correct pin or needle for your work is very important, as the wrong choice can damage fabric or leave small holes. Needles are made from steel and pins from steel or occasionally brass.

Take care of them by keeping pins in a pincushion and needles in a needle case—if kept together in a small container, they could become scratched and blunt.

✕ NEEDLES AND THREADERS

Needles are available for all types of fabrics and projects. A good selection of needles should be at hand at all times, whether it be for emergency mending of tears, sewing on buttons, or adding trims to special-occasion wear. With a special needle threader, inserting the thread through the eye of the needle is simplicity itself.

Sharps
A general-purpose hand-sewing needle with a small, round eye. Available in sizes 1 to 12. For most hand sewing, use a size 6 to 9.

Beading
Long and extremely fine, to sew beads and sequins to fabric. As it is prone to bending, keep it wrapped in tissue when not in use.

Bodkin
A strange-looking needle with a blunt end and a large, fat eye. Use to thread elastic or cord. There are larger eyes for thicker yarns.

Darning
A long, thick needle that is designed to be used with wool or thick yarns and to sew through multiple layers.

Self-threading needle
A needle that has a double eye. The thread is placed in the upper eye through the gap, then pulled into the eye below for sewing.

Crewel
Also known as an embroidery needle, a long needle with a long, oval eye that is designed to take multiple strands of embroidery thread.

Quilting or betweens
Similar to a milliner's needle but very short, with a small, round eye. Perfect for fine hand stitches and favored by quilters.

Tapestry
A medium-length, thick needle with a blunt end and a long eye. For use with wool yarn in tapestry. Also for darning in serger threads.

Wire needle threader
A handy gadget, especially useful for needles with small eyes. Also helpful in threading sewing-machine needles.

Chenille
This looks like a tapestry needle, but it has a sharp point. Use with thick or wool yarns for darning or heavy embroidery.

Milliner's or straw
A very long, thin needle with a small, round eye. Good for hand sewing and basting, as it doesn't damage fabric. A size 8 or 9 is most popular.

Automatic needle threader
This threader is operated with a small lever. The needle, eye down, is inserted and the thread is wrapped around.

✕ PINS

There is a wide variety of pins available in differing lengths and thicknesses and ranging from plain household pins to those with colored balls or flower shapes on their ends.

Straight
General-purpose pins of a medium length and thickness. Can be used for all types of sewing.

Pearl-headed
Longer than straight pins, with a colored pearl head. They are easy to pick up and use.

Extra fine
Extra long and extra fine, this pin is favored by many professional dressmakers because it is easy to use and doesn't damage finer fabrics.

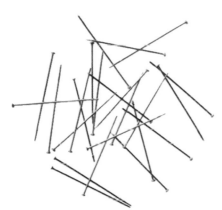

Dressmaker's
Similar to a straight pin in shape and thickness, but slightly longer. These are the pins for beginners to choose.

Glass-headed
Similar to pearl-headed pins but shorter. They have the advantage that they can be pressed over without melting.

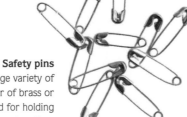

Safety pins
Available in a huge variety of sizes and made either of brass or stainless steel. Used for holding two or more layers together.

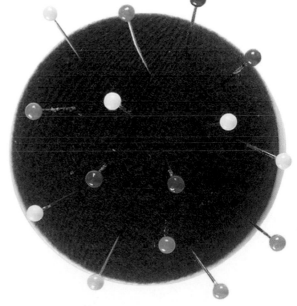

Pincushion
Choose a fabric cover: a foam cushion may blunt pins. Magnetic ones should not be put on a computerized sewing machine.

SEWING MACHINE

A sewing machine will quickly speed up any job, whether it be a quick repair or a huge home-sewing project. Most sewing machines today are aided by computer technology, which enhances stitch quality and ease of use. Always spend time trying out a sewing machine before you buy to really get a feel for it.

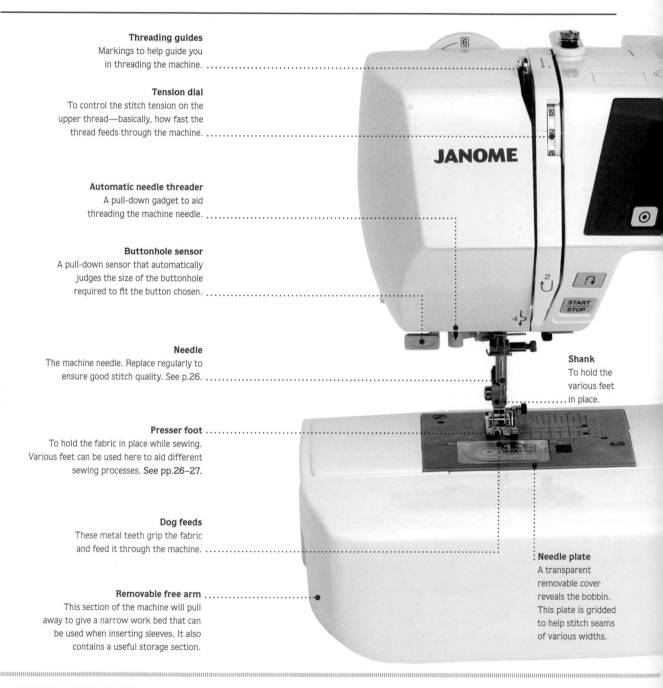

Threading guides
Markings to help guide you in threading the machine.

Tension dial
To control the stitch tension on the upper thread—basically, how fast the thread feeds through the machine.

Automatic needle threader
A pull-down gadget to aid threading the machine needle.

Buttonhole sensor
A pull-down sensor that automatically judges the size of the buttonhole required to fit the button chosen.

Needle
The machine needle. Replace regularly to ensure good stitch quality. See p.26.

Presser foot
To hold the fabric in place while sewing. Various feet can be used here to aid different sewing processes. See pp.26–27.

Dog feeds
These metal teeth grip the fabric and feed it through the machine.

Removable free arm
This section of the machine will pull away to give a narrow work bed that can be used when inserting sleeves. It also contains a useful storage section.

Shank
To hold the various feet in place.

Needle plate
A transparent removable cover reveals the bobbin. This plate is gridded to help stitch seams of various widths.

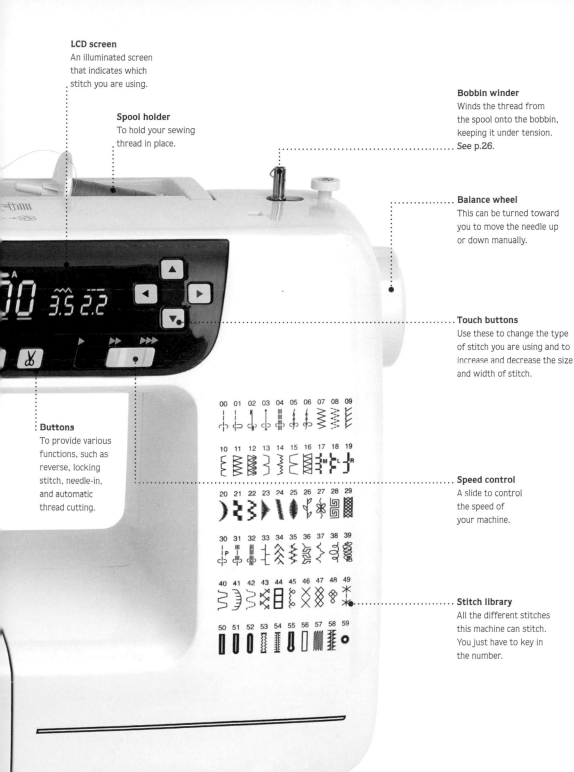

LCD screen
An illuminated screen that indicates which stitch you are using.

Spool holder
To hold your sewing thread in place.

Bobbin winder
Winds the thread from the spool onto the bobbin, keeping it under tension. See p.26.

Balance wheel
This can be turned toward you to move the needle up or down manually.

Touch buttons
Use these to change the type of stitch you are using and to increase and decrease the size and width of stitch.

Buttons
To provide various functions, such as reverse, locking stitch, needle-in, and automatic thread cutting.

Speed control
A slide to control the speed of your machine.

Stitch library
All the different stitches this machine can stitch. You just have to key in the number.

⋊ SEWING-MACHINE ACCESSORIES

Many accessories can be purchased for your sewing machine to make certain sewing processes so much easier. There are different machine needles not only for different fabrics, but also for different types of threads. There is also a huge number of sewing-machine feet, and new feet are constantly coming onto the market. Those shown here are some of the most popular.

PLASTIC BOBBIN

The bobbin is for the lower thread. Some machines take plastic bobbins, others metal. Always check which kind of bobbin your machine uses, as the incorrect choice can cause stitch problems.

METAL BOBBIN

Also known as a universal bobbin, this is used on many types of sewing machines. Be sure to check that your machine needs a metal bobbin before you buy.

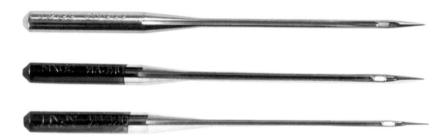

MACHINE NEEDLES

There are different types of sewing machine needles to cope with different fabrics. Machine needles are sized from 60 to 100, a 60 being a very fine needle. There are special needles for machine embroidery and for metallic threads.

EMBROIDERY FOOT

A clear plastic foot with a groove underneath that allows linear machine embroidery stitches to pass under.

BUTTONHOLE FOOT

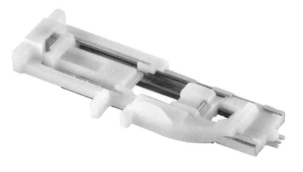

This extends and the button is placed in the back of the foot. The machine will sew a buttonhole to fit due to the buttonhole sensor.

ROLLED HEM FOOT

This foot rolls the fabric while sewing with a straight stitch or a zigzag stitch.

OVEREDGE FOOT

A foot that runs along the raw edge of the fabric and holds it stable while an overedge stitch is worked.

BLIND HEM FOOT

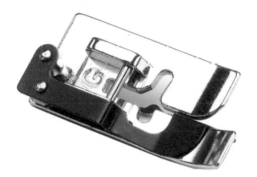

Use this foot in conjunction with the blind hem stitch to create a neat hemming stitch.

WALKING FOOT

This odd-looking foot "walks" across the fabric so that the upper layer of fabric does not push forward. Great for matching checks and stripes and also for difficult fabrics, like quilts.

ZIPPER FOOT

This foot fits to either the right- or left-hand side of the needle to enable you to sew close to a zipper.

INVISIBLE ZIPPER FOOT

A foot that is used to insert a concealed zipper—the foot holds open the coils of the zipper, enabling you to sew behind them.

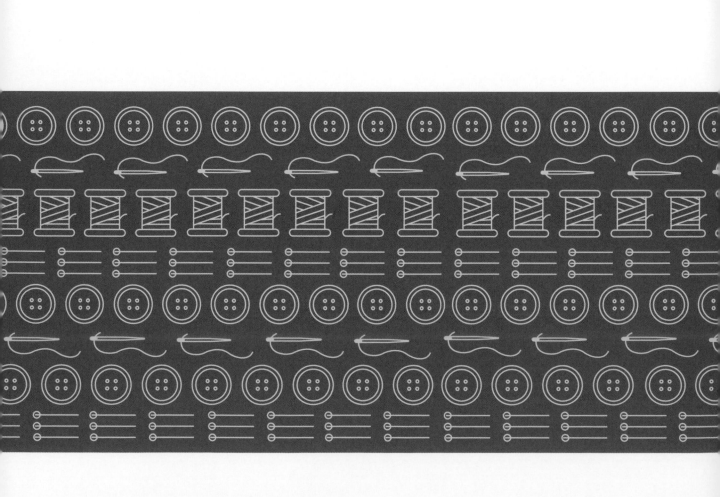

FABRICS

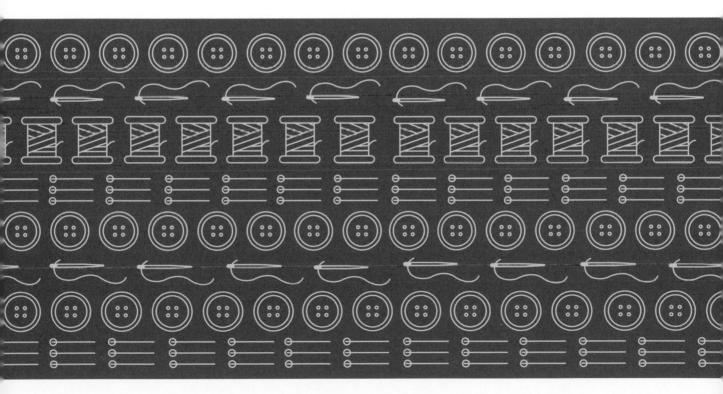

◤ WOOL FABRICS

A natural fiber, wool comes primarily from sheep—Australian merino sheep's wool is considered to be the best. However, we also get wool fibers from goats (mohair and cashmere), rabbits (angora), camels (camel hair), and llamas (alpaca). A wool fiber is either short and fluffy, when it is known as a woollen yarn, or it is long, strong, and smooth, when it is called worsted. The term virgin (or new) wool denotes wool fibers that are being used for the first time. Wool may be reprocessed or reused and is then often mixed with other fibers.

PROPERTIES OF WOOL

- Comfortable to wear in all climates, as it is available in many weights and weaves
- Warm in the winter and cool in the summer, because it will breathe with your body
- Absorbs moisture better than other natural fibers—will absorb up to 30 percent of its weight before it feels wet
- Flame-resistant

- Relatively crease-resistant
- Ideal to tailor, as it can be easily shaped with steam
- Often blended with other fibers to reduce the cost of fabric
- Felts if exposed to excessive heat, moisture, and pressure
- Will be bleached by sunlight with prolonged exposure
- Can be damaged by moths

CASHMERE

Wool from the Kashmir goat and the most luxurious of all the wools. A soft yet hard-wearing fabric available in different weights.

Cutting out: as cashmere often has a slight pile, use a nap layout

Seams: plain, neatened with serger stitch or pinking shears (a zigzag stitch would curl the edge of the seam)

Thread: a silk thread is ideal, or a polyester all-purpose thread

Needle: machine size 12/14, depending on the thickness of the fabric; sharps for hand sewing

Pressing: steam iron on a steam setting with a pressing cloth and seam roll

Use for: jackets, coats, men's wear; knitted cashmere yarn for sweaters, cardigans

CHALLIS

A fine wool fabric made from a worsted yarn that has an uneven surface texture. Challis is often printed, as well as plain.

Cutting out: a nap layout is not required unless the fabric is printed

Seams: plain, neatened with serger or zigzag stitch; a run and fell seam can also be used

Thread: polyester all-purpose thread

Needle: machine size 11/12; sharps for hand sewing

Pressing: steam iron on a steam setting with a pressing cloth; fabric will stretch while warm, so handle with care

Use for: dresses, jackets, garments with pleating or draping detail

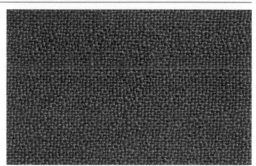

CREPE

A soft fabric made from a twisted yarn, which is what produces the uneven surface. It is important to preshrink this fabric prior to use by giving it a good steaming, because it will have stretched on the bolt and it is prone to shrinkage.

Cutting out: use a regular layout

Seams: plain, neatened with serger (a zigzag stitch may curl the edge of the seam)

Thread: polyester all-purpose thread

Needle: machine size 12; sharps or milliner's for hand sewing

Pressing: steam iron on a wool setting; a pressing cloth is not always required

Use for: all types of clothing

FLANNEL

A wool with a lightly brushed surface, featuring either a plain or twill weave. Used in the past for underwear.
Cutting out: use a nap layout
Seams: plain, neatened with serger or zigzag stitch or Hong Kong finish
Thread: polyester all-purpose thread

Needle: machine size 14; sharps for hand sewing
Pressing: steam iron on a wool setting with a pressing cloth; use a seam roll, as the fabric is prone to marking
Use for: men's wear, bedding, sleepwear

GABARDINE

A hard-wearing suiting fabric with a distinctive weave. Gabardine often has a sheen and is prone to shine. It can be difficult to handle, as it is springy and frays badly.
Cutting out: a nap layout is advisable, as the fabric has a sheen
Seams: plain, neatened with serger or zigzag stitch
Thread: polyester all-purpose thread or 100 percent cotton thread

Needle: machine size 14; sharps for hand sewing
Pressing: steam iron on a wool setting; use just the toe of the iron and a silk organza pressing cloth, as the fabric will mark and may shine
Use for: men's wear, jackets, pants

MOHAIR

From the wool of the Angora goat. A long, straight, and very strong fiber that produces a hairy cloth.
Cutting out: use a nap layout, with the fibers brushing down the pattern pieces in the same direction, from neck to hem
Seams: plain, neatened with serger or pinking shears

Thread: polyester all-purpose thread
Needle: machine size 14; sharps for hand sewing
Pressing: steam iron on a wool setting; "stroke" the iron over the wool, moving in the direction of the nap
Use for: jackets, coats, men's wear, home goods, knitted mohair yarns for sweaters

TARTAN

An authentic tartan belongs to a Scottish clan, and each has its own unique design that can only be used by that clan. The fabric is made using a twill weave from worsted yarns.
Cutting out: examine the design for even/uneven check, as it may need a nap layout or even a single layer layout
Seams: plain, matching the pattern and neatened with serger or zigzag stitch

Thread: polyester all-purpose thread
Needle: machine size 14; sharps for hand sewing
Pressing: steam iron on a wool setting; may require a pressing cloth, so test first
Use for: traditionally kilts, but these days also skirts, pants, jackets, home goods

TWEED, MODERN

A mix of chunky and nubby wool yarns. Modern tweed is often found in contemporary color palettes, as well as plain, and with interesting fibers in the weft such as metallics and paper. It is much favored by fashion designers.

Cutting out: use a nap layout
Seams: plain, neatened with serger or zigzag stitch; the fabric is prone to fraying

Thread: polyester all-purpose thread
Needle: machine size 14; sharps for hand sewing
Pressing: steam iron on a wool setting; a pressing cloth may not be required
Use for: jackets, coats; also skirts, dresses, home goods

TWEED, TRADITIONAL

A rough fabric with a distinctive warp and weft, usually in different colors, and often forming a small check pattern. Traditional tweed is associated with the English countryside.

Cutting out: a nap layout is not required unless the fabric features a check
Seams: plain, neatened with serger or zigzag stitch; can also be neatened with pinking shears

Thread: polyester all-purpose thread or 100 percent cotton thread
Needle: machine size 14; sharps for hand sewing
Pressing: steam iron on a steam setting; a pressing cloth may not be required
Use for: jackets, coats, skirts, men's wear, home goods

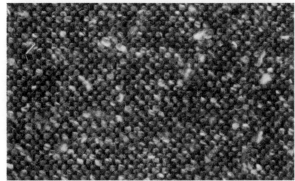

VENETIAN

A wool with a satin weave, making a luxurious, expensive fabric.

Cutting out: use a nap layout
Seams: plain, neatened with serger or zigzag stitch
Thread: polyester all–purpose thread or 100 percent cotton thread

Needle: machine size 14; sharps for hand sewing
Pressing: steam iron on a steam setting with a silk organza cloth to avoid shine; use a seam roll under the seams to prevent them from showing through
Use for: jackets, coats, men's wear

WOOL WORSTED

A light and strong cloth made from good-quality thin, firm filament fibers. Always steam prior to cutting out, as the fabric may shrink slightly after having been stretched around a bolt.

Cutting out: use a nap layout
Seams: plain, neatened with serger or zigzag stitch or Hong Kong finish

Thread: polyester all-purpose thread
Needle: machine size 12/14, depending on fabric; milliner's or sharps for hand sewing
Pressing: steam iron on a wool setting with a pressing cloth; use a seam roll to prevent the seam from showing through
Use for: skirts, jackets, coats, pants

◤ COTTON FABRICS

One of the most versatile and popular of all fabrics, cotton is a natural fiber that comes from the seed pods, or bolls, of the cotton plant. It is thought that cotton fibers have been in use since ancient times. Today, the world's biggest producers of cotton include the United States, India, and countries in the Middle East. Cotton fibers can be filament or staple, with the longest and finest used for top-quality bed linen. Cotton clothing is widely worn in warmer climates, as the fabric will keep you cool.

PROPERTIES OF COTTON

- Absorbs moisture well and carries heat away from the body
- Stronger wet than dry
- Does not build up static electricity
- Dyes well

- Prone to shrinkage unless it has been treated
- Will deteriorate from mildew and prolonged exposure to sunlight
- Creases easily
- Soils easily but launders well

EYELET

A fine, plain-weave cotton that has been embroidered in such a way as to make small holes. Usually white or a pastel color.
Cutting out: may need layout to place embroidery at hem edge
Seams: plain, neatened with serger or zigzag stitch; a French seam can also be used

Thread: polyester all-purpose thread
Needle: machine size 12/14; sharps for hand sewing
Pressing: steam iron on a cotton setting; a pressing cloth is not required
Use for: baby clothes, summer skirts, blouses

CALICO

A plain weave fabric that is usually unbleached and quite stiff. Available in many different weights, from very fine to extremely heavy.
Cutting out: use a regular layout
Seams: plain, neatened with serger or zigzag stitch

Thread: polyester all-purpose thread
Needle: machine size 11/14, depending on thickness of thread; sharps for hand sewing
Pressing: steam iron on a steam setting; a pressing cloth is not required
Use for: toiles (test garments), home goods

CHAMBRAY

A light cotton that has a colored warp thread and white weft thread. Chambray can also be found as a checked or a striped fabric.
Cutting out: use a regular layout
Seams: plain, neatened with serger or zigzag stitch
Thread: polyester all-purpose thread

Needle: machine size 11; sharps for hand sewing
Pressing: steam iron on a cotton setting; a pressing cloth is not required
Use for: blouses, men's shirts, children's wear

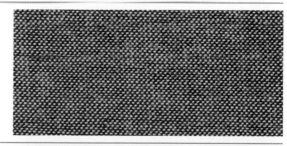

CHINTZ

A floral print or plain cotton fabric with a glazed finish that gives it a sheen. It has a close weave and is often treated to resist dirt.
Cutting out: use a nap layout
Seams: plain, neatened with serger or zigzag stitch; a run and fell seam can also be used

Thread: polyester all-purpose thread or 100 percent cotton thread
Needle: machine size 14; milliner's for hand sewing
Pressing: steam iron on a cotton setting; a pressing cloth may be required due to sheen on fabric
Use for: home goods

CORDUROY

A soft pile fabric with distinctive stripes (known as wales or ribs) woven into it. The name depends on the size of the ribs: baby or pin cord has extremely fine ribs; needle cord has slightly thicker ribs; corduroy has 10–12 ribs per 1in (2.5cm); and elephant or jumbo cord has thick, heavy ribs.

Cutting out: use a nap layout with the pile on the corduroy, brushing the pattern pieces from neck to hem, to give depth

Seams: plain, stitched using a walking foot and neatened with serger or zigzag stitch
Thread: polyester all-purpose thread
Needle: machine size 12/16; sharps or milliner's for hand sewing
Pressing: steam iron on a cotton setting; use a seam roll under the seams with a pressing cloth
Use for: pants, skirts, men's wear

CRINKLE COTTON

Looks like an exaggerated version of seersucker (see p.36), with creases added by a heat process. Crinkle cotton may require careful laundering, as it often has to be twisted into shape when wet to put the creases back in.

Cutting out: a nap layout is not required unless the fabric is printed

Seams: plain, neatened with serger or zigzag stitch
Thread: polyester all-purpose thread
Needle: machine size 12; milliner's for hand sewing
Pressing: steam iron on a cotton setting; take care not to press out the crinkles
Use for: blouses, dresses, children's wear

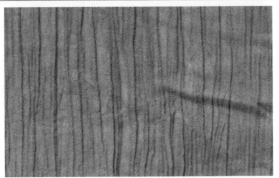

DAMASK

A cotton that has been woven on a jacquard loom to produce a fabric usually with a floral pattern in a uniform color. May have a sheen to the surface. Can also be made of silk or linen.

Cutting out: use a nap layout
Seams: plain, neatened with serger or zigzag stitch

Thread: polyester all-purpose thread or 100 percent cotton thread
Needle: machine size 14; sharps for hand sewing
Pressing: steam iron on a cotton setting; a pressing cloth may be required if the fabric has a sheen
Use for: home furnishings; colored jacquards for jackets, skirts

DENIM

Named after Nîmes in France. A hard-wearing twill-weave fabric with a colored warp and white weft, usually made into jeans. Available in various weights and often mixed with an elastic thread for stretch. Denim is usually blue but is also available in a variety of other colors.

Cutting out: use a regular layout

Seams: run and fell or top-stitched plain
Thread: polyester all-purpose thread with top-stitching thread for detail top-stitching
Needle: machine size 14/16; sharps for hand sewing
Pressing: steam iron on a cotton setting; a pressing cloth should not be required
Use for: jeans, jackets, children's wear

DRILL

A hard-wearing twill or plain-weave fabric with the same color warp and weft. Drill frays badly on the cut edges.

Cutting out: use a regular layout

Seams: run and fell; or plain, neatened with serger or zigzag stitch

Thread: polyester all-purpose thread with top-stitching thread for detail top-stitching

Needle: machine size 14; sharps for hand sewing

Pressing: steam iron on a cotton setting; a pressing cloth is not required

Use for: men's wear, casual jackets, pants

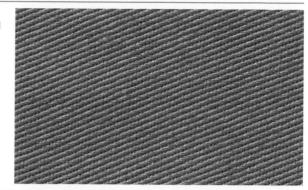

GINGHAM

A fresh, two-color cotton fabric that features checks of various sizes. A plain weave made by having groups of white and colored warp and weft threads.

Cutting out: usually an even check, so nap layout is not required but recommended; pattern will need matching

Seams: plain, neatened with serger or zigzag stitch

Thread: polyester all-purpose thread

Needle: machine size 11/12; sharps for hand sewing

Pressing: steam iron on a cotton setting; a pressing cloth should not be required

Use for: children's wear, dresses, shirts, home furnishings

JERSEY

A fine cotton yarn that has been knitted to give stretch, making the fabric very comfortable to wear. Jersey will also drape well.

Cutting out: a nap layout is recommended

Seams: 4-thread serger stitch; or plain seam stitched with a small zigzag stitch and then seam allowances stitched together with a zigzag

Thread: polyester all-purpose thread

Needle: machine size 12/14; a ballpoint needle may be required for serger and for hand sewing

Pressing: steam iron on a wool setting may shrink on a cotton setting

Use for: underwear, drapey dresses, leisurewear, bedding

MADRAS

A plaid fabric made from a fine cotton yarn, usually from India. Often found in bright colors. An inexpensive cotton fabric.

Cutting out: use a nap layout and match the pattern

Seams: plain, neatened with serger or zigzag stitch

Thread: polyester all-purpose thread

Needle: machine size 12/14; sharps for hand sewing

Pressing: steam iron on a cotton setting; a pressing cloth is not required

Use for: shirts, skirts, home furnishings

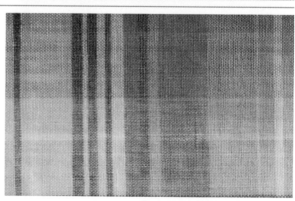

MUSLIN

A fine, plain, open-weave cotton. Can be found in colors but usually sold a natural/unbleached or white. Makes great pressing cloths and interlinings. It is a good idea to wash prior to use.

Cutting out: use a regular layout

Seams: 4-thread serger stitch; or plain seam, neatened with serger or zigzag stitch; a French seam could also be used

Thread: polyester all-purpose thread

Needle: machine size 11; milliner's for hand sewing

Pressing: steam iron on a cotton setting; a cloth is not required

Use for: curtaining and other household uses, as well as test patterns or toiles

SEERSUCKER

A woven cotton that has a bubbly appearance woven into it due to stripes of puckers. Do not overpress, or the surface effect will be damaged.

Cutting out: use a nap layout due to puckered surface effect

Seams: plain, neatened with serger or zigzag stitch

Thread: polyester all-purpose thread

Needle: machine size 11/12; milliner's for hand sewing

Pressing: steam iron on a cotton setting (be careful not to press out the wrinkles)

Use for: summer clothing, skirts, shirts, children's wear

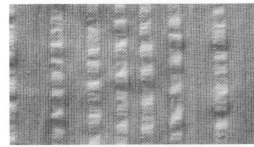

SHIRTING

A closely woven, fine cotton, with colored warp and weft yarns making stripes or checks.

Cutting out: use a nap layout if fabric has uneven stripes

Seams: plain, neatened with serger or zigzag stitch; a run and fell seam can also be used

Thread: polyester all-purpose thread

Needle: machine size 12; milliner's for hand sewing

Pressing: steam iron on a cotton setting; a pressing cloth is not required

Use for: ladies' and men's shirts

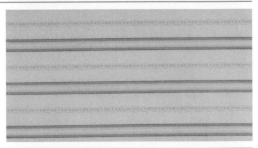

TERRYCLOTH

A cotton fabric with loops on the surface; top-quality terrycloth has loops on both sides. It is highly absorbent. Wash before use to preshrink and make it fluffy.

Cutting out: use a nap layout

Seams: 4-thread serger stitch; or plain seam, neatened with serger or zigzag stitch

Thread: polyester all-purpose thread

Needle: machine size 14; sharps for hand sewing

Pressing: steam iron on a cotton setting; a pressing cloth is not required

Use for: bathrobes, beachwear, towels

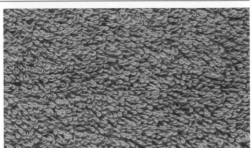

VELVET

A pile-weave fabric made by using an additional yarn that is then cut to produce the pile. Difficult to handle and can be easily damaged if seams have to be unpicked.

Cutting out: use a nap layout with the pile brushing up from hem to neck to give depth of color

Seams: plain, stitched using a walking foot (stitch all seams from hem to neck) and neatened with serger or zigzag stitch

Thread: polyester all-purpose thread

Needle: machine size 14; milliner's for hand sewing

Pressing: only if you have to; use a velvet board, a bit of steam, toe of iron, and silk organza cloth

Use for: jackets, coats

◤ SILK FABRICS

Often referred to as the queen of all fabrics, silk is made from the fibers of the silkworm's cocoon. This strong and luxurious fabric dates back thousands of years to its first development in China, and the secret of silk production was well protected by the Chinese until 300 CE. Silk fabrics can be very fine or thick and chunky. They need careful handling, as some silk fabrics can be easily damaged.

PROPERTIES OF SILK

- Keeps you warm in winter and cool in summer
- Absorbs moisture and dries quickly
- Dyes well, producing deep, rich colors
- Static electricity can build up and fabric may cling
- Will fade in prolonged strong sunlight
- Prone to shrinkage
- Best dry-cleaned
- Weaker when wet than dry
- May water-mark

CHIFFON

A very strong and very fine, transparent silk with a plain weave. Will gather and ruffle well. Difficult to handle.
Cutting out: place tissue paper under the fabric and pin the fabric to the tissue, cutting through all layers if necessary; use extra-fine pins

Seams: French
Thread: polyester all-purpose thread
Needle: machine size 9/11; fine milliner's for hand sewing
Pressing: dry iron on a wool setting
Use for: special-occasion wear, over-blouses

CREPE DE CHINE

Medium weight, with an uneven surface due to the twisted silk yarn used. Drapes well and often used on bias-cut garments.
Cutting out: if to be bias-cut, use a single layer layout; otherwise, use a nap layout

Seams: If to be bias-cut, use a single layer layout; otherwise, use a nap layout
Thread: polyester all-purpose thread
Needle: machine size 11; milliner's or betweens for hand sewing
Pressing: dry iron on a wool setting
Use for: blouses, dresses, special-occasion wear

DUCHESS SATIN

A heavy, expensive satin fabric used almost exclusively for special-occasion wear.
Cutting out: use a nap layout
Seams: plain, with pinked edges
Thread: polyester all-purpose thread

Needle: machine size 12/14; milliner's for hand sewing
Pressing: steam iron on a wool setting with a pressing cloth; use a seam roll under the seams to prevent shadowing
Use for: special-occasion wear

DUPIONI

Similar to shantung (see p.38) but woven using a much smoother yarn to reduce the amount of nubby bits in the weft.
Cutting out: use a nap layout to prevent shadowing
Seams: plain, neatened with serger or zigzag stitch

Thread: polyester all-purpose thread
Needle: machine size 12; milliner's for hand sewing
Pressing: steam iron on a wool setting with a pressing cloth, as fabric may water-mark
Use for: dresses, skirts, jackets, special-occasion wear, home goods

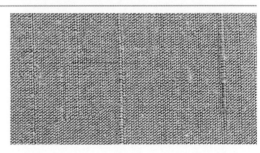

SHANTUNG

The most popular of all the silks. A distinctive weft yarn with many nubby bits. Available in hundreds of colors. Easy to handle, but it does fray badly.

Cutting out: use a nap layout, as the fabric shadows

Seams: plain, neatened with serger or zigzag stitch

Thread: polyester all-purpose thread

Needle: machine size 12; milliner's for hand sewing

Pressing: steam iron on a wool setting with a pressing cloth to avoid water-marking

Use for: dresses, special-occasion wear, jackets, home goods

GEORGETTE

A soft, filmy silk fabric that has a slight transparency. Does not crease easily.

Cutting out: place tissue paper under the fabric and pin fabric to tissue, cutting through all layers if necessary; use extra-fine pins

Seams: French

Thread: polyester all-purpose thread

Needle: machine size 11; milliner's for hand sewing

Pressing: dry iron on a wool setting to avoid damage by steam

Use for: special-occasion wear, loose-fitting overshirts

HABUTAI

Originally from Japan, a smooth, fine silk that can have a plain or a twill weave. Fabric is often used for silk painting.

Cutting out: use a regular layout

Seams: French

Thread: polyester all-purpose thread

Needle: machine size 9/11; very fine milliner's or betweens for hand sewing

Pressing: steam iron on a wool setting

Use for: lining, shirts, blouses

MATKA

A silk suiting fabric with an uneven-looking yarn. Matka can be mistaken for linen.

Cutting out: use a nap layout, as silk may shadow

Seams: plain, neatened with serger or zigzag stitch or Hong Kong finish

Thread: polyester all-purpose thread

Needle: machine size 12/14; milliner's for hand sewing

Pressing: steam iron on a wool setting with a pressing cloth; a seam roll is recommended to prevent the seams from showing through

Use for: dresses, jackets, pants

ORGANZA

A sheer fabric with
a crisp appearance that
will crease easily.
Cutting out: use a regular layout
Seams: French or a seam for
a difficult fabric
Thread: polyester
all-purpose thread

Needle: machine size 11;
milliner's or betweens for
hand sewing
Pressing: steam iron on a
wool setting; a pressing cloth
should not be required
Use for: sheer blouses, shrugs,
interlining, interfacing

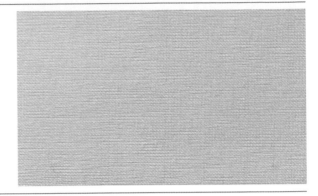

SATIN

A silk with a satin weave that
can be very light to quite heavy
in weight.
Cutting out: use a nap layout in
a single layer, as fabric is slippery
Seams: French; on thicker satins,
a seam for a difficult fabric
Thread: polyester all-purpose
thread (not silk thread, as it
becomes weak with wear)

Needle: machine size 11/12;
milliner's or betweens for
hand sewing
Pressing: steam iron on a
wool setting with a pressing
cloth, as fabric may water-mark
Use for: blouses, dresses,
special-occasion wear

SILK AND WOOL BLEND

A fabric made by mixing wool
and silk fibers or wool and
silk yarns. The fabric made
may be fine in quality or thick,
like a coating.
Cutting out: use a nap layout
Seams: plain, neatened with
serger or zigzag stitch
Thread: polyester
all-purpose thread

Needle: machine size 11/14,
depending on fabric; sharps
for hand sewing
Pressing: steam iron on a
wool setting; seams will
require some steam to
make them lie flat
Use for: suits, skirts,
pants, coats

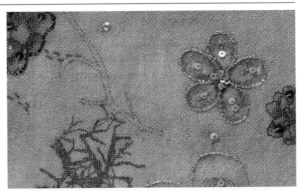

TAFFETA

A smooth, plain-weave fabric
with a crisp appearance. It makes
a rustling sound when worn. Can
require special handling and does
not wear well.
Cutting out: use a nap layout
with extra-fine pins in seams, as
they will mark the fabric
Seams: plain; fabric may pucker,
so sew from the hem upward,

keeping the fabric taut under
the machine; neaten with
serger or pinking shears
Thread: polyester
all-purpose thread
Needle: machine size 11; milliner's
or betweens for hand sewing
Pressing: cool iron, with a
seam roll under the seams
Use for: special-occasion wear

◄ LINEN FABRICS

Linen is a natural fiber that is derived from the stem of the flax plant. It is available in a variety of qualities and weights, from very fine linen to heavy suiting weights. Coarser than cotton, it is sometimes woven with cotton, as well as being mixed with silk.

PROPERTIES OF LINEN

- Cool and comfortable to wear
- Absorbs moisture well
- Shrinks when washed
- Does not ease well
- Has a tendency to wrinkle
- Prone to fraying
- Resists moths but is damaged by mildew

COTTON AND LINEN BLEND

Two fibers may have been mixed together in the yarn or may have mixed warp and weft yarns. It has lots of texture in the weave. Silk and linen mix is treated in the same way.
Cutting out: use a regular layout
Seams: plain, neatened with serger or zigzag stitch
Thread: polyester all-purpose thread
Needle: machine size 14; sharps for hand sewing
Pressing: a steam iron on a steam setting with a silk organza pressing cloth
Use for: summer-weight jackets, tailored dresses

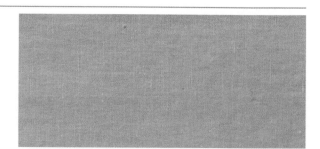

DRESS-WEIGHT LINEN

A medium-weight linen with a plain weave. The yarn is often uneven, which causes slubs in the weave.
Cutting out: use a regular layout
Seams: plain, neatened with serger or zigzag stitch or a Hong Kong finish
Thread: polyester all-purpose thread with a top-stitching thread for top-stitching
Needle: machine size 14; sharps for hand sewing
Pressing: steam iron on a cotton setting
Use for: dresses, pants, skirts

PRINTED LINENS

Many linens today feature prints or even embroidery. The fabric may be light to medium weight, with a smooth yarn that has few slubs.
Cutting out: use a nap layout
Seams: plain, neatened with serger or zigzag stitch
Thread: polyester all-purpose thread
Needle: machine size 14; sharps for hand sewing
Pressing: steam iron on a cotton setting (steam is required to remove creases)
Use for: dresses, skirts

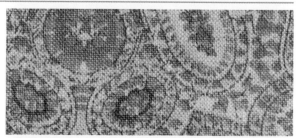

SUITING LINEN

A heavier yarn is used to produce a linen suitable for suits for men and women. Can be a firm, tight weave or a looser weave.
Cutting out: use a regular layout
Seams: plain, neatened with serger or a zigzag stitch and sharps for hand-sewing needle
Thread: polyester all-purpose thread with a top-stitch thread for top-stitching
Needle: machine size 14; sharps for hand sewing
Pressing: steam iron on a cotton setting (steam is required to remove creases)
Use for: men's and women's suits, pants, coats

⊀ LEATHER AND SUEDE

Leather and suede are natural fabrics derived from either a pig or a cow and are sold as skins. Depending on the curing process that has been used, the skin will be either a suede or a leather. The fabrics require special handling.

LEATHER AND SUEDE
As the pattern pieces cannot be pinned onto leather and suede, you will need to draw around them using tailor's chalk. After cutting out, the chalk will rub off and will not damage the skin.
Cutting out: a complete pattern is required, left and right-hand halves; use a nap layout for suede, as it will brush one way
Seams: lapped or plain, using a walking foot or an ultra glide foot; neatening is not required
Thread: polyester all-purpose thread
Needle: machine size 14 (a special leather needle may actually damage the skin); hand sewing is not recommended
Pressing: Avoid steam when ironing; set the iron on the rayon setting and use a 100 percent cotton cloth between the iron and leather
Use for: skirts, pants, jackets, home goods

⊀ MANMADE FABRICS

The term "manmade" applies to any fabric that is not 100 percent natural. Many of these fabrics have been developed over the last hundred years, which means they are new compared to natural fibers. Some manmade fabrics are made from natural elements mixed with chemicals, while others are made entirely from non-natural substances.

ACETATE
Introduced in 1924, acetate is made from cellulose and chemicals. The fabric has a slight shine and is widely used for linings. Acetate can also be woven into fabrics such as acetate taffeta, acetate satin, and acetate jersey.
Properties of acetate:
• Dyes well
• Can be heat-set into pleats
• Washes well
Cutting out: use a nap layout due to sheen on fabric
Seams: plain, neatened with serger or zigzag stitch, or 4-thread serger stitch
Thread: polyester all-purpose thread
Needle: machine size 11; sharps for hand sewing
Pressing: steam iron on a cool setting (fabric can melt)
Use for: special-occasion wear, linings

ACRYLIC
Introduced in 1950, acrylic fibers are made from ethylene and acrylonitrile. The fabric resembles wool and makes a good substitute for machine-washable wool. Often seen as a knitted fabric, the fibers can be mixed with wool.
Properties of acrylic:
• Little absorbency
• Tends to retain odors
• Not very strong
Cutting out: use a regular layout
Seams: 4-thread serger stitch on knitted fabrics; plain seam on woven fabrics
Thread: polyester all-purpose thread
Needle: machine size 12/14, but a ballpoint needle may be required on knitted fabrics; sharps for hand sewing
Pressing: steam iron on a wool setting (fabric can be damaged by heat)
Use for: knitted yarns for sweaters; wovens for skirts, blouses

NYLON
Developed by DuPont in 1938, the fabric takes its name from a collaboration between New York (NY) and London (LON). Nylon is made from polymer chips that are melted and extruded into fibers. The fabric can be knitted or woven.
Properties of nylon:
• Very hard-wearing
• Does not absorb moisture
• Washes easily, although white nylon can discolor easily
• Very strong
Cutting out: a nap layout is not required unless the fabric is printed
Seams: plain, neatened with serger or zigzag stitch
Thread: polyester all-purpose thread
Needle: machine size 14, but a ballpoint needle may be required for knitted nylons; sharps for hand sewing
Pressing: steam iron on a silk setting (fabric can melt)
Use for: sportswear, underwear

POLYESTER

One of the most popular of the manmade fibers, polyester was introduced in 1951 as a washable man's suit. Polyester fibers are made from petroleum by-products and can take on any form, from a very fine sheer fabric to a thick, heavy suiting.

Properties of polyester:
• Nonabsorbent
• Does not crease
• Can build up static
• May "pill"
Cutting out: a nap layout is only required if the fabric is printed
Seams: French, plain, or 4-thread serger, depending on the weight of the fabric

Thread: polyester all-purpose thread
Needle: machine size 11/14; sharps for hand sewing
Pressing: steam iron on a polyester setting
Use for: workwear, school uniforms

RAYON

Also known as viscose and often referred to as artificial silk, this fiber was developed in 1889. It is made from wood pulp or cotton linters mixed with chemicals. Rayon can be knitted or woven and made into a wide range of fabrics. It is often blended with other fibers.

Properties of rayon:
• Is absorbent
• Is not static
• Dyes well
• Frays badly
Cutting out: a nap layout is only required if the fabric is printed
Seams: plain, neatened with serger or zigzag stitch

Thread: polyester all-purpose thread
Needle: machine size 12/14; sharps for hand sewing
Pressing: steam iron on a silk setting
Use for: dresses, blouses, jackets

SPANDEX

Introduced in 1958, this is a lightweight, soft fiber that can be stretched 500 percent without breaking. A small amount of spandex is often mixed with other fibers to produce wovens with a slight stretch.

Properties of spandex:
• Resistant to body oils, detergents, sun, sea, and sand
• Can be difficult to sew
• Can be damaged by heat
• Not suitable for hand sewing
Cutting out: use a nap layout
Seams: 4-thread serger stitch or a seam stitched with a small zigzag

Thread: polyester all-purpose thread
Needle: machine ballpoint size 14 or a machine stretch needle
Pressing: steam iron on a wool setting (spandex can be damaged by a hot iron)
Use for: swimwear, foundation wear, sportswear

SYNTHETIC FURS

Created using a looped yarn that is then cut on a knitted or a woven base, synthetic fur can be made from nylon or acrylic fibers. The furs vary tremendously in quality, and some are very difficult to tell from the real thing.

Properties of synthetic furs:
• Require careful sewing
• Can be heat-damaged by pressing
• Not as warm as real fur
Cutting out: use a nap layout, with the fur pile brushed from the neck to the hem; cut just the backing carefully and not through the fur pile

Seams: plain, with a longer stitch and a walking foot; no neatening is required
Thread: polyester all-purpose thread
Needle: machine size 14; sharps for hand sewing
Pressing: if required, use a cool iron (synthetic fur can melt under a hot iron)
Use for: outerwear

SYNTHETIC LEATHER AND SUEDE

Made from polymers, these are nonwoven fabrics. Some synthetic leathers and suedes can closely resemble the real thing.

Properties of synthetic leather and suede:
• Do not fray
• Do not ease well
• Can be difficult to sew by hand, so this is not recommended
Cutting out: use a nap layout
Seams: plain, stitched using a walking foot and neatened

with pinking shears; can also use top-stitched seams and lapped seams
Thread: polyester all-purpose thread
Needle: machine size 11/14
Pressing: steam iron on a wool setting with a pressing cloth
Use for: jackets, skirts, pants, home goods

◤ FABRIC CONSTRUCTION

Most fabric is made by either knitting or weaving. A knitted fabric is constructed by interlocking looped yarns. For a woven fabric, horizontal and vertical yarns go under and over each other. The warp yarn, which is the strongest, runs vertically and the weft crosses it at right angles. There are also nonwoven fabrics created by a felting process where tiny fibers are mixed and squeezed together, then rolled out.

PLAIN WEAVE
As the name suggests, this is the simplest of all the weaves. The weft yarn passes under one warp yarn, then over another one.

SATIN WEAVE
This has a long strand known as a float on the warp yarn. The weft goes under four warp yarns, then over one. This weave gives a sheen to the fabric.

HERRINGBONE WEAVE
The distinctive herringbone zigzag weave is made by the weft yarn going under and over warp yarns in a staggered pattern.

 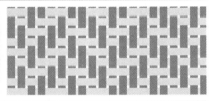

TWILL WEAVE
The diagonal twill weave is made by the weft yarn going under two warp yarns, then over another two, with the pattern moved one yarn across each time.

WARP KNIT
This is made on a knitting machine, where one yarn is set to each needle (latch). The knit is formed in a vertical and diagonal direction.

 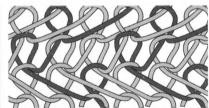

WEFT KNIT
Made in the same way as knitting by hand on needles, this uses one yarn that runs horizontally.

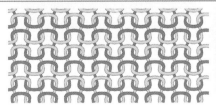 

INTERFACINGS

An interfacing is a piece of fabric that is attached to the main fabric to give it support or structure. An interfacing fabric may be woven, knitted, or nonwoven. It may also be fusible or nonfusible. A fusible interfacing (also called iron-on) can be bonded to the fabric by applying heat, whereas a nonfusible interfacing needs to be sewn to the fabric with a basting stitch. Always cut interfacings on the same grain as the fabric, regardless of its construction.

▶◀ FUSIBLE INTERFACINGS

Be sure to buy fusibles designed for the home sewer, because the adhesive on the back of fusible interfacings for commercial use cannot be released with a normal steam iron. Do all pattern markings after the interfacing has been applied to the fabric.

HOW TO APPLY A FUSIBLE INTERFACING

1 Place fabric on pressing surface, wrong side up, making sure it is straight and not wrinkled.
2 Place the chosen interfacing sticky side down on the fabric. (The sticky side feels gritty.)
3 Cover with a dry pressing cloth and spray the cloth with a fine mist of water.
4 Place a steam iron, on a steam setting, on top of the pressing cloth.

5 Leave the iron in place for at least 10 seconds before moving it to the next area of fabric.
6 Check to see if the interfacing is fused to the fabric by rolling the fabric—if the interfacing is still loose in places, repeat the pressing process.
7 When the fabric has cooled down, the fusing process will be complete. Then pin the pattern back onto the fabric and transfer the pattern markings as required.

WOVEN
A woven fusible is always a good choice for a woven fabric, as the two weaves will work together. Always cut on the same grain as the fabric. This type of interfacing is suitable for crafts and for more structured garments.

LIGHTWEIGHT WOVEN
A very light, woven fusible that is almost sheer, this can be difficult to cut out, as it tends to stick to the scissors. It is suitable for all light to medium-weight fabrics.

KNITTED
A knitted fusible is ideally suited to a knit fabric, as the two will be able to stretch together. Some knitted fusibles only stretch one way, while others will stretch in all directions. A knitted fusible is also a good choice on fabrics that have a percentage of stretch.

NONWOVEN
Nonwoven fusibles are available in a wide variety of weights—choose one that feels lighter than your fabric. You can always add a second layer if one interfacing proves to be too light. This interfacing is suitable for supporting collars and cuffs and facings on garments.

▶◀ NONFUSIBLE INTERFACINGS

These sew-in interfacings require basting to the wrong side of facings or the main garment fabric around the seam allowances. They are useful for sheer or fine fabrics where the adhesive from a fusible interfacing might show through.

HOW TO APPLY A NONFUSIBLE INTERFACING

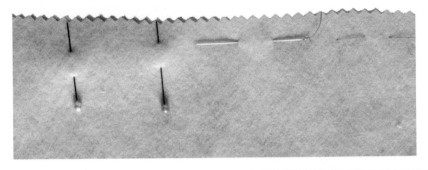

1 Place the interfacing onto the wrong side of the fabric, aligning the cut edges.
2 Pin in place.
3 Using a basting stitch, baste the interfacing to the fabric at ⅜in (1cm) within the seam allowance.

ALPACA
A tailoring canvas made from wool and alpaca, this interfacing is excellent to use in difficult fabrics such as velvet, because the alpaca can be steamed into shape.

VOILE AND BATISTE
Voile (shown) is a lightweight, semisheer, 100 percent cotton fabric. It is perfect as an underlining or for interfacing silks and cotton lawns. It can also be used in heirloom sewing and smocking. Batiste is very similar but slightly firmer and can be used in the same ways.

MUSLIN
A cotton muslin interfacing is a good choice on summer dresses, as well as for special-occasion wear. Muslin can also be used to line fine cotton dresses.

ORGANZA
A pure silk organza makes an excellent interfacing for sheer fabric to give support and structure. It can also be used for structure in much larger areas such as bridal skirts.

NONWOVEN SEW-IN INTERFACING
A nonwoven material is ideal for crafts and small areas of garments, such as cuffs and collars. Use it in garments when a woven or fusible alternative is not available.

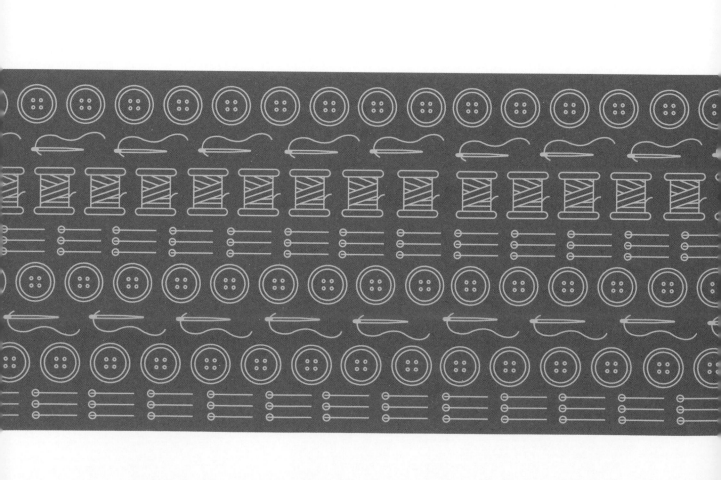

STITCH
ESSENTIALS

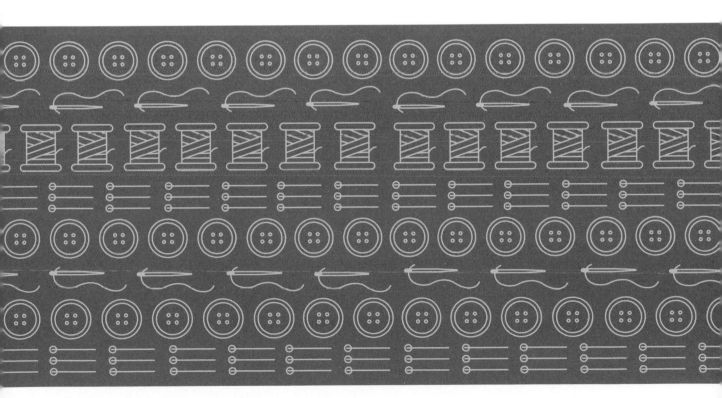

HAND SEWING

It is necessary to use hand sewing to prepare the fabric prior to permanent stitching—these temporary basting stitches will eventually be removed. Permanent hand sewing is used to finish a garment and to attach fasteners, as well as to help out with a quick repair.

⋉ THREADING THE NEEDLE

When sewing by hand, cut your piece of thread to be no longer than the distance from your fingertips to your elbow. If the thread is much longer than this, it will knot as you sew.

HOW TO THREAD A NEEDLE

1 Hold your needle in your right hand and the end of the thread in your left. Keeping the thread still, place the eye of the needle over the thread.

2 If the needle will not slip over the thread, dampen your fingers and run the moisture across the eye of the needle. Pull the thread through.

3 At the other end of the thread, tie a knot as shown (above) or secure the thread as shown opposite.

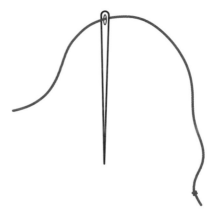

4 You are now ready to start your sewing.

➤ SECURING THE THREAD

The ends of the thread must be secured firmly, especially if the hand sewing is to be permanent. A knot (see opposite page) is frequently used and is the preferred choice for temporary stitches. For permanent sewing, a double stitch is a better option.

DOUBLE STITCH

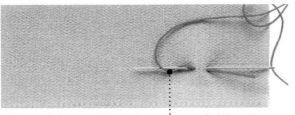

1 Take a stitch. **2** Go back through the stitch with the thread wrapped under the needle. **3** Pull through to make a knot.

BACKSTITCH

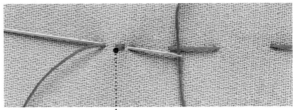

Make two small stitches in the same place.

➤ BASTING STITCHES

Each of the many types of basting stitches has its own individual use. Basic bastes hold two or more pieces of fabric together. Long-and-short bastes are an alternative version of the basic basting stitch, often used when the basting will stay in the work for some time. Diagonal bastes hold folds or overlaid fabrics together, while slip bastes are used to hold a fold in fabric to another piece of fabric.

BASIC BASTES

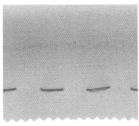

Starting with a knot and, using single thread, make straight stitches, evenly spaced.

LONG-AND-SHORT

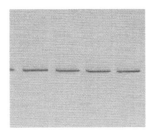

Make long stitches with a short space between each one.

DIAGONAL BASTES

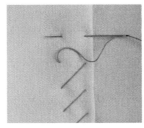

Work vertically, taking horizontal stitches.

SLIP BASTES

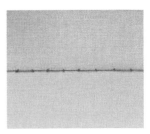

Take a stitch into the fold and then a stitch into the base fabric.

BAR BASTES

1 Using double thread, make two or three loops between the two layers of fabric.

2 Work a buttonhole stitch (see p.50) across the loops.

▶ STITCHES FOR HAND SEWING

There are a number of hand stitches that can be used during construction of a garment or other item. Some are for decorative purposes, while others are more functional.

BACKSTITCH

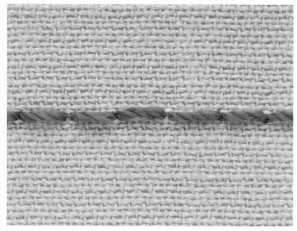

A strong stitch that could be used to construct a piece of work. Work from right to left. Bring the needle up, leaving a space, then take the thread back to the end of the last stitch. Repeat.

RUNNING STITCH

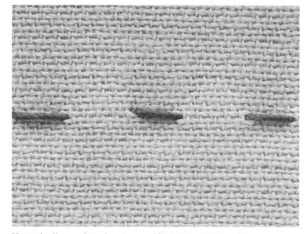

Very similar to basting (see p.49), but used more for decorative purposes. Work from right to left. Run the needle in and out of the fabric to create even stitches and spaces.

WHIP STITCH

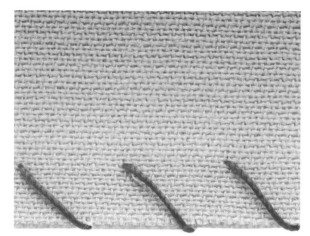

A diagonal stitch sewn with a single thread along a raw edge to prevent fraying. Work from right to left. Take a stitch through the edge of the fabric. The depth of the stitch depends on the thickness of the fabric—for a thin fabric, take a shallow stitch.

BUTTONHOLE STITCH

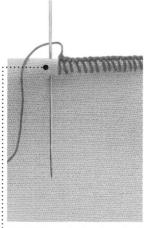
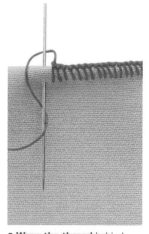

1 Used to make hand-worked buttonholes and also to secure fastenings. It is always stitched on an edge with no spaces between the stitches. Work from right to left. Push the needle from the top edge into the fabric.

2 Wrap the thread behind the needle as the needle goes in and again as the needle leaves the fabric. Pull through, and a knot will appear at the edge. This is an essential stitch for all sewers and is not difficult to master.

HERRINGBONE STITCH

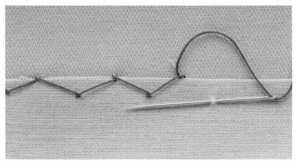

A very useful stitch, as it is secure yet has some movement in it. It is used to secure hems and interlinings. Work from left to right. Take a small (not more than 0.5mm) horizontal stitch into one layer and then the other, so the thread crosses itself.

SLIP HEM STITCH

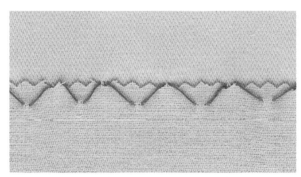

Also called a catch stitch, this is used primarily for securing hems. It looks similar to herringbone (above). Work from right to left. Take a short horizontal stitch into one layer and then the other.

BLANKET STITCH

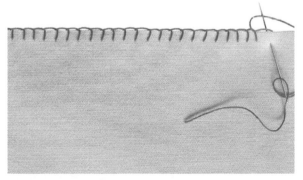

Similar to buttonhole stitch but without the knot. Blanket stitch is useful to neaten edges and for decorative purposes. Always leave a space between the stitches. Push the needle into the fabric and, as it appears at the edge, wrap the thread under the needle.

FLAT FELL STITCH

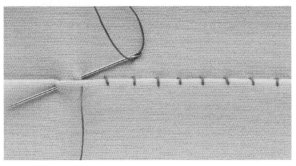

A strong, secure stitch to hold two layers permanently together. This stitch is often used to secure bias bindings and linings. Work from right to left. Make a short, straight stitch at the edge of the fabric.

BLIND HEM STITCH

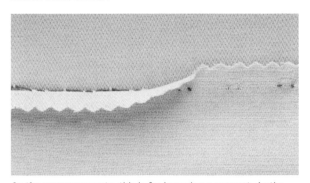

As the name suggests, this is for hemming a garment. As the stitch is under the edge of the fabric, it should be discreet. Work from right to left and use a slip hem stitch (left).

CROSS STITCH

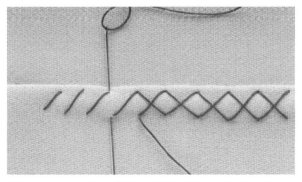

A temporary securing stitch used to hold pleats in place after construction. It can also be used to secure linings. Work a row of even diagonal stitches in one direction and then a row back over them to make crosses.

MACHINE SEWING AND SEAMS

Fabric is joined together using seams—whether it be for an item of clothing, craft work, or home goods. The most common seam is a plain seam, which is suitable for a wide variety of fabrics and items. However, there are many other seams to be used as appropriate, depending on the fabric and item being constructed. Some seams are decorative and can add detail to structured garments.

✕ SECURING THE THREAD

Machine stitches need to be secured at the end of a seam to prevent them from coming undone. This can be done by hand, tying the ends of the thread, or using the machine with a reverse stitch or a locking stitch, which stitches three or four stitches in the same place.

TIE THE ENDS

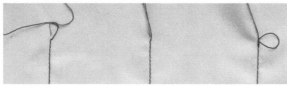

1 Pull on the top thread, and it will pull up a loop—this is the bobbin thread.

2 Pull the loop through to the top.

3 Tie the two threads together.

REVERSE STITCH

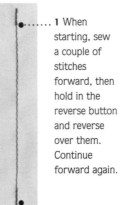

1 When starting, sew a couple of stitches forward, then hold in the reverse button and reverse over them. Continue forward again.

2 At the end of the seam, reverse again to secure the stitches.

LOCKING STITCH

1 When starting, press the locking stitch and stitch, then continue forward.

2 At the end of the seam, press the locking stitch again.

✕ STITCHES MADE WITH A MACHINE

The sewing machine will sew plain seams and decorative seams, as well as buttonholes of various styles. The length and width of all buttonholes can be altered to suit the garment or craft item. Stitch length and width can also be adjusted. On most machines, the number settings equate to millimeters, but some brands use stitches per inch; both types of measurements are included in this book.

STRAIGHT STITCH

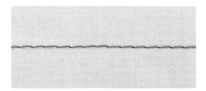

Used for most applications.
The length of the stitch can be altered from 0.5 to 5.0 on most sewing machines.

ZIGZAG STITCH

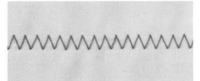

To neaten seam edges and for securing and decorative purposes. Both the width and the length of this stitch can be altered.

3-STEP ZIGZAG STITCH

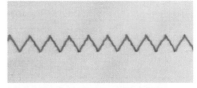

Made up of small, straight stitches.
This stitch is decorative, as well as functional, and is often found in lingerie. The stitch length and width can be altered.

BLIND HEM STITCH

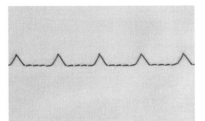

Made in conjunction with the blind hem foot. A combination of straight stitches and a zigzag stitch (see opposite page). Used to secure hems.

OVEREDGE STITCH

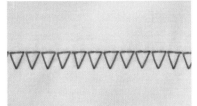

Made in conjunction with the overedge foot. The stitch is used for neatening the edge of fabric. The width and length of the stitch can be altered.

STRETCH STITCH

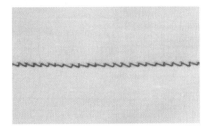

Also known as a lightening stitch. This stitch is recommended for stretch knits but is better used to help control difficult fabrics.

BASIC BUTTONHOLE STITCH

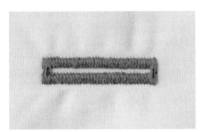

Square on both ends. Used on all styles of garments.

ROUND-END BUTTONHOLE STITCH

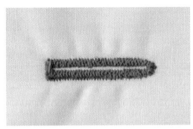

One square end and one round end. Used on jackets.

KEYHOLE BUTTONHOLE STITCH

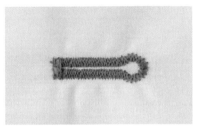

One square end and one end shaped like a loop. Used on jackets.

DECORATIVE STITCHES

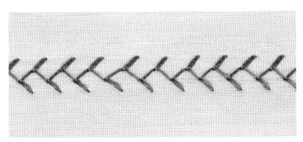

CORN STITCH

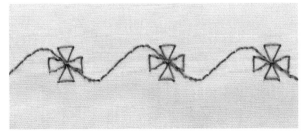

FLOWER STITCH

Sewing machines are capable of producing decorative linear stitches. These can be used to enhance the surface of work or a seam as they add interest to edges. Or, when worked as many rows together, they can be used to create a piece of embroidered fabric.

STAR STITCH

◤ HOW TO MAKE A PLAIN SEAM

A plain seam is ⅝in (1.5cm) wide, but it can be ⅜in (1cm) or even ¼in (6mm). It is important that the seam is stitched at the width indicated on the pattern to ensure the item comes out true to size. There are guides on the plate of the sewing machine that can be used to help align the fabric.

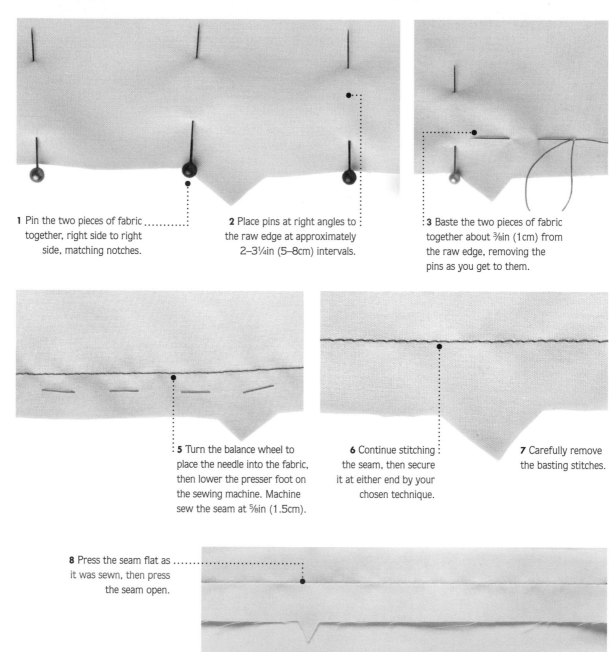

1 Pin the two pieces of fabric together, right side to right side, matching notches.

2 Place pins at right angles to the raw edge at approximately 2–3¼in (5–8cm) intervals.

3 Baste the two pieces of fabric together about ⅜in (1cm) from the raw edge, removing the pins as you get to them.

5 Turn the balance wheel to place the needle into the fabric, then lower the presser foot on the sewing machine. Machine sew the seam at ⅝in (1.5cm).

6 Continue stitching the seam, then secure it at either end by your chosen technique.

7 Carefully remove the basting stitches.

8 Press the seam flat as it was sewn, then press the seam open.

◄ SEAM NEATENING

It is important that the raw edges of the seam are neatened or finished—this will make the seam hard-wearing and prevent fraying.

The method of neatening will depend on the style of item that is being made and the fabric you are using.

PINKED

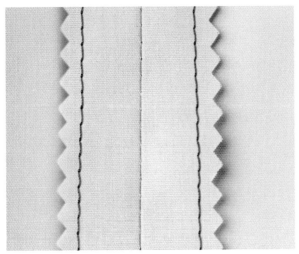

This method of neatening is ideal to use on fabrics that do not fray badly. Stitch ³⁄₁₆in (5mm) away from the raw edge, then use pinking shears to trim as little as possible off the edge.

ZIGZAGGED

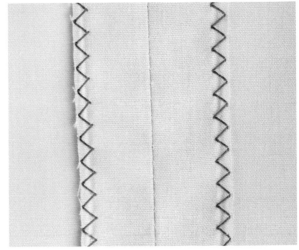

All sewing machines will make a zigzag stitch. It is an ideal stitch to use to stop the edges from fraying and is suitable for all types of fabric. Sew in from the raw edge, then trim back to the zigzag stitch. On most fabrics, use a stitch width of 2.0 and a stitch length of 1.5.

OVEREDGE SEWING

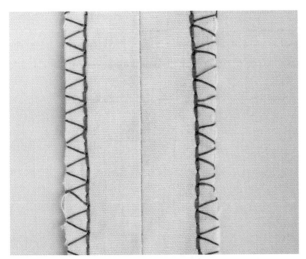

This is found on most sewing machines. Select the overedge stitch on your machine. Using the overedge machine foot and the preset stitch length and width, machine along the raw edge of the seam.

CLEAN FINISHED

This is a very hard-wearing finish and is ideal for cottons and fine fabrics. Using a straight stitch, turn under the raw edge of the seam allowance by ⅛in (3mm) and sew straight along the fold.

◤ HONG KONG FINISH

This is a great finish to use on wools and linens to neaten the seams on unlined jackets. It is made by wrapping the raw edge with bias-cut strips.

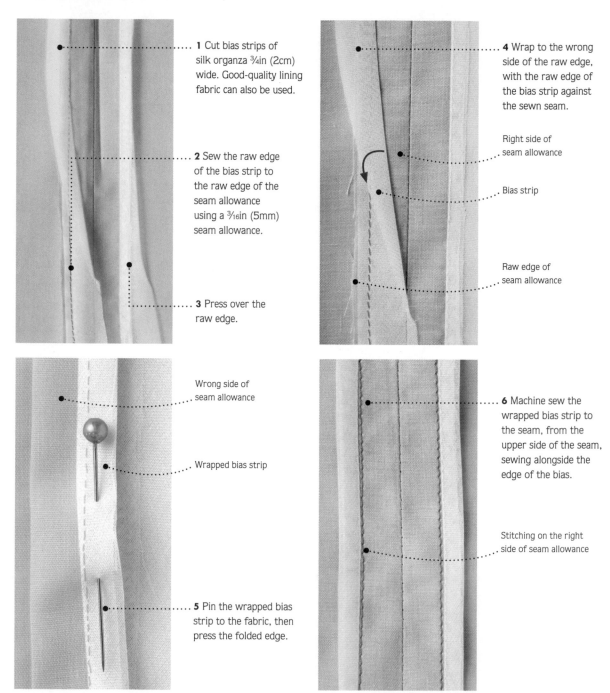

1 Cut bias strips of silk organza ¾in (2cm) wide. Good-quality lining fabric can also be used.

2 Sew the raw edge of the bias strip to the raw edge of the seam allowance using a ³⁄₁₆in (5mm) seam allowance.

3 Press over the raw edge.

4 Wrap to the wrong side of the raw edge, with the raw edge of the bias strip against the sewn seam.

Right side of seam allowance

Bias strip

Raw edge of seam allowance

Wrong side of seam allowance

Wrapped bias strip

5 Pin the wrapped bias strip to the fabric, then press the folded edge.

6 Machine sew the wrapped bias strip to the seam, from the upper side of the seam, sewing alongside the edge of the bias.

Stitching on the right side of seam allowance

✄ FRENCH SEAM

A French seam is a seam that is sewn twice, first on the right side of the work and then on the wrong side, enclosing the first seam. The French seam has traditionally been used on delicate garments such as lingerie and on sheer and silk fabrics.

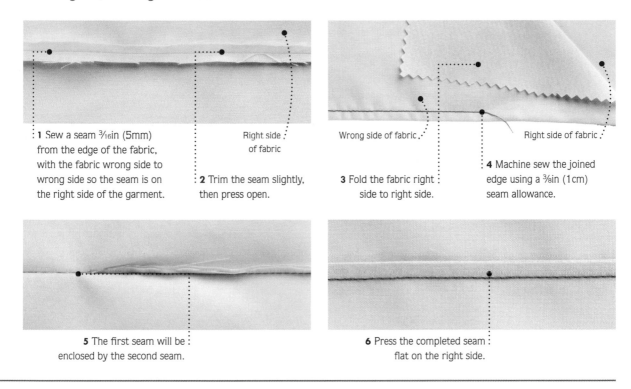

1 Sew a seam ³⁄₁₆in (5mm) from the edge of the fabric, with the fabric wrong side to wrong side so the seam is on the right side of the garment.

Right side of fabric

2 Trim the seam slightly, then press open.

Wrong side of fabric

Right side of fabric

3 Fold the fabric right side to right side.

4 Machine sew the joined edge using a ³⁄₈in (1cm) seam allowance.

5 The first seam will be enclosed by the second seam.

6 Press the completed seam flat on the right side.

✄ FLAT FELL SEAM

Some garments require a strong seam that will withstand frequent washing and wear and tear. A flat fell seam is very strong. It is made on the right side of a garment and is used on the inside leg seam of jeans and on men's tailored shirts.

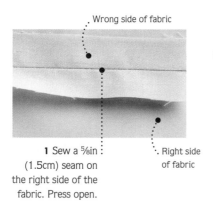

Wrong side of fabric

Right side of fabric

1 Sew a ⅝in (1.5cm) seam on the right side of the fabric. Press open.

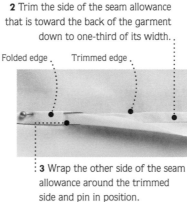

2 Trim the side of the seam allowance that is toward the back of the garment down to one-third of its width.

Folded edge   Trimmed edge

3 Wrap the other side of the seam allowance around the trimmed side and pin in position.

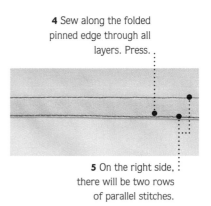

4 Sew along the folded pinned edge through all layers. Press.

5 On the right side, there will be two rows of parallel stitches.

✕ TOP-STITCH SEAM

A top-stitch seam is very useful, as it is both
decorative and practical. This seam is often used
on crafts and home goods, as well as garments.

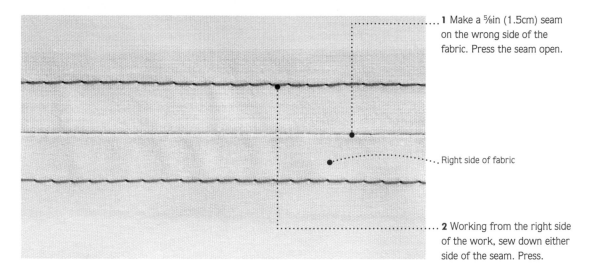

1 Make a ⅝in (1.5cm) seam
on the wrong side of the
fabric. Press the seam open.

Right side of fabric

2 Working from the right side
of the work, sew down either
side of the seam. Press.

✕ LAPPED SEAM

Also called an overlaid seam, a lapped seam is
constructed on the right side of the garment. It
is a very flat seam when it is finished.

1 Press under ⅝in (1.5cm) on one side of
the seamline to the wrong side.

Wrong side
of fabric

3 Sew close to the fold.

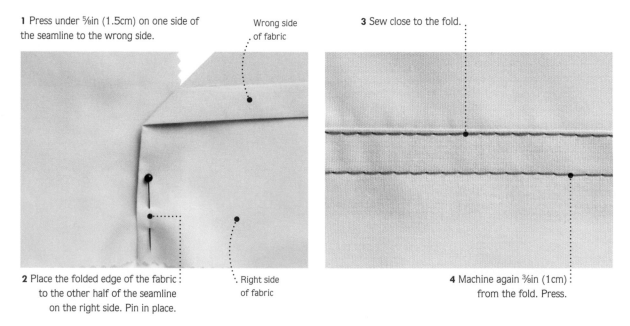

2 Place the folded edge of the fabric
to the other half of the seamline
on the right side. Pin in place.

Right side
of fabric

4 Machine again ⅜in (1cm)
from the fold. Press.

✕ SEWING CORNERS AND CURVES

Not all sewing is straight lines. Most items will have curves and corners that require negotiation to produce sharp, clean angles and curves on the right side. The technique for sewing a corner shown below applies to corners of all angles. On a thick fabric, the technique is slightly different, with a stitch taken across the corner, and on a fabric that frays badly, the corner is reinforced with a second line of stitches.

SEWING A CORNER

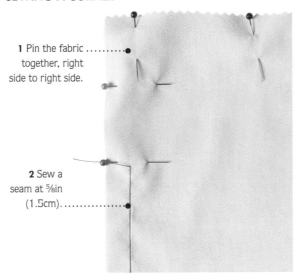

1 Pin the fabric together, right side to right side.

2 Sew a seam at ⅝in (1.5cm).

3 On reaching the corner, insert the machine needle into the fabric.

4 Raise the presser foot and turn the fabric through 90 degrees. (This is pivoting at the corner.)

5 Lower the presser foot and continue sewing in the other direction.

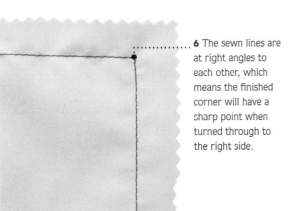

6 The sewn lines are at right angles to each other, which means the finished corner will have a sharp point when turned through to the right side.

SEWING A CORNER ON HEAVY FABRIC

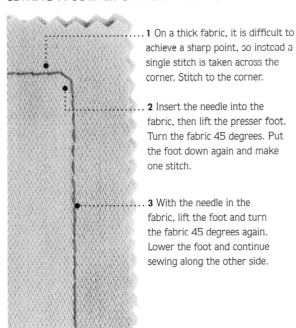

1 On a thick fabric, it is difficult to achieve a sharp point, so instead a single stitch is taken across the corner. Stitch to the corner.

2 Insert the needle into the fabric, then lift the presser foot. Turn the fabric 45 degrees. Put the foot down again and make one stitch.

3 With the needle in the fabric, lift the foot and turn the fabric 45 degrees again. Lower the foot and continue sewing along the other side.

SEWING A REINFORCED CORNER

1 On the wrong side of the fabric, sew along one side of the corner to make a ⅝in (1.5cm) seam.

2 Sew through to the edge of the fabric.

3 Sew the other side of the corner at a ⅝in (1.5cm) seam allowance, again sewing through the edge of the fabric.

6 Rip the surplus stitches in the seam allowance.

4 The two sewn lines will overlap at the corner.

5 Sew exactly over the first two sewn lines, this time pivoting at the corner (see Sewing a corner, steps 3–5, p.59).

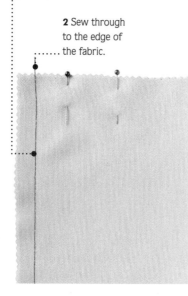

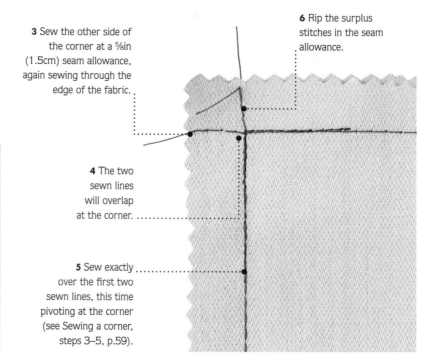

SEWING AN INNER CORNER

1 Sew accurately at ⅝in (1.5cm) from the edge, pivoting at the corner (see Sewing a corner, steps 3–5, p.59).

2 Clip through the seam allowance into the corner.

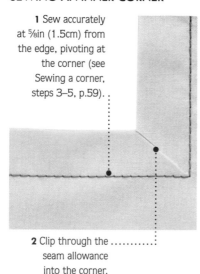

SEWING AN INNER CURVE

1 Place the right sides of the fabric together.

2 Sew a seam at ⅝in (1.5cm) from the edge. Be sure the sewn line follows the curve (use the stitch guides on the plate of the machine to help).

SEWING AN OUTER CURVE

1 Put the right sides of the fabric together and stitch a ⅝in (1.5cm) seam.

2 Follow the curve and keep the sewing line at a uniform distance from the edge.

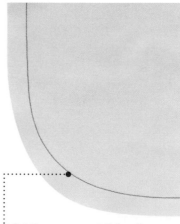

REDUCING SEAM BULK

It is important that the seams used for construction do not cause bulk on the right side. To make sure this does not happen, the seam allowances need to be reduced in size by a technique known as layering a seam. They may also require V shapes to be removed, which is known as notching, or the seam allowance may be clipped.

▶◁ LAYERING A SEAM

On the majority of fabrics, if the seam is on the edge of the work, the fabric in the seam needs reducing. The seam allowance closest to the outside of the garment or item stays full width, while the seam allowance closest to the body or inside is reduced.

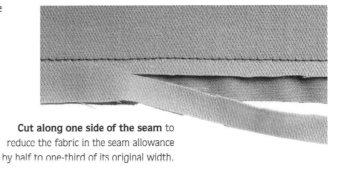

Cut along one side of the seam to reduce the fabric in the seam allowance by half to one-third of its original width.

▶◁ REDUCING SEAM BULK ON AN INNER CURVE

For an inner curve to lie flat, the seam will need to be layered and notched, then understitched to hold it in place (see p.62).

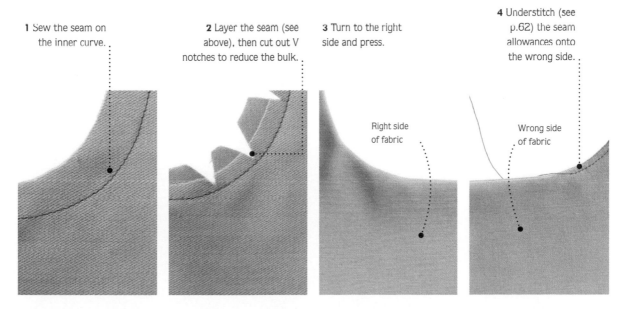

1 Sew the seam on the inner curve.

2 Layer the seam (see above), then cut out V notches to reduce the bulk.

3 Turn to the right side and press.

Right side of fabric

4 Understitch (see p.62) the seam allowances onto the wrong side.

Wrong side of fabric

▶◀ REDUCING SEAM BULK ON AN OUTER CURVE

An outer curve also needs layering and notching or clipping to allow the fabric to turn to the right side, after which it is understitched.

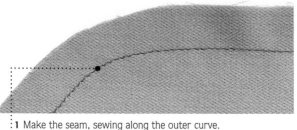

1 Make the seam, sewing along the outer curve.

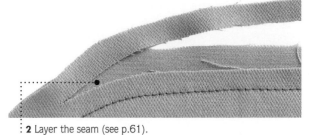

2 Layer the seam (see p.61).

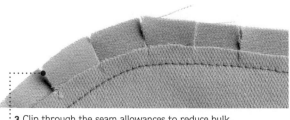

3 Clip through the seam allowances to reduce bulk.

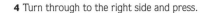

Right side of fabric

4 Turn through to the right side and press.

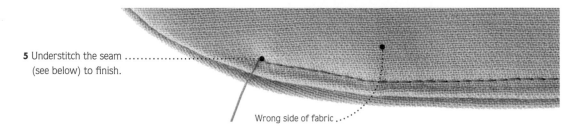

5 Understitch the seam (see below) to finish.

Wrong side of fabric

▶◀ SEWN FINISHES

Top-stitching and understitching are two methods to finish edges. Top-stitching is meant to be seen on the right side of the work, whereas understitching is not visible from the right side.

TOP-STITCHING

A top-stitch is a decorative, sharp finish to an edge. Use a longer stitch length, of 3.0 or 3.5, and machine on the right side of the work, using the edge of the machine foot as a guide.

UNDERSTITCHING

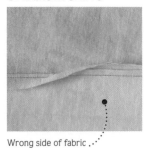

Wrong side of fabric

Understitching is used to secure a seam that is on the edge of a piece of fabric. It helps to stop the seam from rolling to the right side. First make the seam, then layer, turn, and press onto the right side. Open the seam flat again and push the seam allowance to the wrong side. Sew the seam allowance down.

⋊ SEAMS ON DIFFICULT FABRICS

Some fabrics require special care for seam construction because they are very bulky, as you find with a fur fabric, or so soft and delicate that they appear too soft to sew. On a sheer fabric, the seam used is an alternative to a French seam; it is very narrow when finished and presses very flat. Making a seam on suede is done by means of a lapped seam. As some suede-effect fabric has a fake fur on the other side, the seam is reversible.

A SEAM ON SHEER FABRIC

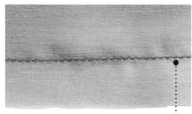

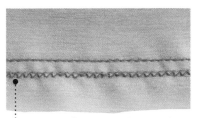

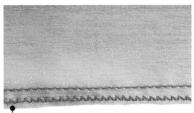

1 On the wrong side of the work, make a ⅝in (1.5cm) seam.

2 Sew again ³⁄₁₆in (5mm) from the first line of stitches, using either a very narrow zigzag stitch or a stretch stitch. Press.

3 Trim the raw edge of the fabric close to the second row of stitches.

A SEAM ON SUEDE OR SUEDE-EFFECT FABRIC

1 On all seams, trace baste the seamline ⅝in (1.5cm) from the edge.

2 Trace baste again ⅝in (1.5cm) away from the first row of stitching.

3 Overlap one side of the seam over the other, matching the ⅝in (1.5cm) baste lines. The raw edge should touch the second row of bastes.

5 Sew again ⅜in (1cm) from the first line of stitches.

6 Trim the raw edge by about ⅛in (3mm).

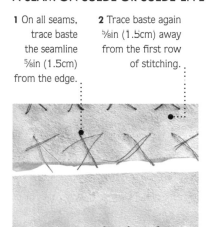

4 Using a walking foot and a longer than normal stitch length of 3.5, sew the two layers together along the bastes marking the ⅝in (1.5cm) seam allowance.

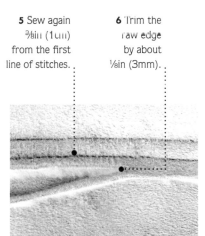

A SEAM ON FUR FABRIC

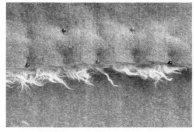

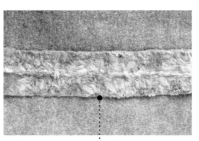

1 Pin the fabric together right side to right side, placing the pins in alternate directions to stop the fur moving.

2 Using a walking foot and a longer than normal stitch length, sew the seam.

3 Finger press the seam open.

4 Trim the surplus fur fabric off the seam allowances.

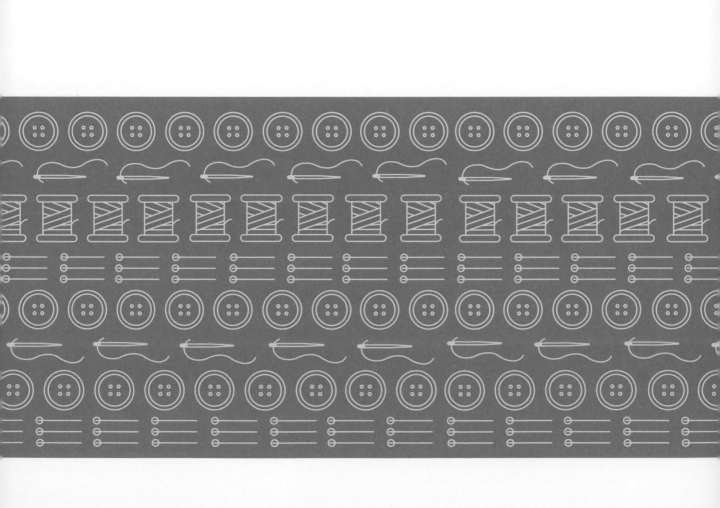

PATTERNS

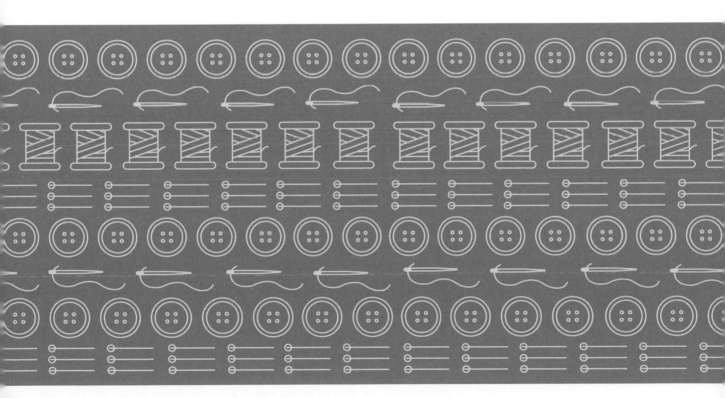

READING PATTERNS

Paper patterns are available for clothing, crafts, and home furnishings. A pattern has three main components: the envelope, the pattern, and the instructions. The envelope gives an illustration of the item together with fabric suggestions and requirements. The pattern sheets inside the envelope contain a wealth of information, while the instructions tell you how to construct the item.

READING A PATTERN ENVELOPE

The envelope front illustrates the finished item that can be made from its contents. This may be a line drawing or a photograph. Different versions will be labeled as views. The back of the envelope usually depicts an illustration of the back view and the body measurement chart used for that pattern. There is also a chart to help you purchase the correct amount of fabric. Suitable fabrics are also listed alongside "notions," or haberdashery. Smaller independent pattern companies may list this information differently.

Number of pattern pieces

Code number for ordering

Description of garment or item, giving details of style and different views included in pattern

List of pattern sizes in imperial and metric measurements for bust, waist, and hips in each size

Suggested fabrics suitable for garment or item, as well as unsuitable fabrics

Notions required for each view

5678
15 pieces

MISSES' UNLINED JACKET, SKIRT, SHORTS, AND PANTS. Unlined, semifitted, V-neck jacket has short sleeves, front buttons, optional waistline darts, and optional breast pocket. Straight skirt, above midknee, and pants or shorts with straight legs, have waistband, front pleats, side seam pockets, and back zipper.

FABRICS: Jacket, skirt, shorts, and pants: wool crepe, soft cottons, sheeting, linen, silk, silk types, and lightweight woolens. Skirt, shorts, and pants also challis, jacquards, and crepe. Unsuitable for fabrics printed with obvious diagonals. Allow extra fabric in order to match plaids, stripes, or one-way design fabrics.

Use nap yardages/layouts for shaded, pile, or one-way design fabrics. *with nap. ** without nap
NOTIONS: Thread. Jacket: three ⅞ in (1.2 cm) buttons; ¼ in (6 mm) shoulder pads. Skirt, pants: pkg of 1¼ in (3.2 cm) waistband interfacing; 7 in (18 cm) zipper; and one hook and one hook and eye closure.

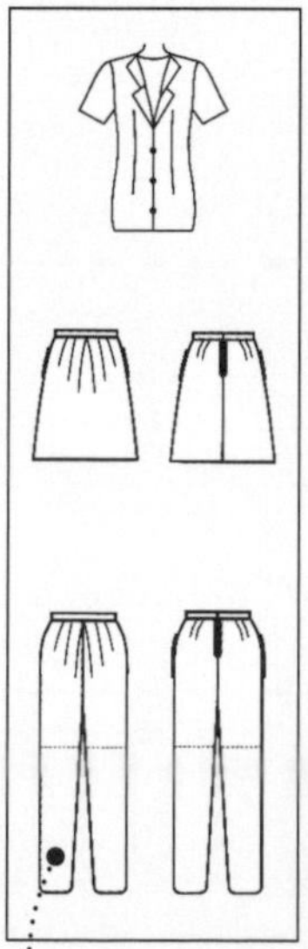

METRIC

Body measurements	(6	8	10)	(12	14	16)	(18	20	22)
Bust	78	80	83	87	92	97	102	107	112 cm
Waist	58	61	63.5	66	71	76	81	86	94 cm
Hip	81	84	86	91	96.5	102	107	112	117 cm

Fabric needed		(6	8	10)	(12	14	16)	(18	20	22)
Jacket	115 cm*/**	1.70	1.70	1.70	1.80	1.80	2.10	2.20	2.20	2.20 m
	150 cm*/**	1.30	1.30	1.30	1.40	1.70	1.70	1.70	1.80	1.80 m
Interfacing	1 m of 55–90 cm lightweight fusible or nonfusible									
Skirt A	115 cm*/**	1.6	1.6	1.6	1.6	1.9	1.9	1.9	1.9	2 m
	150 cm*/**	1.2	1.2	1.3	1.3	1.3	1.3	1.4	1.4	1.5 m
Shorts B	115 cm*/**	1.6	1.6	1.6	1.6	1.9	1.9	1.9	1.9	2 m
	150 cm*/**	1.2	1.2	1.3	1.3	1.3	1.3	1.4	1.4	1.5 m
Pants B	115 cm*/**	2.4	2.4	2.4	2.4	2.4	2.4	2.4	2.7	2.7 m
	150 cm*	2	2	22	2.1	2.1	2.2	2.3	2.3 m	
	150 cm**	1.6	1.6	1.8	2 2	2.1	2.2	2.3	2.3 m	

Garment measurements	(6	8	10)	(12	14	16)	(18	20	22)
Jacket bust	92	94.5	97	101	106	111	116	121	126 cm
Jacket waist	81	83	86	89.5	94.5	100	105	110	116 cm
Jacket back length	73	73.5	74	75	75.5	76	77	77.5	78 cm
Skirt A lower edge	99	101	104	106	112	117	122	127	132 cm
Skirt A length	61	61	61	63	63	63	65	65	65 cm
Shorts B leg width	71	73.5	76	81	86.5	94	99	104	109 cm
Shorts B side length	49.5	50	51	51.5	52	52.5	53.5	54	54.5 cm
Pants B leg width	53.5	53.5	56	56	58.5	58.5	61	61	63.5 cm
Pants B side length	103	103	103	103	103	103	103	103	103 cm

IMPERIAL

Body measurements	(6	8	10)	(12	14	16)	(18	20	22)
Bust	30½	31½	32½	34	36	38	40	42	44 in
Waist	23	24	25	26½	28	30	32	34	37 in
Hip	32½	33½	34½	36	38	40	42	44	46 in

Fabric needed		(6	8	10)	(12	14	16)	(18	20	22)
Jacket	45 in*/**	1⅞	1⅞	1⅞	1⅞	2	2⅜	2⅜	2⅜	2⅜ yd
	60 in*/**	1⅜	1⅜	1⅜	1½	1⅞	1⅞	1⅞	1⅞	2 yd
Interfacing	1⅛ yd of 22–36 in lightweight fusible or nonfusible									
Skirt A	45 in*/**	1¾	1⅞	1⅞	1⅞	2	2	2	2	2⅛ yd
	60 in*/**	1¼	1¼	1⅜	1⅜	1⅜	1⅜	1½	1½	1⅝ yd
Shorts B	45 in*/**	1¾	1¾	1¾	1¾	2	2	2	2	2⅛ yd
	60 in*/**	1¼	1¼	1⅜	1⅜	1⅜	1⅜	1½	1½	1⅝ yd
Pants B	45 in*/**	2⅝	2⅝	2⅝	2⅝	2⅝	2⅝	2⅝	2⅞	2⅞ yd
	60 in*	2⅛	2⅛	2⅛	2⅛	2¼	2¼	2⅜	2½	2½ yd
	60 in **	1¾	1¾	1⅞	2⅛	2⅛	2¼	2⅜	2½	2½ yd

Garment measurements	(6	8	10)	(12	14	16)	(18	20	22)
Jacket bust	36¼	37¼	38¼	39¾	41¾	43¾	45¼	47¾	49¾ in
Jacket waist	31¾	32¾	33¾	35¼	37¼	39¼	41¼	43¼	45¼ in
Jacket back length	28¾	29	29¼	29½	29¾	30	30¼	30½	30¾ in
Skirt A lower edge	39	40	41	42	44	46	48	50	52 in
Skirt A length	24	24	24	24¾	24¾	24¾	25½	25½	25½ in
Shorts B leg width	28	29	30	32	34	37	39	41	43 in
Shorts B side length	19½	19¾	20	20¼	20½	20¾	21	21¼	21½ in
Pants B leg width	21	21	22	22	23	23	24	24	25 in
Pants B side length	40½	40½	40½	40½	40½	40½	40½	40½	40½ in

Outline drawing of garment or item, including back views, with darts and zipper positions

Garment measurements box gives actual size of finished garment

Chart to follow for required fabric quantity, indicating size across top, and chosen view and correct width down the side

SINGLE-SIZE PATTERNS

Some patterns contain a garment or craft project of one size only. If you are using a single-size pattern, cut around the tissue on the thick black cutting line before making any alterations.

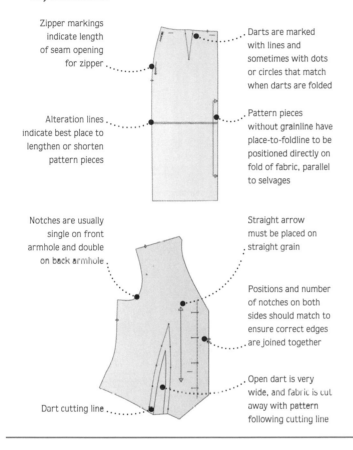

Zipper markings indicate length of seam opening for zipper

Darts are marked with lines and sometimes with dots or circles that match when darts are folded

Alteration lines indicate best place to lengthen or shorten pattern pieces

Pattern pieces without grainline have place-to-foldline to be positioned directly on fold of fabric, parallel to selvages

Notches are usually single on front armhole and double on back armhole

Straight arrow must be placed on straight grain

Positions and number of notches on both sides should match to ensure correct edges are joined together

Open dart is very wide, and fabric is cut away with pattern following cutting line

Dart cutting line

MULTISIZE PATTERNS

Many patterns today have more than one size printed on the tissue. Each size is clearly labeled, and the cutting lines are marked with a different type of line for each size.

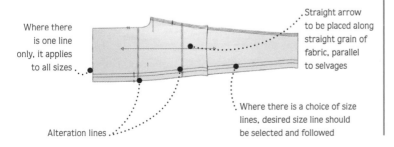

Where there is one line only, it applies to all sizes

Straight arrow to be placed along straight grain of fabric, parallel to selvages

Where there is a choice of size lines, desired size line should be selected and followed

Alteration lines

PATTERN MARKINGS

Each pattern piece will have a series of lines, dots, and other symbols printed on it. These symbols are to help you alter the pattern and join the pattern pieces together.

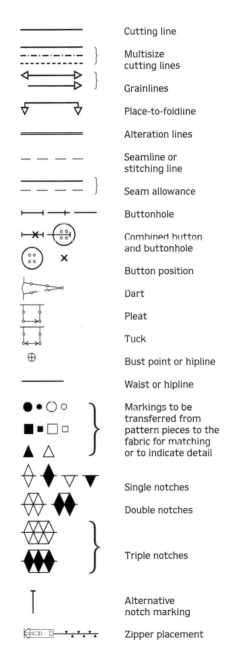

Symbol	Meaning
	Cutting line
	Multisize cutting lines
	Grainlines
	Place-to-foldline
	Alteration lines
	Seamline or stitching line
	Seam allowance
	Buttonhole
	Combined button and buttonhole
	Button position
	Dart
	Pleat
	Tuck
	Bust point or hipline
	Waist or hipline
	Markings to be transferred from pattern pieces to the fabric for matching or to indicate detail
	Single notches
	Double notches
	Triple notches
	Alternative notch marking
	Zipper placement

BODY MEASURING

Accurate body measurements are needed to determine the correct pattern size to use and if any alterations are required. Pattern sizes are usually chosen by the hip or bust measurement.

For tops, follow the bust measurement; for skirts or pants, use the hip measurement. If you are choosing a dress pattern, go by whichever measurement is the largest.

TAKING BODY MEASUREMENTS

1 You'll need a tape measure and ruler, as well as a helper for some of the measuring, and a hard chair or stool.

2 Wear underwear that fits you well, especially a well-fitting bra.

3 Tie a piece of elastic or ribbon snugly around your waist prior to taking any measurements. The elastic will find your natural waist, which may not be where you think it is.

4 Do not wear any shoes.

HOW TO MEASURE YOUR HEIGHT

Most paper patterns are designed for a woman 5ft 5in to 5ft 6in (165 to 168cm). If you are shorter or taller than this, you may need to adjust the pattern prior to cutting out your fabric.

1 Remove your shoes.

2 Stand straight, with your back against the wall.

3 Place a ruler flat on your head, touching the wall, and mark the wall at this point.

4 Step away and measure the distance from the floor to the marked point.

CHEST

Measure above the bust, high under the arms, keeping the tape measure flat and straight across the back.

FULL BUST

Make sure you are wearing a well-fitting bra and measure over the fullest part of the bust. If your cup size is in excess of a B, you will probably need to do a bust alteration, although some patterns are now cut to accommodate larger cup sizes.

WAIST

This is the measurement around the smallest part of your waist. Wrap the tape around first to find your natural waist, then measure.

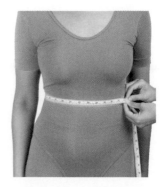

HIPS

This measurement must be taken around the fullest part of the hips, between the waist and legs.

HIGH HIP

Take this just below the waist and just above the hip bones to give a measurement across the stomach.

SHOULDER

Hold the end of the tape measure at the base of your neck (where a necklace would lie) and measure to the dent at the end of your shoulder. To find this dent, raise your arm slightly.

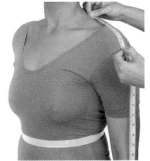

NECK

Measure around the neck—snugly but not too tight—to determine collar size.

ARM

Bend your elbow and place your hand on your hip, then measure from the end of the shoulder over the elbow to the wrist bone.

BACK WAIST

Take this measurement down the center of the back, from the bumpy bit at the top of the spine, in line with the shoulders, to the waist.

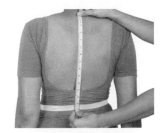

OUTSIDE LEG

Measure the side of the leg from the waist, over the hip, and straight down the leg to the ankle bone.

INSIDE LEG

Stand with your legs apart and measure the inside of one leg from the crotch to the ankle bone.

CROTCH DEPTH

Sit upright on a hard chair or stool and measure from the waist vertically down to the chair.

CUTTING OUT

Cutting out correctly can make or break your project. But first you need to examine the fabric in the store, looking for any flaws, such as a crooked pattern, and checking to see if the fabric has been cut properly from the roll—that is at a right angle to the selvage. If not, you will need to straighten the edge. If the fabric is creased, press it; if washable, wash it to avoid shrinkage later. After this preparation, you will be ready to lay the pattern pieces on the fabric, pin in place, and cut out.

▶ FABRIC GRAIN AND NAP

It is important that the pattern pieces are cut on the correct grain, as this will make the fabric hang correctly and produce a longer-lasting item. The grain of the fabric is the direction in which the yarns or threads that make up the fabric lie. The majority of pattern pieces need to be placed with the straight of grain symbol running parallel to the warp yarn. Some fabrics have a nap due to the pile, which means the fabric shadows when it is smoothed in one direction. A fabric with a one-way design or uneven stripes is also described as being with nap. Fabrics with nap are generally cut out with the nap running down, whereas those without nap can be cut out either way.

GRAIN ON WOVEN FABRICS

The selvage is the woven, nonfrayable edge that runs parallel to the warp grain.

Yarns that run the length of the fabric are called warp yarns. They are stronger than weft yarns and less likely to stretch.

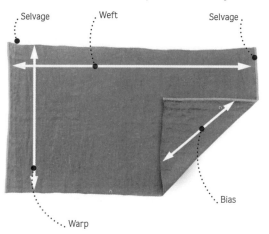

Selvage   Weft   Selvage

Warp

Bias

Weft yarns run crossways, over and under the warp yarns.

The bias grain is diagonal—running at 45 degrees to the warp and weft. A garment cut on the bias will follow the contours of the body.

GRAIN ON KNITTED FABRICS

A knitted fabric also has a grain. Some knit fabrics stretch only one way while others stretch in both directions. Patterns for knit fabrics often need to be cut following the direction of the greatest stretch.

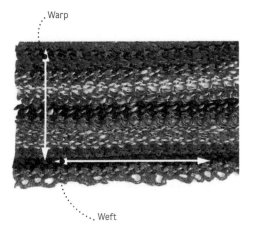

Warp

Weft

NAP DUE TO PILE

Fabrics such as velvet (shown here), corduroy, and velour will show a difference in color, depending on whether the nap is running up or down.

NAP IF ONE-WAY DESIGN

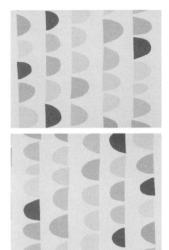

A one-way pattern that runs lengthwise in the fabric will be upside-down on one side if the pieces are cut when the fabric is folded across the warp grainline.

NAP IF STRIPED

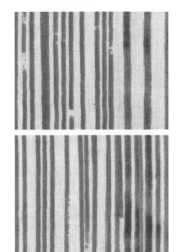

If the stripes do not match on both sides when the fabric is folded across the warp grainline, they are uneven and the fabric will need a nap layout.

✂ PATTERN PREPARATION

Before cutting out, sort out all the pattern pieces that are required for the item you are making. Check them to see if any have special cutting instructions. Make pattern alterations, if necessary. If there are no alterations, just trim patterns to your size.

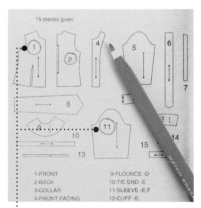

1 Using the pattern instruction sheet, which has drawings of the pattern pieces, select the pieces you require.

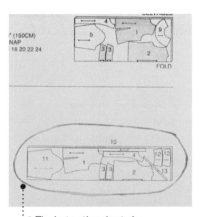

2 The instruction sheet also shows a suggested cutting-out layout for the item you are making, on different widths of fabric, with or without nap.

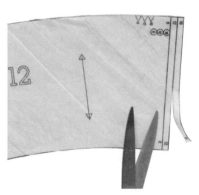

3 Trim multisize pattern pieces according to the chosen size.

▶< PATTERN LAYOUT

Fabric is usually folded selvage to selvage. With the fabric folded, the pattern is pinned on top, and both the right and left side pieces are cut at the same time. If pattern pieces have to be cut from single layer fabric, remember to cut matching pairs. For a fabric with a design, it is a good idea to have this on the outside so that you can arrange the pattern pieces to show off the design. If you have left and right side pattern pieces, they are cut on single fabric with the fabric right side up and the pattern pieces right side up.

PINNING THE PATTERN TO THE FABRIC

1 The "to fold" symbol indicates the pattern piece is to be pinned carefully to the folded edge of the fabric.

2 To check the straight of grain on the other pattern pieces, place the grain arrow so that it looks parallel to the selvage, then pin to secure at one end of the arrow.

3 Measure from the pinned end to the selvage.

4 Measure from the other end of the arrow to the selvage.

5 Move the pattern piece slightly until this measurement is the same as the pinned end, then pin in place.

6 Once it is straight, pin around the rest of the pattern piece, placing pins in the seam allowances.

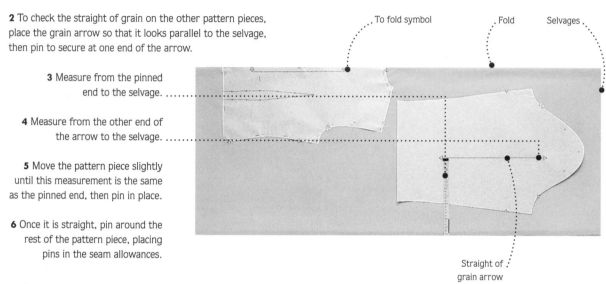

To fold symbol · Fold · Selvages ·

Straight of · grain arrow

GENERAL GUIDE TO LAYOUT

On single layer fabrics

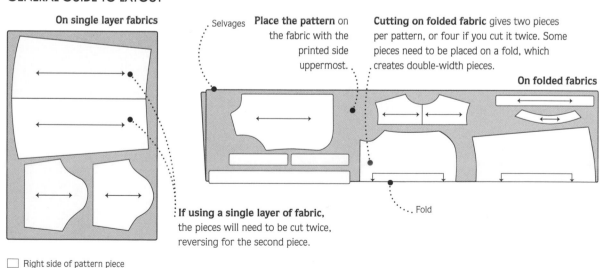

Selvages

Place the pattern on the fabric with the printed side uppermost.

Cutting on folded fabric gives two pieces per pattern, or four if you cut it twice. Some pieces need to be placed on a fold, which creates double-width pieces.

On folded fabrics

If using a single layer of fabric, the pieces will need to be cut twice, reversing for the second piece.

Fold

☐ Right side of pattern piece
☐ Wrong side of pattern piece

LAYOUT FOR FABRICS WITH A NAP OR A ONE-WAY DESIGN

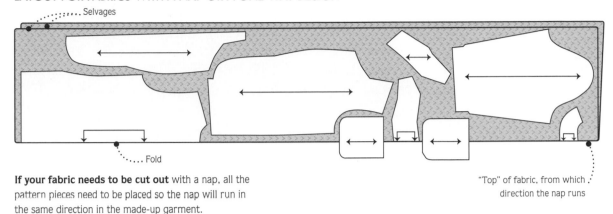

Selvages

Fold

"Top" of fabric, from which direction the nap runs

If your fabric needs to be cut out with a nap, all the pattern pieces need to be placed so the nap will run in the same direction in the made-up garment.

LAYOUT ON A CROSSWISE FOLD

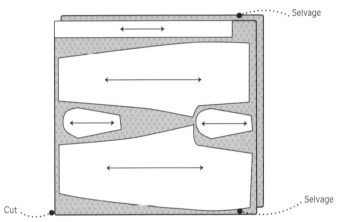

Selvage

Fold

Selvage

Occasionally a fabric is folded across the grain. This is usually done to accommodate very large pattern pieces.

LAYOUT ON A CROSSWISE FOLD WITH A NAP

Selvage

Selvage

Cut

If a crosswise fold is required in a fabric with a nap, fold the fabric with the wrong sides together, then cut into two pieces. Turn one around to make sure that the nap is running in the same direction on both pieces. Place the two pieces of fabric together, wrong side to wrong side.

LAYOUT ON A PARTIAL FOLD

The fabric is folded partway to enable you to cut some pattern pieces on a fold and the remainder from single fabric.

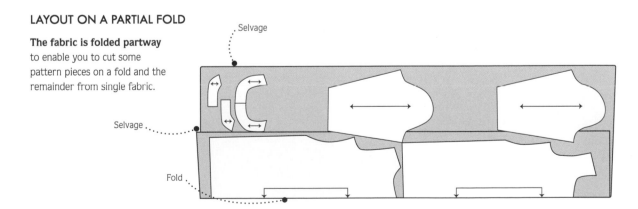

Selvage

Selvage

Fold

◥ STRIPES AND PLAID

For fabrics with a stripe or plaid pattern, a little more care is needed when laying out the pattern pieces. If the stripes and plaid are running across or down the length of the fabric when cutting out, they will run the same direction in the finished garment. So it is important to place the pattern pieces to ensure that the plaid and stripes match and that they run together at the seams. If possible, try to place the pattern pieces so each has a stripe down the center. With plaid, be aware of the hemline placement on the pattern.

EVEN STRIPES

When a corner of the fabric is folded back diagonally, the stripes will meet up at the fold.

UNEVEN STRIPES

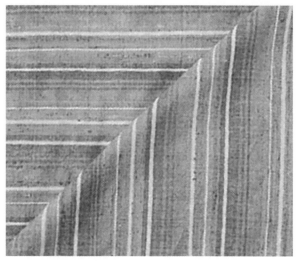

When a corner of the fabric is folded back diagonally, the stripes will not match at the fold.

EVEN PLAID

When a corner is folded back diagonally, the plaid will be symmetrical on both of the fabric areas.

UNEVEN PLAID

When a corner of the fabric is folded back diagonally, the plaid will be uneven lengthwise, widthwise, or both.

LAYOUT FOR EVEN PLAID ON FOLDED FABRIC

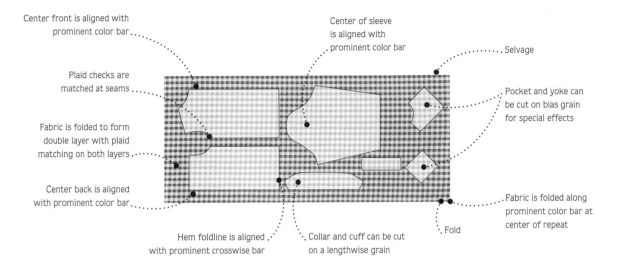

Center front is aligned with prominent color bar

Center of sleeve is aligned with prominent color bar

Selvage

Plaid checks are matched at seams

Pocket and yoke can be cut on bias grain for special effects

Fabric is folded to form double layer with plaid matching on both layers

Center back is aligned with prominent color bar

Fabric is folded along prominent color bar at center of repeat

Hem foldline is aligned with prominent crosswise bar

Collar and cuff can be cut on a lengthwise grain

Fold

LAYOUT FOR EVEN STRIPES ON FOLDED FABRIC

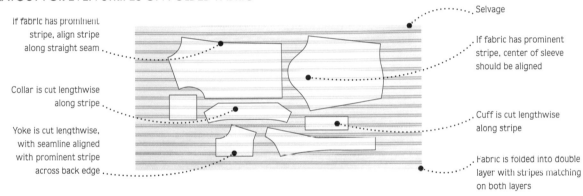

If fabric has prominent stripe, align stripe along straight seam

Selvage

If fabric has prominent stripe, center of sleeve should be aligned

Collar is cut lengthwise along stripe

Cuff is cut lengthwise along stripe

Yoke is cut lengthwise, with seamline aligned with prominent stripe across back edge

Fabric is folded into double layer with stripes matching on both layers

LAYOUT FOR UNEVEN PLAID OR STRIPES ON UNFOLDED FABRIC

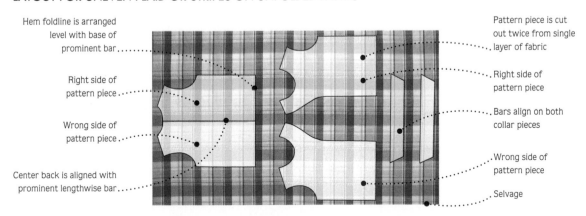

Hem foldline is arranged level with base of prominent bar

Pattern piece is cut out twice from single layer of fabric

Right side of pattern piece

Right side of pattern piece

Wrong side of pattern piece

Bars align on both collar pieces

Center back is aligned with prominent lengthwise bar

Wrong side of pattern piece

Selvage

MATCHING STRIPES OR PLAID ON A SKIRT

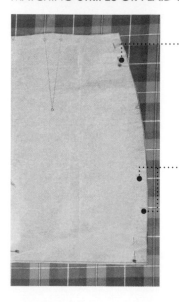

1 Place one of the skirt pattern pieces on the fabric and pin in place.

2 Mark on the tissue the position of the boldest lines of the plaid or stripes.

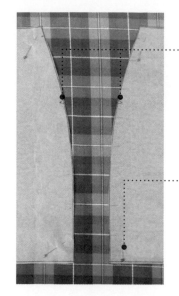

3 Place the adjoining skirt pattern piece alongside, with notches matching and side seams even. Transfer the marks across.

4 Move the second pattern piece away, matching up the bold lines, and pin it in place.

MATCHING STRIPES OR PLAID AT THE SHOULDER

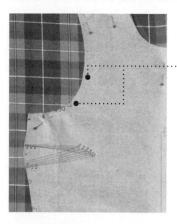

1 Mark the boldest lines of the stripes or plaid around the armhole on the front bodice pattern.

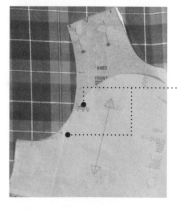

2 Place the sleeve pattern onto the armhole, matching the notches, and copy the marks onto the sleeve pattern.

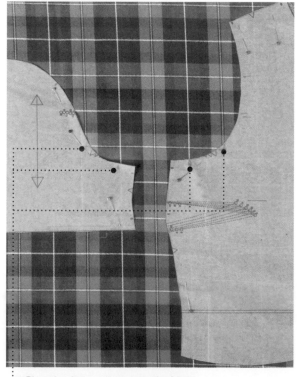

3 Place the sleeve pattern onto the fabric, matching the marks to the corresponding bold lines, and pin in place.

►< CUTTING OUT ACCURATELY

Careful, smooth cutting around the pattern pieces will ensure that they join together accurately. Always cut out on a smooth, flat surface such as a table—the floor is not ideal—and be sure your scissors are sharp. Use the full blade of the scissors on long, straight edges, sliding the blades along the fabric; use smaller cuts around curves. Do not nibble or snip at the fabric.

HOW TO CUT

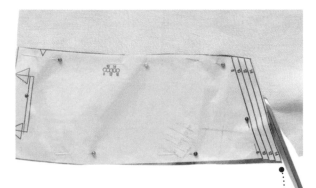

If you are right-handed, place your left hand on the pattern and fabric to hold them in place, and cut cleanly with the scissor blades at a right angle to the fabric.

MARKING DOTS

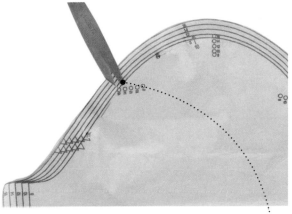

You can cut a small clip into the fabric to mark the dots that indicate the top of the shoulder on a sleeve. Alternatively, these can be marked with tailor's tacks (see p.78).

MARKING NOTCHES

These symbols need to be marked onto the fabric, as they are matching points. One of the easiest ways to do this is to cut the mirror image of the notches out into the fabric. Rather than cutting out each notch separately, cut straight across from point to point.

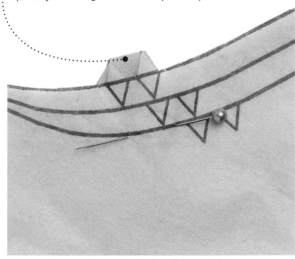

CLIPPING LINES

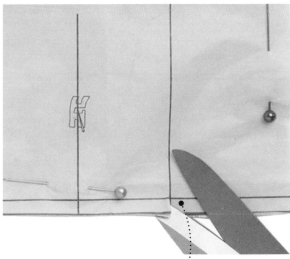

A small clip or snip into the fabric is a useful way to mark some of the lines that appear on a pattern, such as the center front line and foldlines.

◄ PATTERN MARKING

Once the pattern pieces have been cut out, you will need to mark the symbols shown on the tissue through to the fabric. There are various methods to do this. Tailor's tacks are good for circles and dots, or mark these with a water/ air-soluble pen. (When using a pen, it's a good idea to test it on a piece of scrap fabric first.) For lines, you can use trace basting or a tracing wheel with dressmaker's carbon paper.

TAILOR'S TACKS

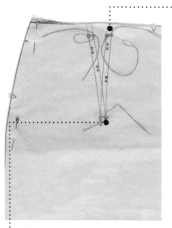

1 As there are often dots of different sizes, it is a good idea to choose a different colored thread for each dot size. It is then easy to match the colors, as well as the dots. Have double thread in your needle, unknotted. Insert the needle through the dot from right to left, leaving a tail of thread. Be sure to go through the tissue and both layers of fabric.

2 Now stitch through the dot again, this time from top to bottom to make a loop. Cut through the loop, then snip off excess thread to leave a tail.

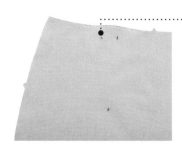

3 Carefully pull the pattern tissue away. On the top side, you will have four threads marking each dot. When you turn the fabric over, the dot positions will be marked with an X.

4 Gently turn back the two layers of fabric to separate them, then cut through the threads so that thread tails are left in both pieces of fabric.

TRACING PAPER AND WHEEL

1 This method is not suitable for all fabrics, as the marks may not be able to be removed easily. Slide dressmaker's carbon paper against the wrong side of the fabric.

2 Run a tracing wheel along the pattern lines. (A ruler will help you make straight lines.)

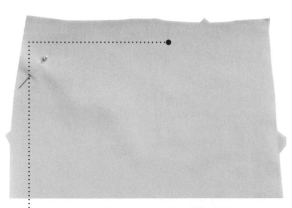

3 Remove the carbon paper and carefully pull off the pattern tissue. You will have dotted lines marked on your fabric.

MARKERS

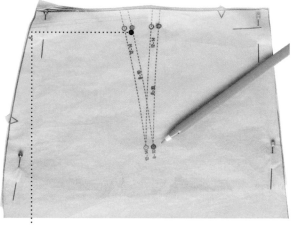 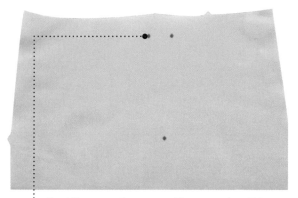

1 This method can only be used with a single layer of fabric. Press the point of the pen into the center of the dot marked on the pattern piece.

2 Carefully remove the pattern. The pen marks will have gone through the tissue onto the fabric. Be sure not to press the fabric before the pen marks are removed or they may become permanent.

TRACE TACKING

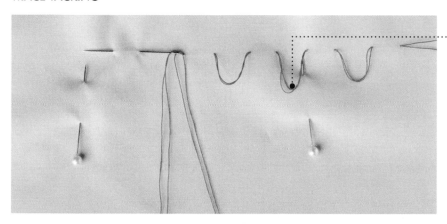

1 This is a really useful technique to mark center front lines, foldlines, and placement lines. With double thread in your needle, stitch a row of loopy stitches, sewing along the line marked on the pattern.

2 Carefully pull away the tissue. Cut through the loops, then gently separate the layers of fabric to show the threads. Snip apart to leave thread tails in both of the fabric layers.

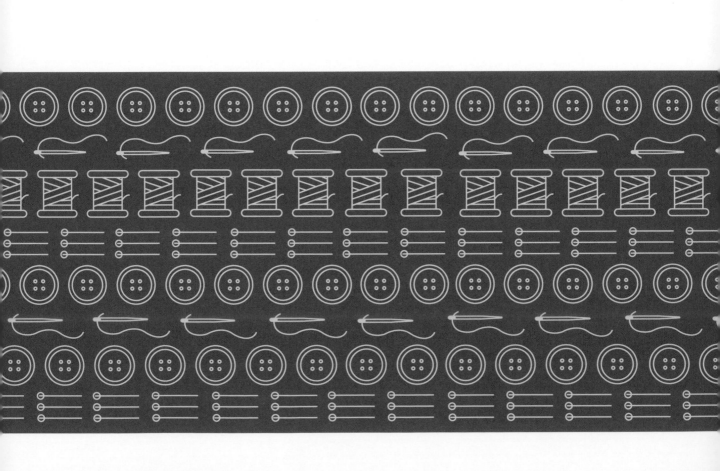

GATHERS, RUFFLES, TUCKS, DARTS, AND PLEATS

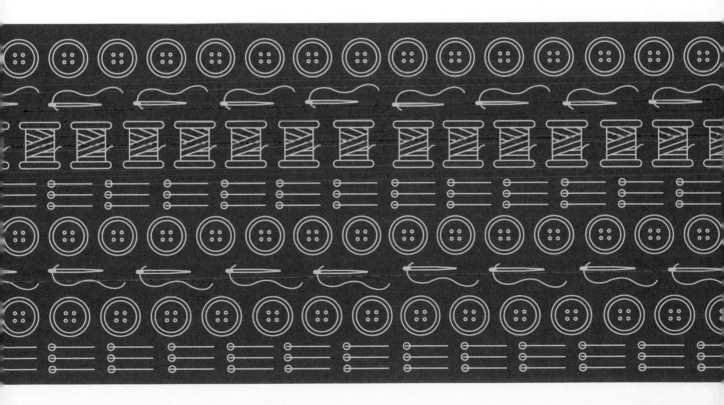

GATHERS

Gathers are an easy way to draw up a piece of larger fabric so that it will fit onto a smaller piece of fabric. The gather stitch is inserted after the major seams have been constructed, and it is best worked on the sewing machine using the longest stitch length that is available. On the majority of fabrics, two rows of gather stitches are required, but for very heavy fabrics, it is advisable to make three rows. Try to stitch the rows so that the stitches line up under one another.

►◄ DIRECTORY OF GATHERS

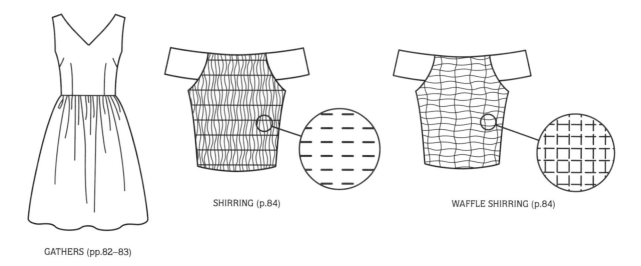

GATHERS (pp.82–83)

SHIRRING (p.84)

WAFFLE SHIRRING (p.84)

►◄ HOW TO MAKE AND FIT GATHERS

Once all the main seams have been sewn, stitch the two rows of gathers so that the stitches are inside the seam allowance. This should avoid the need to remove them, because removing gathers after they have been pulled up can damage the fabric.

1 Sew one row of gathers at ⅜in (1cm) and the second row at ½in (1.2cm) from the raw edge. Leave long tails of thread for gathering. Break the sewn lines at the seams.

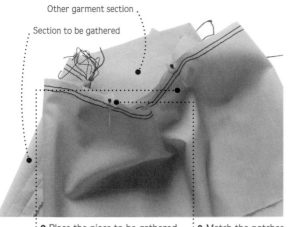

Other garment section

Section to be gathered

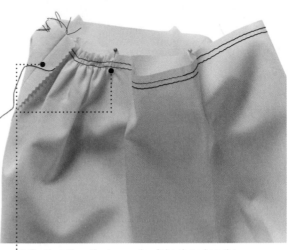

2 Place the piece to be gathered to the other garment section, right side to right side.

3 Match the notches and seams and pin these first.

4 Gently pull on the two ends of the thread on the wrong side—the fabric will gather along the thread.

5 Secure the threads at the one end to prevent the stitches from pulling out.

6 Even out the gathers and pin.

7 When all the gathers are in place, use a standard machine stitch to sew a ⅝in (1.5cm) wide seam.

8 Sew with the gathers uppermost and keep pulling them to the side to stop them from creasing up.

Seam pressed up

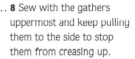

9 Turn the other garment section inside. Using a mini iron or the tip of a regular iron, press the seam very carefully to avoid creasing the gathers.

10 Neaten the seam by sewing both edges together. Use either a zigzag stitch or a 3-thread serger stitch.

11 Press the seam up.

12 Press the gathers using the mini iron or the tip of a regular iron.

⨯ SHIRRING

Shirring is the name given to multiple rows of gathers. It is an excellent way to give fullness in a garment. If made using shirring elastic in the bobbin, shirring gathers can stretch. On heavier fabrics, such as for home goods, static shirring is more suitable.

MACHINE SHIRRING

1 Hand wind shirring elastic onto the bobbin.

2 Insert the bobbin into the sewing machine and pull the elastic through the tension on the bobbin case. Use the all-purpose thread on the top.

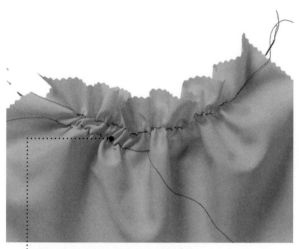

3 Set the machine to a stitch length of 5.0. Sew a row of machining across the fabric.

4 Sew a second row of machining, ⅝in (1.5cm) from seam. Make sure the rows of sewing are parallel.

WAFFLE SHIRRING

1 For this, two rows of shirring cross each other at right angles. Sew horizontal rows of shirring using shirring elastic in the bobbin (see above).

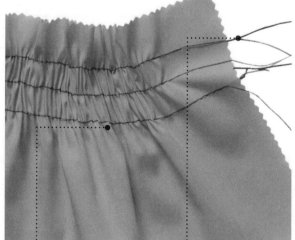

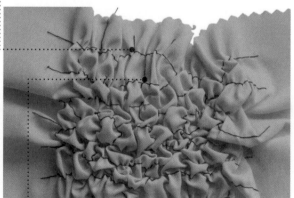

5 Continue sewing as many rows of shirring as required.

6 Knot the ends of the elastic together.

2 Cross these with vertical rows of shirring.

RUFFLES

Ruffles can be single layer or double layer and are used to give a decorative gathered effect to a garment. The amount of fullness in a ruffle depends on the fabric used—to achieve a similar result, a fine, thin fabric will need twice the fullness of a thicker fabric.

▶ DIRECTORY OF RUFFLES

PLAIN RUFFLE (p.85)

DOUBLE RUFFLE (p.86)

GATHERED RUFFLE (p.86)

▶ PLAIN RUFFLE

A plain ruffle is normally made from a single layer of fabric cut on the straight of the grain. The length of the fabric needs to be at least two and a half times the length of the seam into which it is to be inserted or of the edge to which it is to be attached. The width of the ruffle depends on where it is to be used.

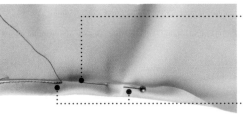

1 Turn under one long edge ³⁄₁₆in (5mm), then turn under again by the same amount.

2 Pin in place, then sew with a straight stitch.

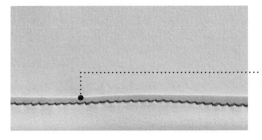

3 Press the sewn edge flat.

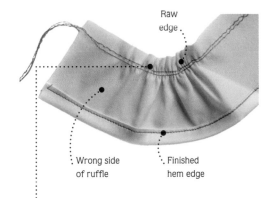

Raw edge

Wrong side of ruffle

Finished hem edge

4 Place two rows of gather stitches along the raw edge—one row at ³⁄₈in (1cm) and the second row at ½in (1.2cm). Pull the threads to gather the fabric. The ruffle is now ready to be attached.

⋈ DOUBLE RUFFLE

This is a useful ruffle on a fabric that is prone to fraying.

1 Cut the fabric for the ruffle twice the required depth.

2 Fold the fabric lengthwise, wrong side to wrong side.

3 Pin the raw edges together.

4 Insert gathers along the raw edge.

5 Pull up the gathers to fit.

⋈ GATHERED RUFFLE

This type of ruffle can give a decorative effect on clothing and home goods.

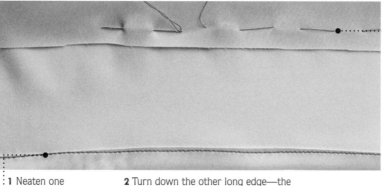

3 Baste the heading in place.

1 Neaten one long edge as for a plain ruffle (see steps 1–3, p.85).

2 Turn down the other long edge—the amount of the turn down is the depth of the required heading plus a seam allowance of ⅝in (1.5cm).

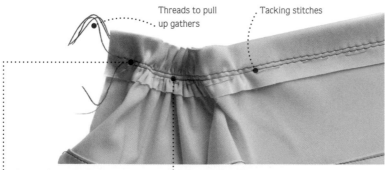

Threads to pull up gathers

Tacking stitches

4 Insert the two rows of gather stitches.

5 Pull up the stitches to make the gathers.

6 After gathering, there will be gathers with a ruffle on one side of the stitch line and a short gathered heading on the other. Pull out the basting stitches.

✂ SEWING A RUFFLE

Once the ruffle has been constructed, it can either be inserted into a seam or attached to the edge of the fabric (see p.88). The two techniques below apply to both single and double ruffles.

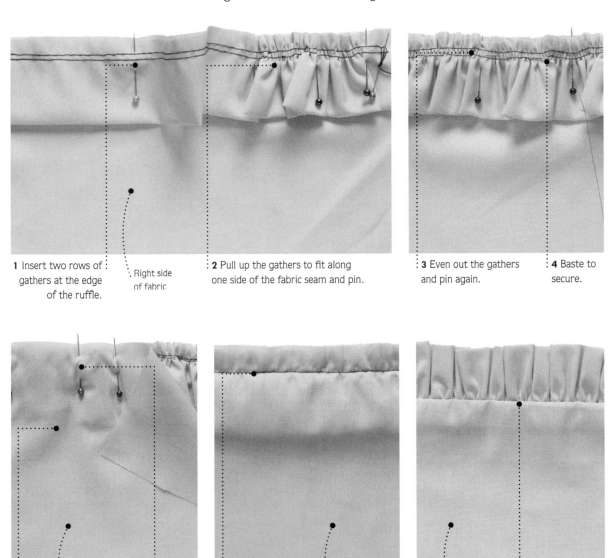

1 Insert two rows of gathers at the edge of the ruffle.

Right side of fabric

2 Pull up the gathers to fit along one side of the fabric seam and pin.

3 Even out the gathers and pin again.

4 Baste to secure.

5 Place the other piece of fabric over the ruffle, right side to right side.

Wrong side of fabric

6 Pin all the layers together.

7 Sew through all the layers using a ⅝in (1.5cm) seam allowance.

Wrong side of fabric

8 Layer the seam to reduce bulk.

Right side of fabric

9 Turn the fabric and ruffle through to the right side.

◄ SEWING A RUFFLE TO AN EDGE

If a ruffle is not in a seam, then it will be attached to an edge. The edge of the seam will require neatening, which is often best done by using a binding method, as it is more discreet. A self-bound edge, where the seam is wrapped onto itself, is suitable for fine, delicate fabrics. For thicker fabrics, use a bias binding to finish the edge.

SELF-BOUND FINISH

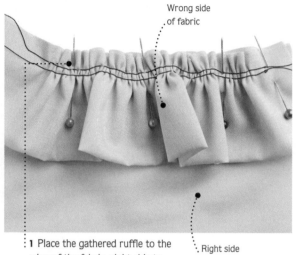

Wrong side of fabric

Right side of fabric

1 Place the gathered ruffle to the edge of the fabric, right side to right side. Pin in place.

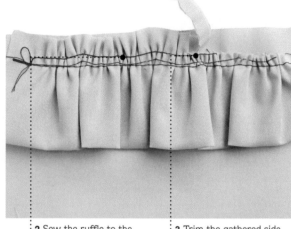

2 Sew the ruffle to the fabric using a ⅝in (1.5cm) seam allowance.

3 Trim the gathered side of the seam allowance down to half.

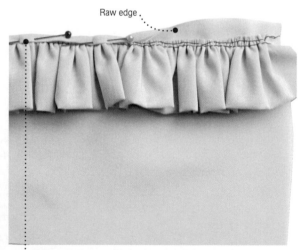

Raw edge

4 Wrap the longer, fabric side of the seam over the gathered seam, tucking under the raw edge. Pin in place.

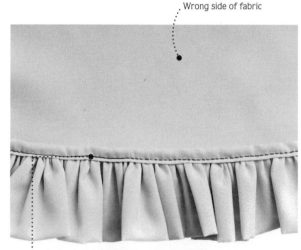

Wrong side of fabric

5 Sew the wrapped seam to secure. Make sure it is attached to the seam only.

BIAS-BOUND FINISH

1 Sew the gathered ruffle to the edge of the fabric, right side to right side, using a ⅝in (1.5cm) seam allowance (see steps 1 and 2, opposite).

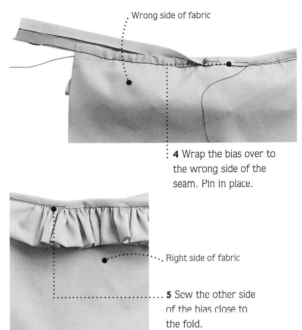

Wrong side of fabric

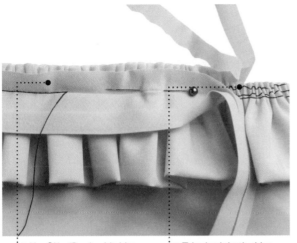

4 Wrap the bias over to the wrong side of the seam. Pin in place.

Right side of fabric

2 Use ¾in (2cm) wide bias binding. Sew the crease in the bias over the stitches of the ruffle.

3 Trim back both sides of the seam allowance.

5 Sew the other side of the bias close to the fold.

✂ SEWING AROUND A CORNER

It can be difficult to sew a ruffle to a corner and achieve a sharp point. It is easier to fit the gathers into a tight curve, which can be done as the ruffle is being applied to the corner.

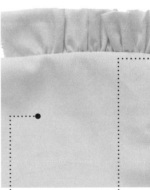

1 Pull up the gathers to fit along one side of the fabric seam and pin in place.

2 Fit the gathers into a tight curve at the corner.

3 Sew the ruffle in place.

4 Attach the other piece of fabric and sew in place. Layer the seam.

5 Turn the fabric and ruffle through to the right side. The corner will have a tight curve.

TUCKS

A tuck is a decorative addition to any piece of fabric and can be big and bold or very delicate. Tucks are made by sewing evenly spaced folds into the fabric on the right side, normally on the straight grain of the fabric. As the tucks take up additional fabric, it is advisable to make them prior to cutting out.

▶◀ DIRECTORY OF TUCKS

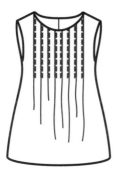

PLAIN TUCKS (p.91)

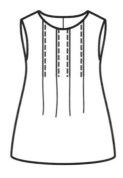

SPACED TUCKS (p.91)

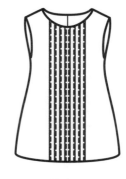

PIN TUCKS (p.91)

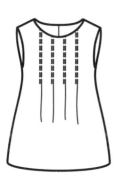

TWIN NEEDLE TUCKS (p.91)

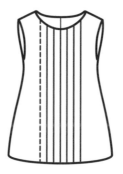

BLIND TUCKS (p.91)

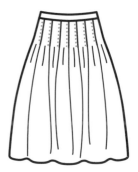

DARTED TUCKS (p.92)

CROSS TUCKS (p.92)

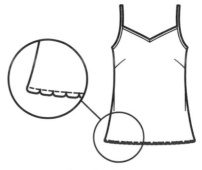

SHELL TUCKS (p.93)

✕ PLAIN TUCKS

A plain tuck is made by marking and creasing the fabric at regular intervals. A row of machine stitches are then worked adjacent to the fold.

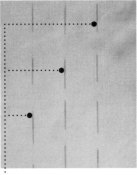

1 Mark the position of the tucks lightly with chalk on the right side of the fabric. Make sure the lines are parallel.

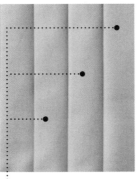

2 Fold along the chalk lines, making sure the folds are straight, and press in place.

3 Machine sew close to the foldline, using the edge of the machine foot as a guide or as indicated on your pattern.

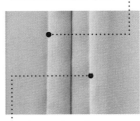

4 Repeat along the next fold, and continue until all the folds are stitched.

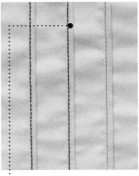

5 Press the tucks all in the same direction.

✕ OTHER SIMPLE TUCKS

These tucks are also made by marking and creasing the fabric. The positioning of the sewn line determines the type of tuck.

SPACED TUCKS

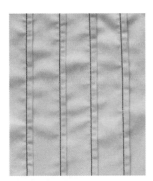

These are similar to a plain tuck but with wider regular spacing. Press the tucks in place along the foldlines and pin. Sew ⅜in (1cm) from the foldline. Press all the tucks in one direction.

PIN TUCKS

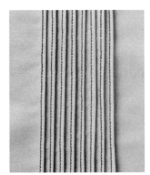

These narrow, regularly spaced tucks are stitched very close to the foldline, which may require moving the machine needle closer to the fold. Use the pintuck foot on the sewing machine.

TWIN NEEDLE TUCKS

For these regularly spaced tucks, use the twin needle on the sewing machine. The twin needle produces a shallow tuck that looks very effective when multiple rows are stitched.

BLIND TUCKS

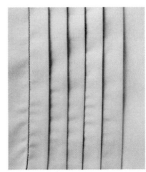

These are wide tucks that are stitched so that no machining shows—the fold of each tuck covers the stitching of the previous tuck.

▶ DARTED TUCKS

A tuck that stops to release the fullness is known as a darted tuck. It can be used to give fullness at the bust or hip. The shaped darted tuck is sewn at an angle to release less fabric, while the plain darted tuck is sewn straight on the grainline.

SHAPED DARTED TUCKS

1 Transfer any pattern markings to the fabric.

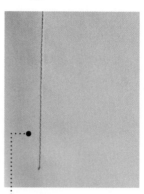

3 Stop at the point indicated on your pattern.

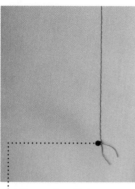

2 Fold the fabric right side to right side. On the wrong side of the fabric, sew at an angle to the folded edge.

4 Secure the stitches.

PLAIN DARTED TUCKS

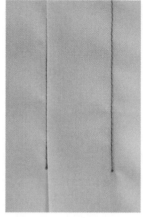

1 Make in the same way as a shaped darted tuck (see left), but sew parallel to the folded edge.

2 Stop as indicated on the pattern.

3 The tuck as seen from the right side.

▶ CROSS TUCKS

These are tucks that cross over each other by being sewn in opposite directions.

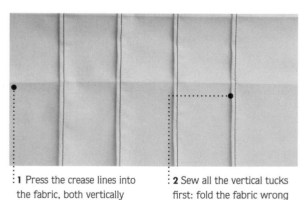

1 Press the crease lines into the fabric, both vertically and horizontally.

2 Sew all the vertical tucks first: fold the fabric wrong side to wrong side along the crease lines. Sew ³⁄₁₆in (5mm) from the folded edge.

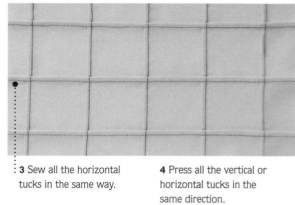

3 Sew all the horizontal tucks in the same way.

4 Press all the vertical or horizontal tucks in the same direction.

◄ SHELL TUCKS

A shell tuck is very decorative, as it has a scalloped edge. Shell tucks can be easily sewn using the sewing machine. On heavy fabric and delicate fabrics, it may be preferable to make the tucks by hand.

MACHINE SHELL TUCKS

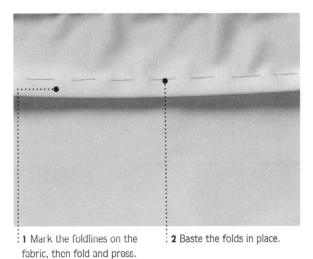

1 Mark the foldlines on the fabric, then fold and press.

2 Baste the folds in place.

3 Use the embroidery foot on the sewing machine and set the sewing machine to a shell hem stitch.

4 Sew along the fold, keeping the fold close to the inside opening of the machine foot.

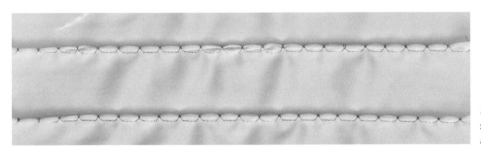

5 The finished tucks should be stitched at regular intervals.

SHELL TUCKS BY HAND

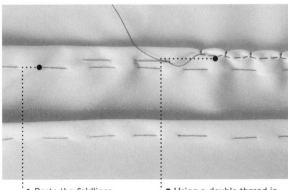

1 Baste the foldlines for the tucks in place.

2 Using a double thread in the needle, make two or three running stitches.

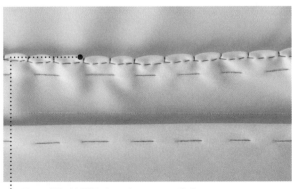

3 Every ½in (1.25cm), make an overstitch through the fold to produce a scallop.

DARTS

A dart is used to give shape to a piece of fabric so that it can fit around the contours of the body. Some darts are sewn using straight sewn lines, and other darts are stitched using a slightly curved line. Always sew a dart from the point to the wide end because you are able to sink the machine needle into the point accurately and securely.

▶ DIRECTORY OF DARTS

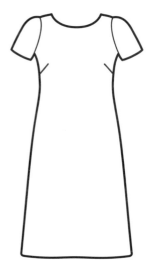

PLAIN DART ON BUST (p.95)

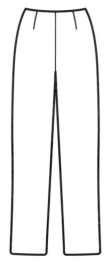

PLAIN DART ON WAIST (p.95)

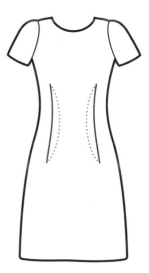

CONTOUR OR DOUBLE-POINTED DART (p.96)

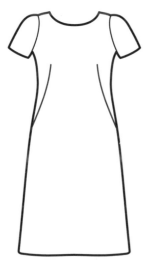

FRENCH DART (p.97)

◤ PLAIN DART

This is the most common type of dart and is used to give shaping to the bust in the bodice. It is also found at the waist in skirts and pants to give shape from the waist to the hip.

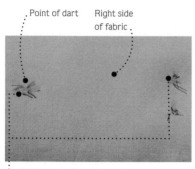

Point of dart

Right side of fabric

1 Tailor tack the points of the dart as marked on the pattern, making one tack at the point and two to mark the wide ends.

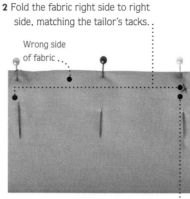

2 Fold the fabric right side to right side, matching the tailor's tacks.

Wrong side of fabric

3 Pin through the tailor's tacks to match them.

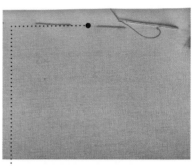

4 Baste along the dart line, joining the tailor's tacks. Remove the pins.

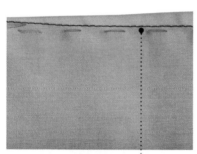

5 Machine sew alongside the basting line. Remove the bastes.

6 Sew the machine threads back into the line of the dart to secure them.

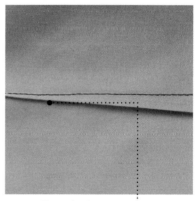

7 Press the dart to one side (see p.97).

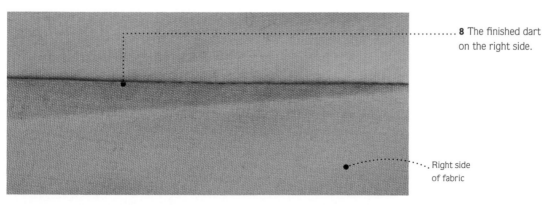

8 The finished dart on the right side.

Right side of fabric

▶◀ CONTOUR OR DOUBLE-POINTED DART

This type of dart is like two darts joined together at the fat end. It is used to give shape at the waist of a garment. It will contour the fabric from the bust into the waist and then out again for the hip.

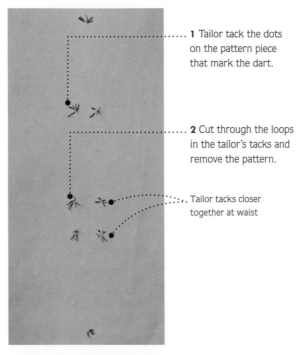

1 Tailor tack the dots on the pattern piece that mark the dart.

2 Cut through the loops in the tailor's tacks and remove the pattern.

Tailor tacks closer together at waist

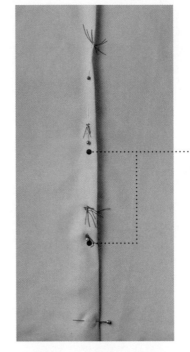

3 Bring the tailor's tacks together, keeping the fabric right side to right side, and pin the tacks together.

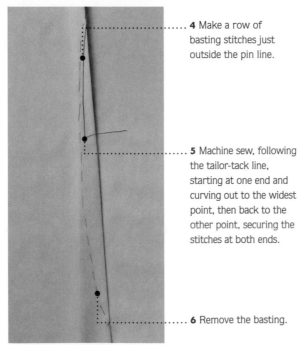

4 Make a row of basting stitches just outside the pin line.

5 Machine sew, following the tailor-tack line, starting at one end and curving out to the widest point, then back to the other point, securing the stitches at both ends.

6 Remove the basting.

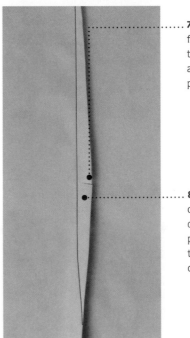

7 Clip across the fold in the fabric at the widest point to allow the dart to be pressed to one side.

8 Press the dart to one side. Contour darts are normally pressed toward the center front or center back.

▶< FRENCH DART

A French dart is used on the front of a garment only. It is a curved dart that extends from the side seam at the waist to the bust point. As this is a long dart that is shaped, it will need to be slashed prior to construction in order for it to fit together and then lie flat when pressed.

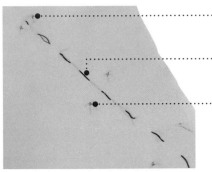

1 Mark all the dots on the pattern piece using tailor's tacks.

2 Mark the slash line with trace basting and a different colored thread.

3 Cut through the loops in the tailor's tacks and remove the pattern.

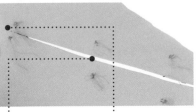

4 Slash between the tailor's tacks along the slash line.

5 Stop at the end of the slash line.

6 Bring the tailor's tacks together, right side to right side, and pin.

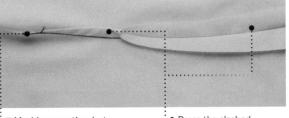

7 Machine sew the dart, starting at the point and securing the stitches, then continue stitching to the fat end.

8 Press the slashed part of the dart open and the nonslashed part of the dart to the one side.

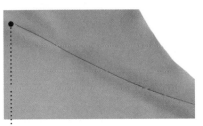

9 On the right side of the piece, the pressed finished dart gives fullness at the point.

▶< PRESSING A DART

If a dart is pressed incorrectly, this can spoil the look of a garment. For successful pressing, you will need a tailor's ham and a steam iron on a steam setting. A pressing cloth may be required for delicate fabrics such as silk, satin, and chiffon and for lining fabrics.

1 Place the fabric piece, right side down, on the tailor's ham. The point of the dart should be over the end of the ham.

2 Press the fabric around the point of the dart.

3 Move the iron from the point toward the wide end of the dart to press the dart flat, open, or to one side, depending on the type of dart.

PLEATS

A pleat is a fold or series of folds in fabric. Pleats are most commonly found in skirts where the pleats are made to fit around the waist and hip and then left to fall in crisply pressed folds, giving fullness at the hemline. It is important that pleats are made accurately; otherwise, they will not fit the body and will look uneven. Foldlines and placement lines, or foldlines and crease lines, are marked on the fabric from the pattern. It is by using a combination of these lines and the spaces between them that the pleats are made.

▶◀ DIRECTORY OF PLEATS

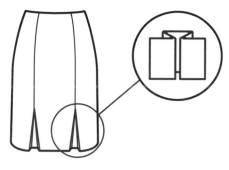

KNIFE PLEATS (pp.99, 101)

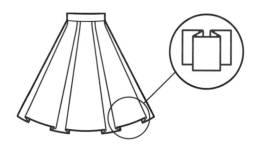

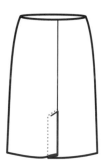

BOX PLEATS (pp.100–101)

INVERTED PLEATS (pp.100–101)

KICK PLEAT (p.101)

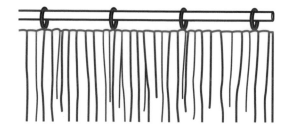

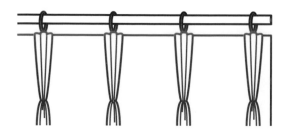

PENCIL PLEATS (p.103)

PINCH PLEATS (p.103)

▶◀ PLEATS ON THE RIGHT SIDE

Knife pleats are normally formed on the right side of fabric. They can all face the same direction or may face opposite directions from opposite sides of the garment. Knife pleats have foldlines and placement lines.

1 Mark the placement lines and foldlines with trace tacks. Use one color thread, such as light blue, for placement lines.

2 Use a contrasting color thread, such as yellow, to mark foldlines.

3 Cut through the thread loops and remove the pattern pieces carefully.

Placement line ⋅ ⋅ ⋅ ⋅ Foldline

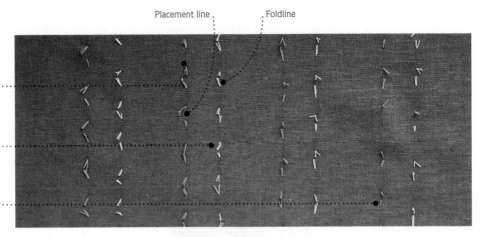

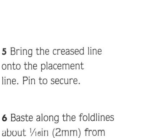

4 Fold the fabric along the foldline, creasing accurately along the trace tacks.

5 Bring the creased line onto the placement line. Pin to secure.

6 Baste along the foldlines about 1/16in (2mm) from the folded edge, through all the layers.

7 Remove the pins and the trace basting on this part of the pleat.

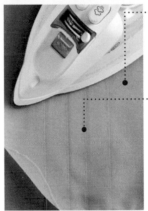

8 With the right side of the fabric uppermost, cover with a silk organza pressing cloth.

9 Using a steam iron on a steam setting, press the pleats in place. Keep the iron still as opposed to moving it around, and eject a shot of steam each time you lift it to a new position. Repeat this action across all of the pleats.

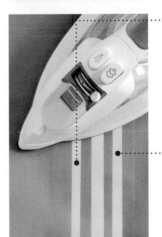

10 Turn the fabric to the wrong side and insert thin strips of construction paper under the pleat fabric.

11 Press again with the steam iron and a silk organza cloth. The paper will prevent the fabric from leaving an imprint on the right side.

▶◀ PLEATS ON THE WRONG SIDE

Some pleats, including box (shown below) and inverted pleats, are formed on the wrong side of the fabric. As the pleats are made on the wrong side, you can mark the crease lines and foldlines with a tracing wheel and dressmaker's carbon paper. Use a ruler to guide the tracing wheel, because these pleats need to be straight lines.

1 Mark the crease lines and foldlines on the wrong side of the fabric using different colors for the different lines. The lines must be marked down the full length of the fabric.

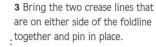
Foldline

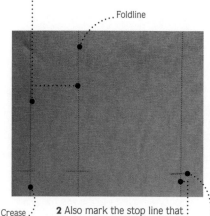

Crease line

2 Also mark the stop line that shows where to stop stitching. Remove the pattern pieces.

3 Bring the two crease lines that are on either side of the foldline together and pin in place.

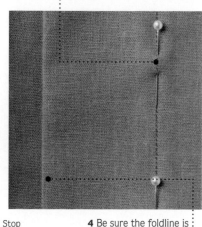

Stop line

4 Be sure the foldline is along the fold in the fabric.

5 Tack through the two layers of fabric where the crease lines have been pinned together, along the entire length of the pleat.

Foldline

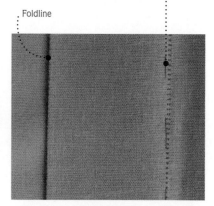

6 Sew along the crease lines.

7 Stop at the stop line. Secure the machine stitches.

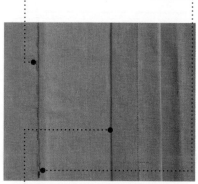

8 Flatten the pleat on the wrong side so that the foldline is lying on top of the machine stitches. Make sure that the fabric on either side of this foldline to the crease line is equal on both sides.

9 Cover the pleats on the wrong side with a silk organza pressing cloth and press, using a steam iron with a shot of steam.

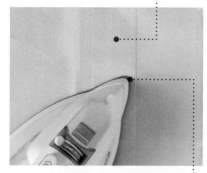

10 Press each section of the pleat in turn, lifting the iron rather than moving it on the fabric.

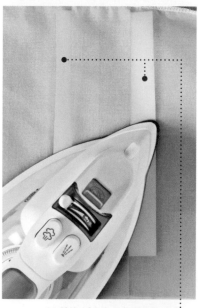

11 If the fabric is in danger of being marked on the right side with the pleats, place some strips of construction paper under the pleats on the wrong side, then press again on the wrong side.

⫷ TOP-STITCHING AND EDGE-STITCHING PLEATS

If a pleat is top-stitched or edge-stitched, it will hang correctly and always look crisp. It will also help the pleats on the skirt to keep their shape when you are sitting.

TOP-STITCHING KNIFE PLEATS

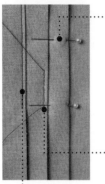

1 Once the knife pleats have been pressed and all bastes and markings removed, place some pins across the pleat to stop it from moving.

2 Machine sew from the right side approximately ¹⁄₁₆in (2mm) from the fold.

3 Start sewing at the lower end of the pleat and sew to the waist.

TOP-STITCHING BOX PLEATS THAT HAVE A SQUARE END

1 This requires sewing down on either side of the foldline. Sew down one side about ³⁄₁₆in (5mm) from the foldline.

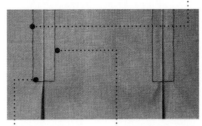

2 Pivot and sew horizontally across the end of the pleat stitches.

3 Pivot again and sew up the other side of the foldline about ³⁄₁₆in (5mm) from the foldline.

TOP-STITCHING BOX PLEATS THAT HAVE A POINTED END

1 Sew down one side ³⁄₁₆in (5mm) from the foldline, then pivot and sew diagonally to the center.

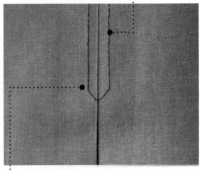

2 Pivot again and sew diagonally the other side and back to the waist ³⁄₁₆in (5mm) from the foldline.

EDGE-STITCHING KNIFE PLEATS

1 After pressing the pleats into shape, stitch ¹⁄₁₆in (2mm) from the fold.

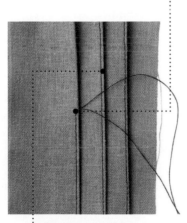

2 Sew along the entire length of the fold.

EDGE-STITCHING AND TOP-STITCHING PLEATS

1 Edge-stitch first the edge of the pleat about ¹⁄₁₆in (2mm) from the folded edge.

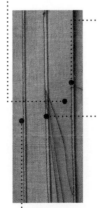

2 Stop the edge-stitching just above the point where the pleat is to be top-stitched.

3 Place the machine needle into the pleat, through all layers, four or five stitches below where the edge-stitch stops.

4 Top-stitch through all the layers, continuing at ¹⁄₁₆in (2mm) from the fold, to the waist.

TOP-STITCHING KICK PLEATS OR INVERTED PLEATS

1 This pleat is pressed to the right. Just below the sewn line that makes the pleat, sew a line diagonally to secure the pleat fabric at the back.

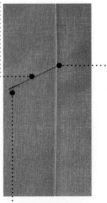

2 Make sure the sewn line finishes exactly on the foldline.

3 Pull the ends of the machine stitching through to the reverse.

⟩⟨ PLEATS ON CURTAINS

Pleats are used in home goods, particularly at the top of curtains, to reduce the fabric so that the curtain will fit onto its track and fit the window. The easiest way to pleat the upper edge of a curtain is to apply a curtain tape. Tapes are available in various depths and will pull the curtain into pencil pleats or goblet pleats. The most common tape used for pencil pleating is 3¼in (8cm) deep. A curtain is normally cut two and a half to three times the width of the window. The curtain tape will reduce the fabric by this much as it pleats up.

PREPARING THE CURTAIN TO TAKE THE TAPE

1 Turn under the two side edges of the curtain by using a double hem of 1in (2.5cm)—so turn the fabric 1in (2.5cm) once and then the same again.

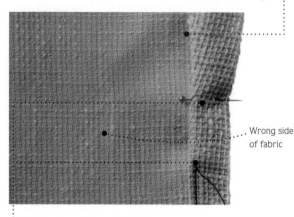

Wrong side of fabric

2 Pin the hem edges on the sides of the curtains, then sew.

Side edge of curtain

3 Turn the top of the curtain down by 1in (2.5cm) and pin.

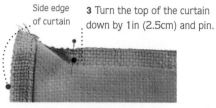

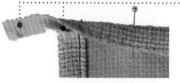

4 Reduce the bulk at the top edge on the corners by trimming away the side hem.

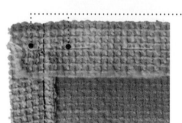

5 Baste the upper edge of the curtain down into place.

MAKING A POCKET FOR THE STRINGS

1 A small pocket needs to be made to take the strings that are used to pull up the tape. Cut a rectangle of spare fabric 6 x 3¼in (15 x 8cm).

2 Turn one short edge wrong side to wrong side and sew to make a single hem.

3 Fold the rectangle right side to right side with a ¾in (2cm) seam at the upper edge free.

4 Sew down the sides and clip the corners.

5 Turn through to the right side and press.

PENCIL PLEATS

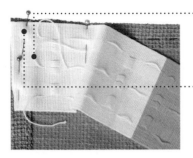

1 Take the curtain tape and release the strings at the one end, making sure they are all visible on the same side.

2 Place the top of the tape ³/₁₆in (5mm) down from the folded edge of the curtain. Pin in place, stretching the tape as you do so. Turn under the short end, avoiding the strings, and pin.

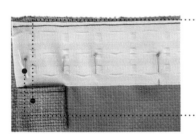

3 Sew the upper edge of the tape to the curtain fabric. Make sure the strings stay free.

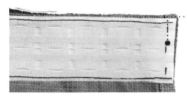

4 Before sewing the lower edge of the tape, place the pocket you made under the end of the tape.

5 Pin the tape and the pocket in place. Sew the tape and pocket.

6 At the opposite end of the tape, sew across each string individually to prevent it from being pulled out.

7 Pull up the strings in the tape from the end with the pocket to make the pleats.

8 Tie the strings together and place in the pocket.

9 Turn the curtain over to check that the pencil pleats are evenly spaced and will fit the window. Adjust if necessary.

PINCH PLEATS

1 Pinch pleats are three pleats together at regular intervals. When the tape is pulled up, the pleats are close together at the base and fan out at the top. Prepare the curtain to take the tape and make the pocket (see opposite page).

2 Attach the tape in the same way as for pencil pleats (left).

3 After pulling up the tape, secure it by hand on the right side at the base of the tape.

4 Hand sew the upper edge of the pleats at the back.

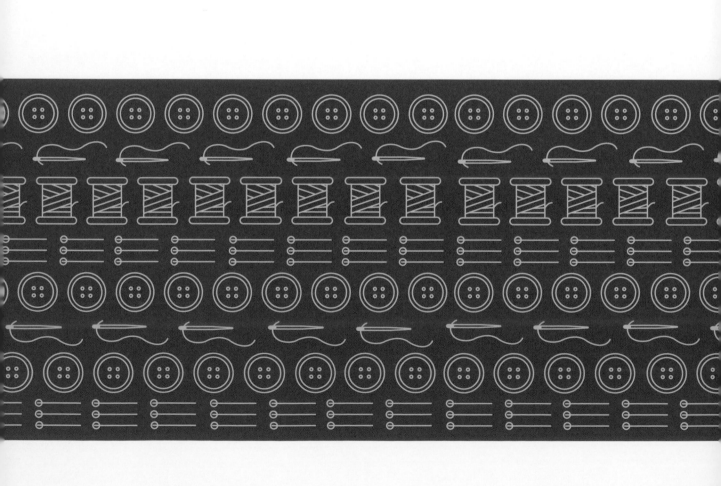

HEMS AND EDGES

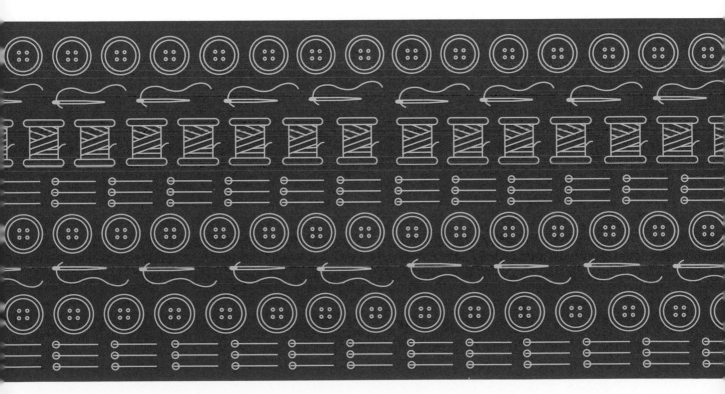

HEMS AND EDGES

The edge of a piece of fabric can be finished with a hem—which is normally used on garments—or with a decorative edge, which is used for crafts and home goods, as well as garments. Sometimes the style of what is being constructed dictates the finish that is used, and sometimes it is the fabric.

▶ DIRECTORY OF HEMS

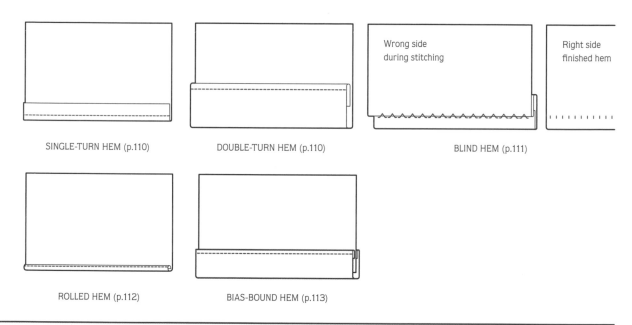

SINGLE-TURN HEM (p.110)

DOUBLE-TURN HEM (p.110)

Wrong side during stitching

Right side finished hem

BLIND HEM (p.111)

ROLLED HEM (p.112)

BIAS-BOUND HEM (p.113)

▶ MARKING A HEMLINE

On a garment such as a skirt or a dress, it is important that the hemline is level all around. Even if the fabric has been cut straight, some styles of skirt—such as A-line or circular—will "drop," which means that the hem edge is longer in some places. This is due to the fabric stretching where it is not on the straight of the grain. Poor posture will also cause a hem to hang unevenly.

USING A RULER

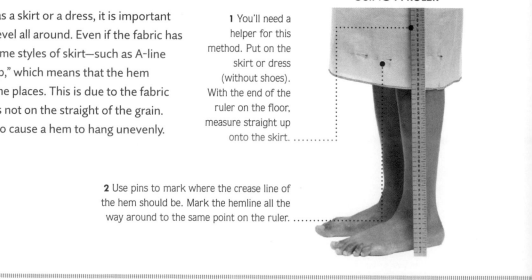

1 You'll need a helper for this method. Put on the skirt or dress (without shoes). With the end of the ruler on the floor, measure straight up onto the skirt. ....

2 Use pins to mark where the crease line of the hem should be. Mark the hemline all the way around to the same point on the ruler. ....

▶◀ TURNING UP A STRAIGHT HEM

Once the crease line for the hem has been marked by the pins, you need to trim the hem allowance to a reasonable amount. Most straight hems are about 1½in (4cm) deep.

1 Gently press the crease line of the hem with the iron. Don't press too hard, as you do not want a sharp crease.

2 Trim the seam allowance back to reduce the bulk. If you wish, neaten the raw edge.

3 Turn up the hem at the crease. Match the seams together.

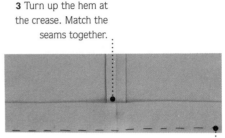

4 Baste the hem into position close to the crease line. The hem is now ready to be sewn in place by hand or machine.

▶◀ HAND-SEWN HEMS

One of the most popular ways to secure a hem edge is by hand. Hand sewing is discreet and, if a fine hand sewing needle is used, the stitches should not show on the right side of the work.

TIPS FOR SEWING HEMS BY HAND

1 Always use a single thread in the needle—a polyester all-purpose thread is ideal for hemming.
2 Once the raw edge of the hem allowance has been neatened (see below and p.108), secure it using a slip hem stitch. For this, take half of the stitch into the neatened edge and the other half into the wrong side of the garment fabric.

3 Start and finish the hand sewing with a double stitch, not a knot, because knots will catch and pull on the hem.
4 It is a good idea to take a small backstitch every 4in (10cm) or so to make sure that if the hem does come loose in one place, it will not all unravel.

CLEAN FINISH

1 This is suitable for fine and lightweight fabrics. Lightly press the hem into position.

2 Turn the raw edge of the hem allowance to itself, wrong side to wrong side. Baste the edge and then sew.

4 Fold the hem back up and tack in place.

5 Roll the edge sewn back and sew underneath it.

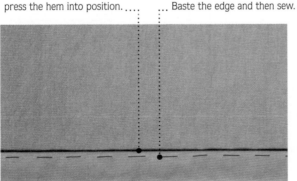

3 Open out the hem and machine sew the tacked edge.

6 Using a small slip hem stitch, secure the edge of the hem to the wrong side of the fabric. Roll the edge back into place.

7 Remove the basting and press lightly.

BIAS-BOUND FINISH

1 This is a good finish for fabrics that fray or that are bulky. Turn up the hem onto the wrong side of the garment and baste close to the crease line.

4 Turn down the bias over the raw edge and press.

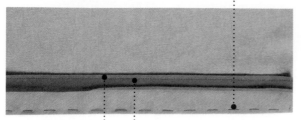

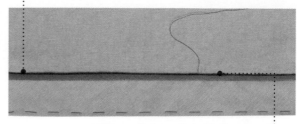

2 Pin the bias binding to the raw edge of the hem allowance.

3 Open out the crease in the bias and stitch along the crease line, keeping the raw edges level.

5 Using a slip hem stitch, join the edge of the bias to the wrong side of the fabric. Remove the basting and press lightly.

ZIGZAG FINISH

1 Use this to neaten the edge of the hem on fabrics that do not fray too badly. Set the sewing machine to a zigzag stitch, width 4.0 and length 3.0. Sew along the raw edge. Trim the fabric edge back to the zigzag stitch.

3 Fold back the zigzag-stitched edge. Using a slip hem stitch, sew the hem into place.

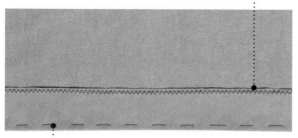

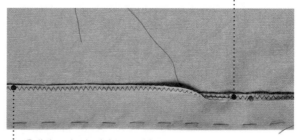

2 Turn the hem onto the wrong side of the garment and tack in place close to the crease line.

4 Roll the edge back into position. Remove the basting and lightly press.

PINKED FINISH

1 Pinking shears can give an excellent hem finish on difficult fabrics. Sew a row of straight stitches along the raw edge, ⅜in (1cm) from the edge. Pink the raw edge.

3 Fold back the edge along the sewn line and hand sew the hem in place with a slip hem stitch.

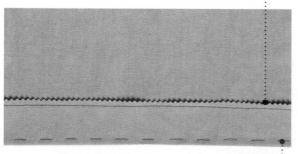

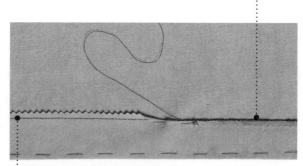

2 Turn up the hem to the wrong side of the garment and baste in place close to the crease line.

4 Roll the hem edge back into place. Remove the basting and lightly press.

✕ TURNING UP A CURVED HEM

When the hem on a shaped skirt is turned up, it will be fuller at the upper edge. This fullness will need to be eased out before the hem is sewn.

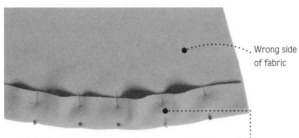

1 Mark the hemline, placing the pins vertically to avoid squashing the fullness out of the upper raw edge.

Wrong side of fabric

2 Baste the hem into position close to the crease line. Remove the pins.

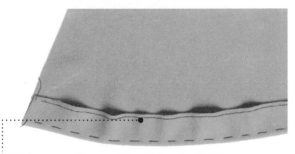

3 Make a row of long machine stitches, length 5.0, close to the raw upper edge of the turned-up hem.

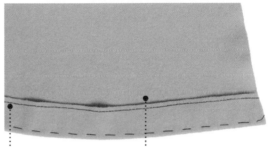

4 Pull on one of the threads of the long stitches to tighten the fabric and ease out the fullness.

5 Use the steam iron to shrink out the remainder of the fullness. The hem is now ready to be sewn in place by hand or machine.

CURVED HEM FINISH

1 With a curved hem on a cotton or firm fabric, it is important that any fullness does not bulge onto the right side. Prior to turning up the hem into position, zigzag stitch the raw edge, using stitch width 4.0 and stitch length 3.0.

4 Baste the hem into position close to the crease line.

5 Pull on the straight stitching to tighten the fabric.

2 Sew a row of straight stitches ⅛in (3mm) below the row of zigzag stitching, using stitch length 5.0.

3 Pin the hem into position, placing the pins vertically.

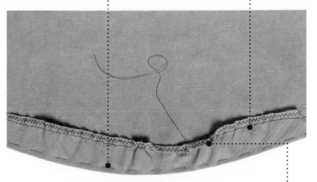

6 Roll the zigzagged edge back to the straight stitched line and hand sew the hem in place using a slip hem stitch. Remove the basting and press lightly.

⊠ MACHINE-SEWN HEMS

On many occasions, the hem or edge of a garment or other item is turned up and secured using the sewing machine. It can be sewn with a straight stitch, a zigzag stitch, or a blind hem stitch. Hems can also be made on the serger.

SINGLE-TURN HEM

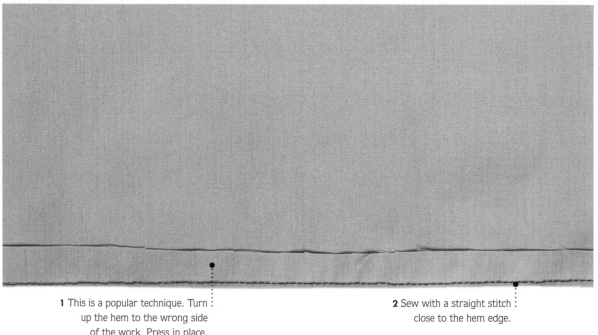

1 This is a popular technique. Turn up the hem to the wrong side of the work. Press in place.

2 Sew with a straight stitch close to the hem edge.

DOUBLE-TURN HEM

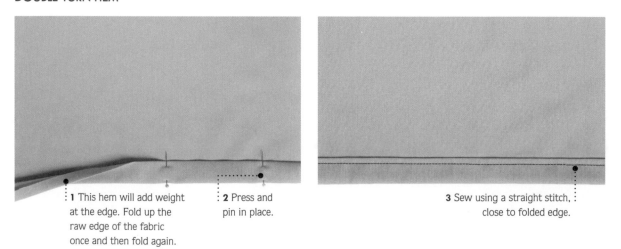

1 This hem will add weight at the edge. Fold up the raw edge of the fabric once and then fold again.

2 Press and pin in place.

3 Sew using a straight stitch, close to folded edge.

BLIND HEM

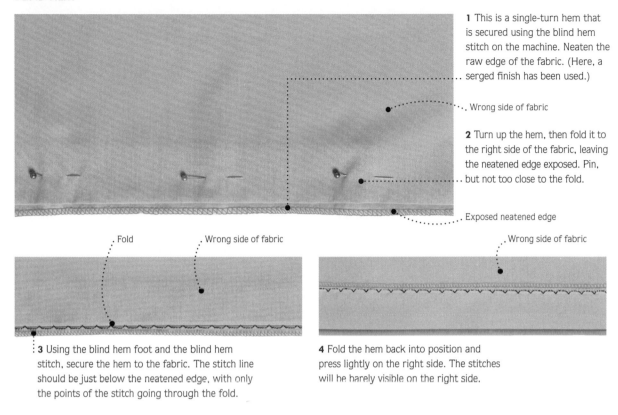

1 This is a single-turn hem that is secured using the blind hem stitch on the machine. Neaten the raw edge of the fabric. (Here, a serged finish has been used.)

Wrong side of fabric

2 Turn up the hem, then fold it to the right side of the fabric, leaving the neatened edge exposed. Pin, but not too close to the fold.

Exposed neatened edge

Fold   Wrong side of fabric

Wrong side of fabric

3 Using the blind hem foot and the blind hem stitch, secure the hem to the fabric. The stitch line should be just below the neatened edge, with only the points of the stitch going through the fold.

4 Fold the hem back into position and press lightly on the right side. The stitches will be barely visible on the right side.

⊁ HEMS ON DIFFICULT FABRICS

Some very fine fabrics or fabrics that fray badly require more thought when a hem is to be made. This technique works very well on delicate fabrics.

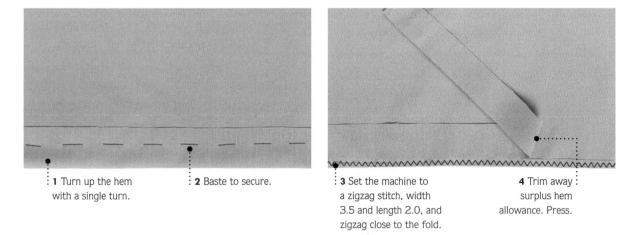

1 Turn up the hem with a single turn.

2 Baste to secure.

3 Set the machine to a zigzag stitch, width 3.5 and length 2.0, and zigzag close to the fold.

4 Trim away surplus hem allowance. Press.

⋊ ROLLED HEMS

A rolled hem is used on lightweight fabrics. It is often found on home goods, as well as garments. To make it, the fabric is rolled to the wrong side by using the rolled hem foot on the sewing machine.

STRAIGHT-STITCHED ROLLED HEM

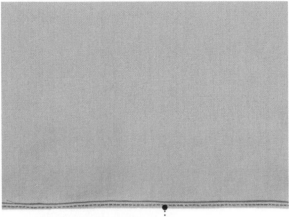

Use the rolled hem foot on the sewing machine and a straight stitch.

ZIGZAG-STITCHED ROLLED HEM

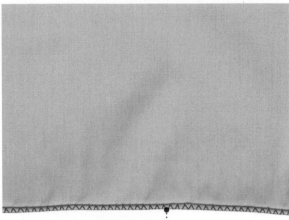

Use the rolled hem foot on the sewing machine and a zigzag stitch.

⋊ FUSED HEM

A fused hem is useful for a fabric that is difficult to hand sew, as well as for an emergency hem repair. It uses a fusible web that has a fusible adhesive on both sides.

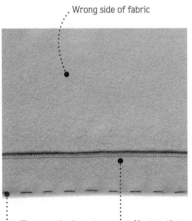

. Wrong side of fabric

1 Turn up the hem to the wrong side of the fabric. Baste the hem in place close to the crease line.

2 Neaten the raw edge with a serger or zigzag stitch.

3 Insert the fusible hemming tape between the hem and the wrong side of the garment. Make sure the tape sits just below the serger or zigzag stitch. Pin the tape in place.

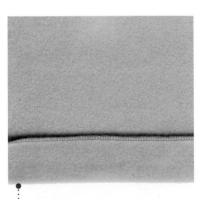

4 Cover the hem allowance with a pressing cloth and, using a steam iron, press the edge of the hem to fuse the tape to the fabric. Once cool, the hem will be stuck in place. Remove the basting stitches and pins.

◤ BIAS-BOUND HEMS

A bias-bound hem will give a narrow decorative edge to a garment or an item of home furnishing. It is particularly useful for curved shapes, to finish them neatly and securely. On a chunky or bulky fabric, a double bias is used so that it will be more substantial and hold its shape better. A double bias is also used on sheer fabrics, as there will be no visible raw edges. The bias strip can be made from purchased bias binding or cut from a matching or contrasting fabric.

SINGLE BIAS-BOUND HEM

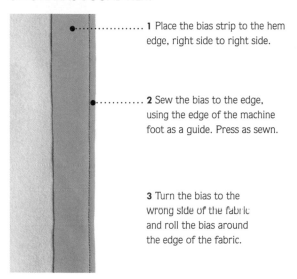

1 Place the bias strip to the hem edge, right side to right side.

2 Sew the bias to the edge, using the edge of the machine foot as a guide. Press as sewn.

3 Turn the bias to the wrong side of the fabric and roll the bias around the edge of the fabric.

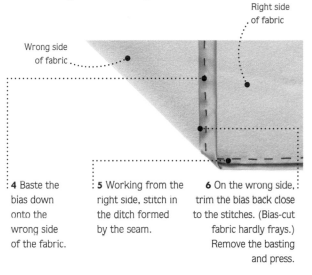

Right side of fabric

Wrong side of fabric

4 Baste the bias down onto the wrong side of the fabric.

5 Working from the right side, stitch in the ditch formed by the seam.

6 On the wrong side, trim the bias back close to the stitches. (Bias-cut fabric hardly frays.) Remove the basting and press.

DOUBLE BIAS-BOUND HEM

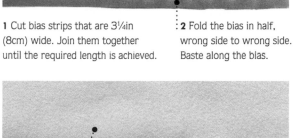

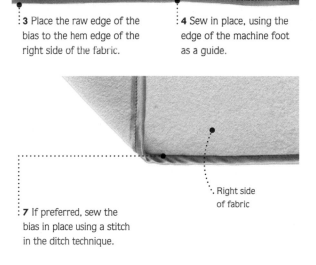

Right side of fabric

1 Cut bias strips that are 3¼in (8cm) wide. Join them together until the required length is achieved.

2 Fold the bias in half, wrong side to wrong side. Baste along the bias.

3 Place the raw edge of the bias to the hem edge of the right side of the fabric.

4 Sew in place, using the edge of the machine foot as a guide.

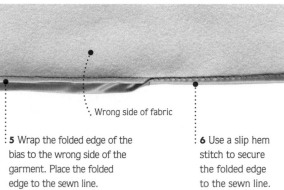

Wrong side of fabric

Right side of fabric

5 Wrap the folded edge of the bias to the wrong side of the garment. Place the folded edge to the sewn line.

6 Use a slip hem stitch to secure the folded edge to the sewn line.

7 If preferred, sew the bias in place using a stitch in the ditch technique.

▶ ATTACHING A LACE TRIM

A lace edge can give a look of luxury to any garment. There are many ways of applying lace, depending on how the lace has been made. A heavy lace trim has a definite edge to be sewn onto the fabric. Lace edging has a decorative edge and an unfinished edge, whereas a galloon lace has decorative scallops on both edges.

HEAVY LACE TRIM

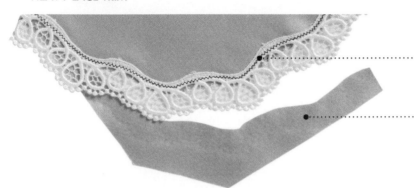

1 Pin the lace to the right side of the fabric.

2 Using a small zigzag stitch, sew along the edge of the lace. All of the stitches should be on the lace.

3 Trim away surplus fabric behind.

LACE EDGING

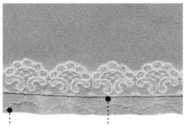

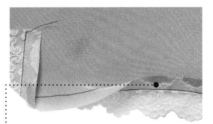

1 Place the lace to the fabric, right side to right side. Align the raw edges.

2 Sew using a straight stitch.

3 Turn the raw edges to the wrong side of the fabric. Press in place onto the wrong side.

4 Working from the right side of the fabric, zigzag stitch close to the fabric edge.

5 Trim away surplus fabric on the reverse side.

GALLOON LACE

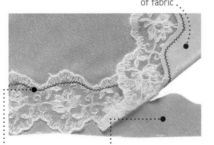

Wrong side of fabric

1 Place the complete piece of lace to the right side of the fabric. Align the edge of the lace with the raw edge of the fabric. Pin in place.

2 Sew along the upper edge of the lace, following the shape.

3 Trim away surplus fabric, following the shape of the stitches.

4 The lace trim on the right side.

▶ APPLYING A FLAT TRIM

On some items, a flat trim braid or ribbon is added for a decorative effect. This may be right on the hem or edge or placed just above it. To achieve a neat finish, any corners should be mitered.

1 Pin the trim to the fabric, wrong side of the trim to right side of the fabric.

2 At the corner point where the trim is to be mitered, fold the trim back on itself and secure with a pin.

3 Sew across the trim at 45 degrees from the edge of the fold, through all layers.

4 Remove excess trim from the corner.

5 Open the trim out and press.

6 Sew the inner and outer sides of the trim to the fabric, close to the edge. Be sure the stitches at the corners are sharp.

▶ PIPED EDGES

A piped edge can look very effective on a garment, especially if it is made in a contrasting color or fabric. Piping is also an excellent way of finishing special-occasion wear, as well as home goods. The piping may be single, double, or gathered.

SINGLE PIPING

1 Just one piece of piping is used. Cut a bias strip 1½in (4cm) wide.

2 Wrap the binding, wrong side to wrong side, around the piping cord. Pin in place.

3 Sew along the binding, close to the cord, using the zipper foot.

4 Pin the raw edge of the piping to the raw edge of the right side of the work.

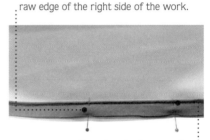

5 Sew close to the sewn line on the piping, using the zipper foot.

6 Place the other side of the fabric over the piping, right side to right side.

Piping

7 Sew in place close to the piping, using the zipper foot.

8 On the right side of the work, the piping can be seen at the edge. Press to finish.

DOUBLE PIPING

1 Different thicknesses of piping cord can be used for this. Make up single piping (see steps 1–3, p.115).

2 Cut another bias strip, in a contrasting color if you like.

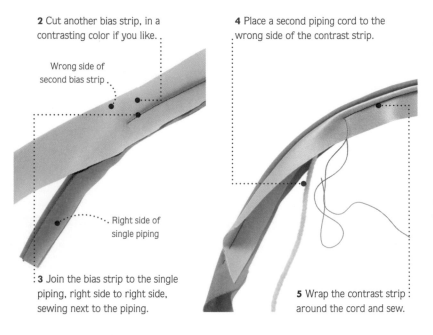

Wrong side of second bias strip

Right side of single piping

3 Join the bias strip to the single piping, right side to right side, sewing next to the piping.

4 Place a second piping cord to the wrong side of the contrast strip.

5 Wrap the contrast strip around the cord and sew.

6 Attach to the edge of the work as for single piping (see steps 4–7, p.115). On the right side, there is a double row of piping at the edge.

GATHERED PIPING

1 This is a great technique to try on cushions. Cut a bias strip 2in (5cm) wide. Sew the bias strip loosely around a piece of piping cord. Secure the cord to the bias at one end.

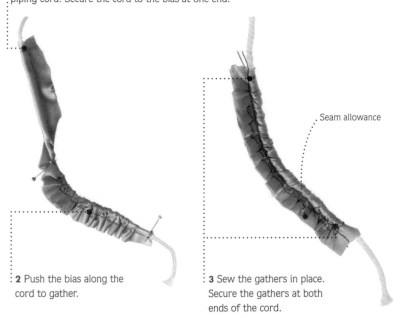

Seam allowance

2 Push the bias along the cord to gather.

3 Sew the gathers in place. Secure the gathers at both ends of the cord.

Gathered piping

4 Attach to the edge of the work as for single piping (see steps 4–7, p.115).

▶ APPLYING OTHER TRIMS

There are many kinds of trims—ribbons, braids, beads, feathers, sequins, fringes, and so on—that can be applied to a fabric edge. If a trim is made on a narrow ribbon or braid, it can often be inserted into a seam during construction. Other trims are attached after the garment or item has been completed.

INSERTING A TRIM IN A SEAM

1 Place the trim to the right side of one piece of fabric, with the beaded or other decorative edge pointing away from the raw edge. The edge of the trim should be on the ⅝in (1.5cm) sewn line. Baste in place.

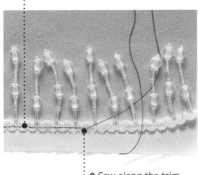

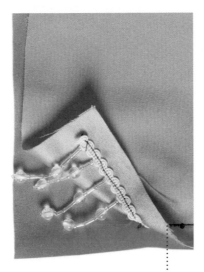

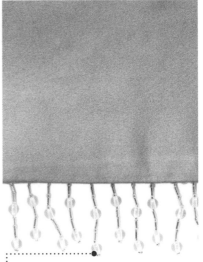

2 Sew along the trim using the zipper foot.

3 Place the other piece of fabric to the first one, right side to right side. Sew again to join them.

4 Turn to the right side. Press carefully. The trim should hang free.

ATTACHING A TRIM TO AN EDGE

1 Pin the trim in position along the finished edge of the work. Be sure the trim is aligned to the edge. Baste in place.

2 Using the zipper foot, sew in place close to the upper edge, leaving the lower edge of the trim free.

HAND STITCHING A TRIM

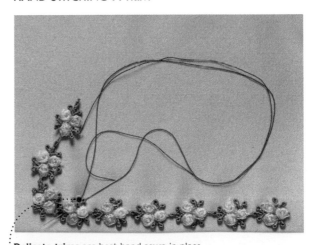

Delicate trims are best hand sewn in place because machine sewing the trim may damage it. Place the trim in position and carefully sew down with a flat fell stitch.

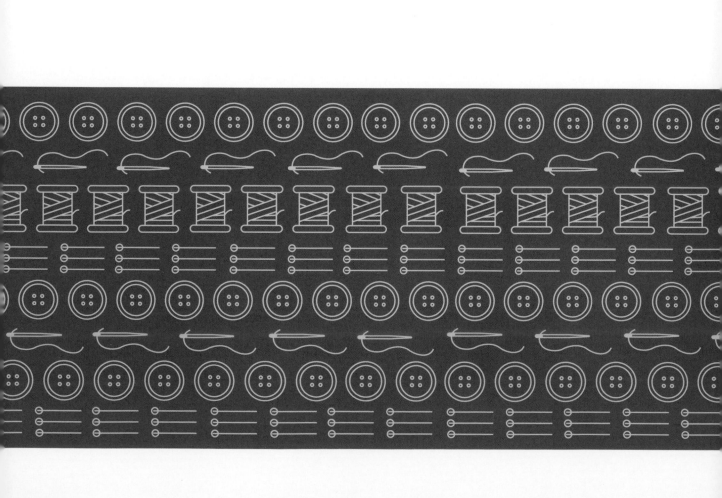

FASTENINGS

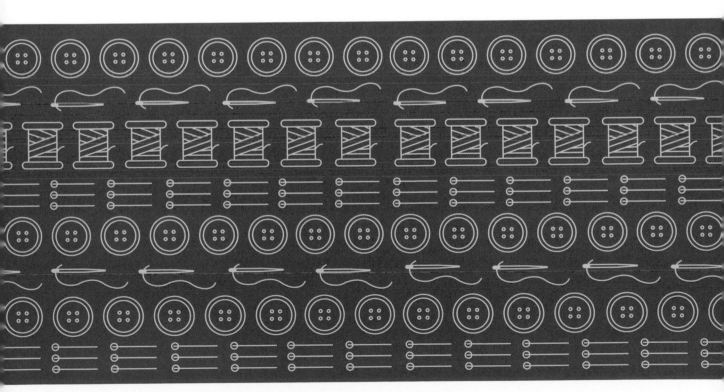

BUTTONS

Buttons are one of the oldest forms of fastening. They come in many shapes and sizes and can be made from a variety of materials, including shell, bone, plastic, nylon, and metal. Buttons are sewn to the fabric either through holes on their face or through a hole in a stalk called a shank, which is on the back. Buttons are normally sewn on by hand, although a two-hole button can be sewn on by machine.

▶ DIRECTORY OF BUTTONS

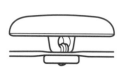

TWO-HOLE BUTTON (p.120) FOUR-HOLE BUTTON (p.121) SHANKED BUTTON (p.121) REINFORCED BUTTON (p.122) COVERED BUTTON (p.122)

▶ SEWING ON A TWO-HOLE BUTTON

This is the most popular type of button and requires a thread shank to be made when sewing in place.

A toothpick will help you to sew on this type of button.

1 Position the button on the fabric. Start with a double stitch and double thread in the needle.

3 Remove the toothpick.

5 Take the thread through to the back of the fabric.

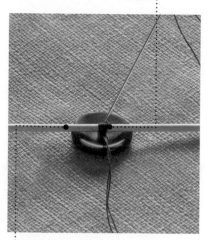

2 Place the toothpick on top of the button. Sew up and down through the holes, going over the stick.

4 Wrap the thread around the thread loops under the button to make a shank.

6 Buttonhole stitch over the loop of threads on the back of the work.

✕ SEWING ON A FOUR-HOLE BUTTON

This is stitched in the same way as for a two-hole button except that the threads make an "X" over the button on the front.

1 Position the button on the fabric. Place a toothpick on the button.

3 Remove the toothpick.

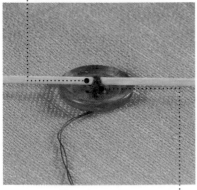

2 Using double thread, sew up and down through alternate sets of holes, over the toothpick. Make an "X" shape as you stitch.

4 Wrap the thread around the thread loops under the button to make the shank.

5 On the reverse of the fabric, buttonhole sew over the thread loops in an X shape.

✕ SEWING ON A SHANKED BUTTON

When sewing this type of button in place, use a toothpick under the button to enable you to make a thread shank on the underside of the fabric.

1 Position the button on the fabric. Hold a toothpick on the other side of the fabric, behind the button.

2 Using double thread, sew the button to the fabric, through the shank.

3 Be sure each stitch goes through the fabric and around the toothpick beneath.

4 Remove the toothpick. Work buttonhole stitch over the looped thread shank.

⋉ SEWING ON A REINFORCED BUTTON

A large, heavy button often features a second button sewn to it on the wrong side and sewn on with the same threads that secure the larger button. The smaller button helps support the weight of the larger button.

1 Position the large button on the right side of the fabric. Hold a smaller button beneath the fabric, in line with the large button.

2 Sew on the large button, sewing through both buttons to secure.

3 When the sewing is complete, wrap the thread around the thread loops beneath the larger button. Secure with a double stitch.

⋉ COVERED BUTTONS

Covered buttons are often found on expensive clothes and will add a professional finish to any jacket or other garment you make. A purchased button-making tool will enable you to create covered buttons very easily.

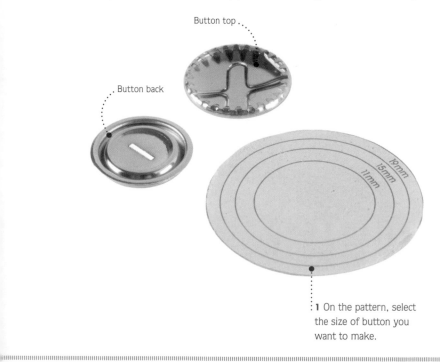

Button top

Button back

19mm
15mm
11mm

1 On the pattern, select the size of button you want to make.

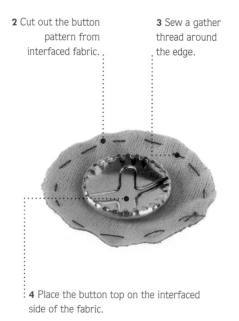

2 Cut out the button pattern from interfaced fabric.

3 Sew a gather thread around the edge.

4 Place the button top on the interfaced side of the fabric.

Shank of button top

5 Pull up the gathers and secure with a double stitch around the shank of the button top.

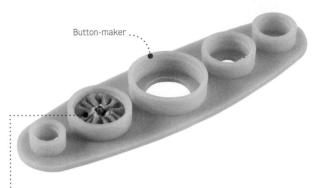

Button-maker

6 Put the button in the correct hole in the button-maker. Push well in.

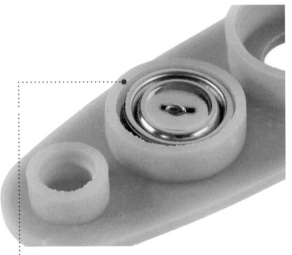

7 Place the button back on top of the button.

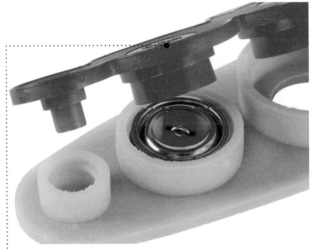

8 Take the other side of the button-maker and press down on the button back until it clicks into position.

9 Remove the button from the button-maker and check to be sure the back is firmly in place.

10 The finished covered button.

BUTTONHOLES

A buttonhole is essential if a button is to be truly functional, although for many oversized buttons, a snap fastener on the reverse is a better option, because the buttonhole would be just too big and could cause the garment to stretch.

◤ DIRECTORY OF BUTTONHOLES AND BUTTON LOOPS

BASIC BUTTONHOLE (p.126)

ROUND-END BUTTONHOLE (p.126)

KEYHOLE BUTTONHOLE (p.126)

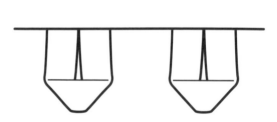

BUTTON LOOPS (p.127)

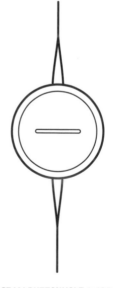

IN-SEAM BUTTONHOLE (p.126)

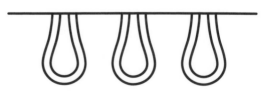

CORDED LOOP (p.128)

✕ STAGES OF A BUTTONHOLE

A sewing machine stitches a buttonhole in three stages. The stitch can be slightly varied in width and length to suit the garment or craft item, but it needs to be tight and close together.

 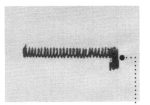 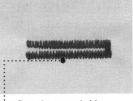 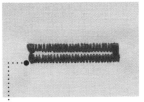

1 Sew the first side of the buttonhole.

2 Sew a bar baste at one end.

3 Sew the second side below the first.

4 Bar tack at the other end.

✕ POSITIONING BUTTONHOLES

The size and position of the buttonhole is determined by the button size and needs to be worked out prior to any type of buttonhole being made.

1 Place the button on a sewing gauge and use the slider to measure the button's diameter.

2 On the right-hand side of the garment, work a row of basting stitches along the center front line.

3 Work a second row of bastes the diameter of the button away.

4 Position the buttons between the baste lines. Sew lines at right angles where the buttonholes are to be placed.

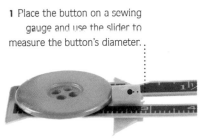 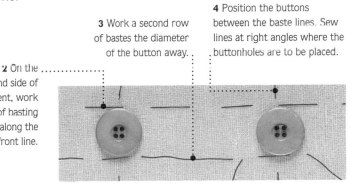

✕ VERTICAL OR HORIZONTAL?

As a general rule, buttonholes are only vertical on a garment when there is a placket or a strip into which the buttonhole fits. All other buttonholes should be horizontal. Any strain on the buttonhole will then pull to the end and prevent the button from coming undone.

HORIZONTAL BUTTONHOLES

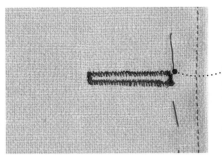

These are positioned with the end on the basted center line.

VERTICAL BUTTONHOLES

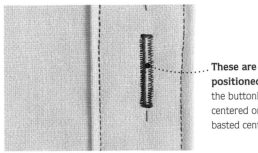

These are positioned with the buttonhole centered on the basted center line.

⋊ MACHINE-MADE BUTTONHOLES

Modern sewing machines can sew various types of buttonhole, suitable for all kinds of garments. On many machines, the button fits into a special foot and a sensor on the machine determines the correct size of buttonhole. The width and length of the stitch can be altered to suit the fabric. Once the buttonhole has been stitched, always cut through with a buttonhole cutter to ensure that the cut is clean.

BASIC BUTTONHOLE

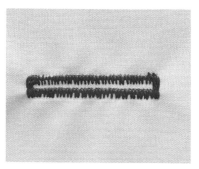

The most popular shape for a buttonhole is square on both ends.

ROUND-END BUTTONHOLE

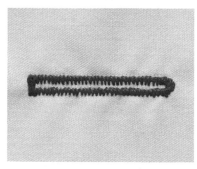

A buttonhole featuring one rounded end and one square end is used on lightweight jackets.

KEYHOLE BUTTONHOLE

This is also called a tailor's buttonhole. It has a square end and a keyhole end and is used on jackets and coats.

⋊ IN-SEAM BUTTONHOLE

This is a buttonhole formed in a seam allowance. It is found down decorative center fronts that feature seam detailing. It is a very discreet buttonhole.

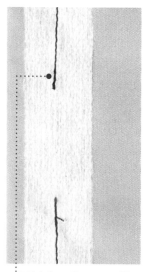

1 Reinforce the seam with a fusible tape on one side.

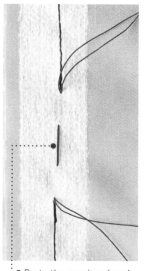

2 Baste the opening closed.

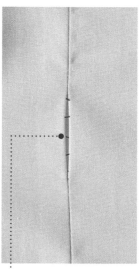

3 Press the seam open. The bastes will show.

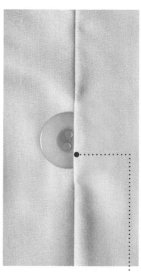

4 Remove the basting stitches to form the buttonhole.

BUTTON LOOPS

A buttonhole is not the only way of using buttons. Buttons can also be fastened by means of a fabric loop, which is usually attached at the edge of a garment. Fabric loops are often found on the back of special-occasion wear, where multiple loops secure rows of small, often covered buttons.

⋈ FABRIC BUTTON LOOP

This button loop is formed from a bias strip. Choose a smooth fabric for the strip, as it will be easier to turn through. A fabric loop is used with a round ball-type button.

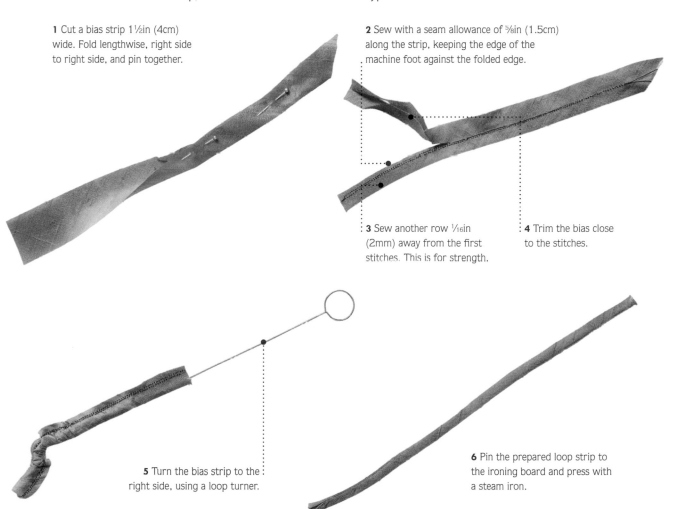

1 Cut a bias strip 1½in (4cm) wide. Fold lengthwise, right side to right side, and pin together.

2 Sew with a seam allowance of ⅝in (1.5cm) along the strip, keeping the edge of the machine foot against the folded edge.

3 Sew another row ¹⁄₁₆in (2mm) away from the first stitches. This is for strength.

4 Trim the bias close to the stitches.

5 Turn the bias strip to the right side, using a loop turner.

6 Pin the prepared loop strip to the ironing board and press with a steam iron.

▶ SPACING THE LOOPS

Once the loops have been made, the next step is to attach them to the garment. It is important that all the loops are the same size and positioned the same distance apart. To achieve this, you will need to baste your fabric to mark the placement lines. The loops go on the right-hand front or the left-hand back of the work.

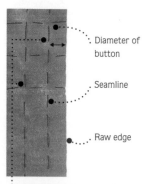

.... Diameter of button

.... Seamline

.... Raw edge

1 Mark the placement lines on the fabric using basting stitches. Be sure the horizontal lines are equally spaced.

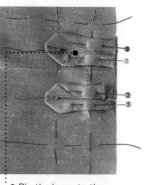

2 Pin the loops to the fabric. The folded end of the loop should be on the inner basting line and the cut ends to the raw edge. Center the loop over the baste line.

3 Sew the loops just inside the seam allowance at the center line.

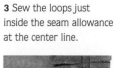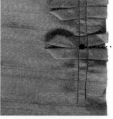

4 Sew another row to ensure the loops are secure.

5 Place the facing or lining over the loops to finish.

6 The completed loop will extend from the edge of the fabric.

▶ CORDED LOOP

It is possible to make a very fine button loop that has a cord running through it. This type of loop is suitable for lightweight fabrics. Use a shanked button with a corded loop.

1 Cut a bias strip 1½in (4cm) wide and any length. Cut a piece of cord twice the length of the strip.

3 Sew along the bias strip, next to, but not too close to, the cord.

4 Sew another row ¹⁄₁₆in (2mm) away from the first stitches.

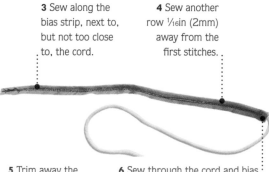

2 Wrap the cord in the bias strip, folded right side to right side. Pin. Make sure the bias strip is close to one end of the cord.

5 Trim away the bias strip close to the stitches.

6 Sew through the cord and bias strip in the center of the cord and near the end of the bias strip.

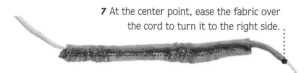

7 At the center point, ease the fabric over the cord to turn it to the right side.

8 Trim off the exposed ends of cord from the fabric loop.

OTHER FASTENINGS

There are many alternative ways to fasten garments, craft projects, and other items, some of which can be used instead of or in conjunction with other fasteners. These include hooks and eyes, snaps, and tape fasteners.

◤ DIRECTORY OF OTHER FASTENINGS

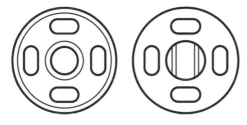

SNAP FASTENER (p.130)

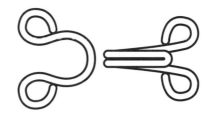

HOOK AND EYE (p.131)

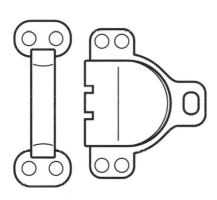

WAISTBAND HOOK AND BAR (p.131)

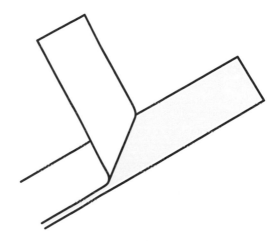

VELCRO™ (p.132)

GROMMETS (p.132)

⋈ SNAPS

A snap is a ball and socket fastener that is used to hold two overlapping edges closed. The ball side goes on top and the socket side underneath. Snaps can be round or square and can be made from metal or plastic.

1 Baste the ball and socket halves of the snap in place. . . . .

2 Secure permanently using a buttonhole stitch through each hole in the outer edge of the snap half. .

3 Remove the bastes.

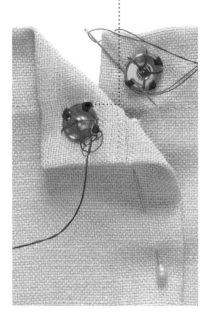

PLASTIC SNAPS

A plastic snap may be white or clear plastic and is usually square in shape. Sew in place as for a metal snap (see above).

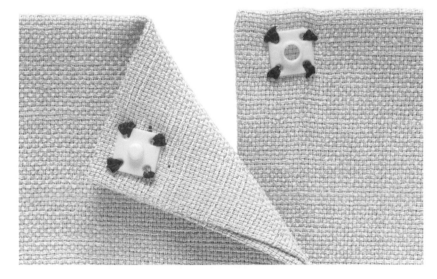

↗ HOOKS AND EYES

There are a multitude of different types of hook and eye fasteners. Purchased hooks and eyes are made from metal and are normally silver or black in color. Different-shaped hooks and eyes are used on different garments—large, broad hooks and eyes can be decorative and sewn to show on the outside, while the tiny fasteners are meant to be discreet. A hook that goes into a hand-worked eye produces a neat, close fastening.

ATTACHING HOOKS AND EYES

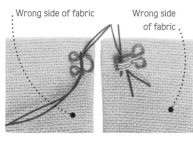
Wrong side of fabric   Wrong side of fabric

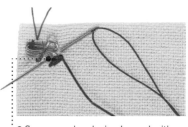

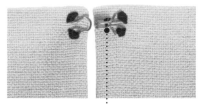

1 Working on the wrong side of the fabric, secure the eye and hook in place with a basting stitch. Make sure they are in line with each other.

2 Sew around each circular end with a buttonhole stitch on both hook and eye.

3 Place a few overstitches under the hook to stop it from moving.

HAND-WORKED EYE

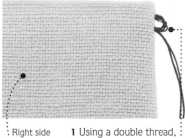
Right side of fabric

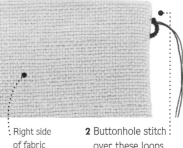
Right side of fabric

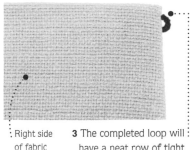
Right side of fabric

1 Using a double thread, work several small loops into the edge of the fabric.

2 Buttonhole stitch over these loops.

3 The completed loop will have a neat row of tight buttonhole stitches.

WAISTBAND HOOK AND BAR

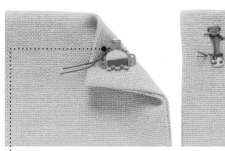

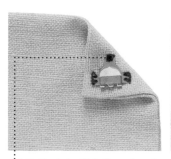

1 The hook and bar fastener for pant and skirt waistbands is large and flat. Baste the hook and bar in position. Do not baste through the holes that are used for securing.

2 Buttonhole stitch through each hole on the hook and bar.

⋈ TAPE FASTENERS

In addition to individual small fasteners, there are fasteners in the form of tapes that can be sewn or stuck on. Velcro™, a hook and loop tape, is available in many colors and types. Sewn-on Velcro™ is ideal for both clothing and soft furnishings, while the stick-on variety can be used to fix curtain valances and blinds to battens on windows. Plain cotton tape with snap fasteners is used primarily in home goods. Hook and eye tape is found in underwear or down the front of a shirt or jacket, where it can be very decorative.

VELCRO™

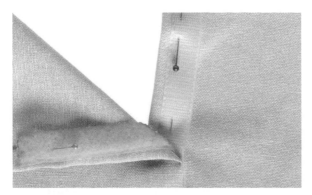

1 Pin the Velcro™ in place. The loop side should be underneath and the hook side on top.

2 Sew around all the edges.

⋈ GROMMETS

A grommet fastening can be decorative and is often found on bridal wear and prom dresses. A piece of boning needs to be inserted into the fabric between the edge and the grommets to provide strength. You will require grommet pliers to punch the holes and then insert the grommets.

1 Using the pliers, punch out the holes for the grommets at 1¼–1½in (3–4cm) intervals.

3 Insert a row of grommets on either side of the back opening. ...... Boning channel

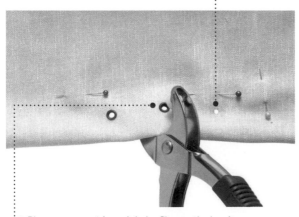

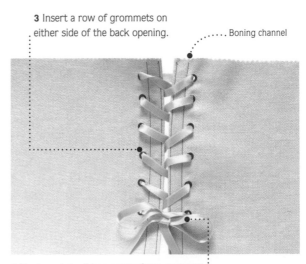

2 Place a grommet in each hole. Change the heads on the pliers and squeeze the grommet in place.

4 To close, lace ribbon across from grommet to grommet and finish with a bow.

ZIPPERS

The zipper is probably the most used of all fastenings. There are many types available in a variety of lengths, colors, and materials, but they all fall into one of five categories: skirt or pant zippers, metal or jeans zippers, invisible zippers, open-ended zippers, and decorative zippers. Before attaching any zipper, apply ¾in (2cm) wide strips of fusible interfacing to the zipper seam allowances on the wrong side of the fabric.

◤ DIRECTORY OF ZIPPERS

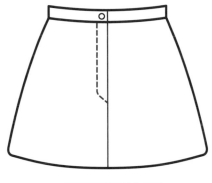

LAPPED ZIPPER (p.135)

OPEN-ENDED ZIPPER (p.136)

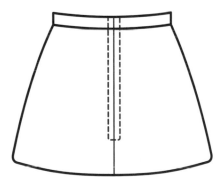

CENTERED ZIPPER (p.137)

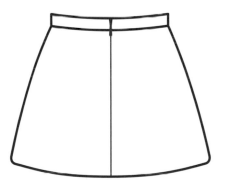

CONCEALED OR INVISIBLE ZIPPER (p.138)

▶ HOW TO SHORTEN A ZIPPER

Zippers do not always come in the length that you need, but it is easy to shorten them. Skirt or pant zippers and invisible zippers are all shortened by sewing across the teeth or coils, whereas an open-ended zipper is shortened at the top and not at the bottom.

SHORTENING A SKIRT/PANT OR INVISIBLE ZIPPER

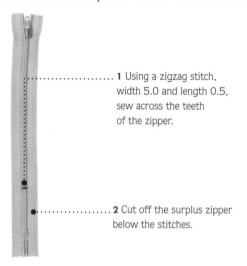

1 Using a zigzag stitch, width 5.0 and length 0.5, sew across the teeth of the zipper.

2 Cut off the surplus zipper below the stitches.

SHORTENING AN OPEN-ENDED ZIPPER

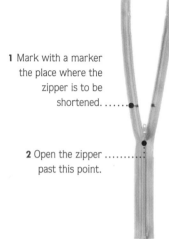

1 Mark with a marker the place where the zipper is to be shortened.

2 Open the zipper past this point.

3 Using a zigzag stitch, width 3.0 and length 0.5, machine sew across each side of the opened zipper. Cut off the surplus.

▶ MARKING FOR PLACING ZIPPERS

For a zipper to sit accurately in the seam, the seam allowances where the zipper will be inserted need to be marked. The upper seam allowance at the top of the zipper also needs marking to ensure that the zipper pull sits just fractionally below the sewn line.

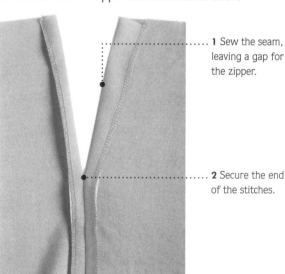

1 Sew the seam, leaving a gap for the zipper.

2 Secure the end of the stitches.

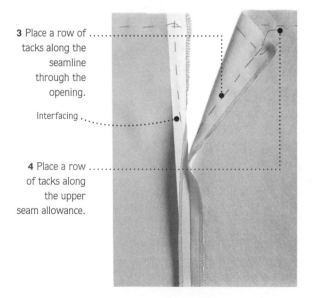

3 Place a row of tacks along the seamline through the opening.

Interfacing

4 Place a row of tacks along the upper seam allowance.

◣ LAPPED ZIPPER

A zipper in a skirt or a dress is usually put in by means of a lapped technique or a centered zipper technique (see p.137). For both of these techniques, you will require the zipper foot on the sewing machine. A lapped zipper features one side of the seam—the left-hand side—covering the teeth of the zipper to conceal them.

1 Sew the seam, leaving enough of the seam open to accommodate the zipper.

Interfacing

2 Secure the end of the stitches.

Wrong side of fabric

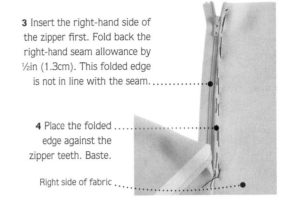

3 Insert the right-hand side of the zipper first. Fold back the right-hand seam allowance by ½in (1.3cm). This folded edge is not in line with the seam.

4 Place the folded edge against the zipper teeth. Baste.

Right side of fabric

5 Using the zipper foot, sew along the baste line to secure the zipper tape to the fabric. Sew from the bottom of the zipper to the top.

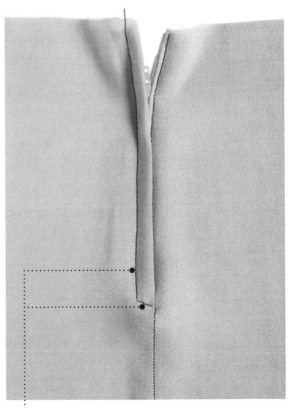

6 Fold back the left-hand seam allowance by ⅝in (1.5cm) and press. Place the folded edge over the sewn line of the other side. Pin and then hand baste along foldline.

7 Starting at the bottom of the zipper, sew across from the center seamline and then up the side of the zipper. The finished zipper should have the teeth covered by the fabric.

✕ OPEN-ENDED ZIPPER

The open-ended zipper is used on garments where the two halves need to be fully opened in order to put the garment on—for example, on a jacket or cardigan.

1 On both pieces of fabric, turn under the seam allowance at the center front and baste. Neaten by preferred method. ....

Wrong side of fabric .

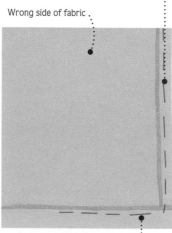

2 Turn up the hem allowance and baste in place.

3 Place the folded edge of the center front about ⅛in (3mm) from the zipper teeth to allow for the pull to move up and down. Pin in place. .

Right side of fabric .

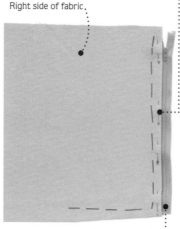

4 Place the bottom of the zipper at the hem edge.

5 Using the zipper foot, sew the zipper in place. Start with the zipper open. Sew 2in (5cm), then place the needle in the work, raise the zipper foot, and close the zipper.

Right side of fabric .

6 Sew to the end of the zipper tape and secure.

7 Pin the other side of the zipper in place on the other piece of fabric. Make sure the fabric lines up top and bottom. .

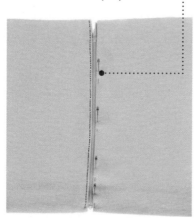

8 Undo the zipper and, using the zipper foot, sew in place as you did on the first side.

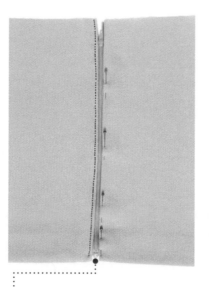

9 Once the zipper is sewn in place, check that the hems line up. If they do not, you will have to rip the seam and start again.

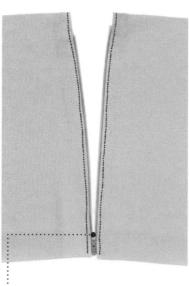

10 The zipper should open completely.

◣ CENTERED ZIPPER

With a centered zipper, the two folded edges of the seam allowances meet over the center of the teeth to conceal the zipper completely.

1 Sew the seam, leaving a gap for the zipper.

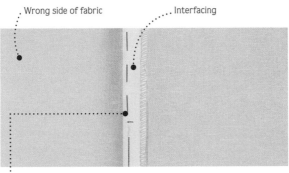

Wrong side of fabric · · · · · · · · Interfacing

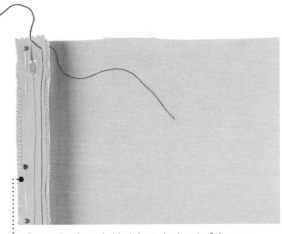

2 Baste the rest of the seam allowance.

3 Press the seam open lightly.

4 Center the zipper behind the tacked part of the seam. Pin and then baste in place along both sides.

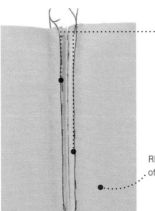

5 On the wrong side, lift the seam allowance and the zipper tape away from the main fabric. Pin.

6 Sew the zipper tape to the seam allowance. Make sure both sides of the zipper tape are secured to the seam allowances. Sew through to the end of the zipper tape.

7 Working from the right side of the work, sew down one side, across the bottom, and up the other side of the zipper.

8 Remove the tacks and press.

Right side of fabric

9 The finished zipper from the right side.

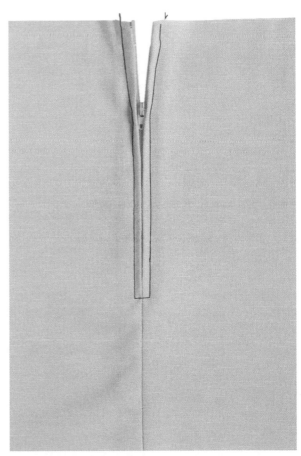

⋉ CONCEALED OR INVISIBLE ZIPPER

This type of zipper looks different from other zippers because the teeth are on the reverse and nothing except the pull is seen on the front. The zipper is inserted before the seam is sewn. A special invisible zipper foot is required.

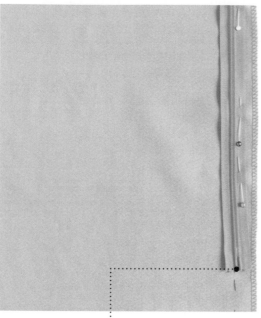

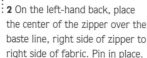

1 Mark the seam allowance with basting stitches.

2 On the left-hand back, place the center of the zipper over the baste line, right side of zipper to right side of fabric. Pin in place.

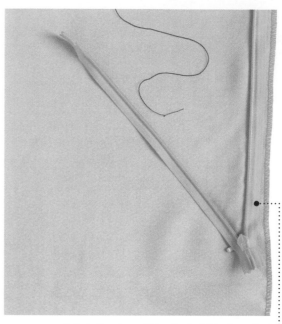

3 Undo the zipper. Using the invisible zipper foot, sew from the top of the zipper down as far as possible. Stitch under the teeth. Stop when the foot hits the zipper pull.

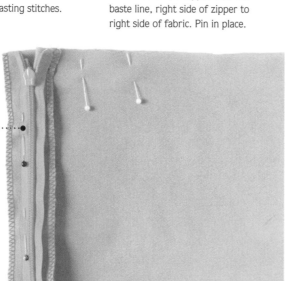

4 Do the zipper up. Place the other piece of fabric to the zipper. Match along the upper edge. Pin the other side of the zipper tape in place.

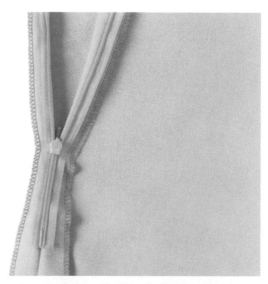

5 Open the zipper again. Using the invisible zipper foot, sew down the other side of the zipper to attach to the right-hand side. Remove any basting stitches.

6 Close the zipper. On the wrong side at the bottom of the zipper, the two rows of stitching that hold in the zipper should be finishing at the same place.

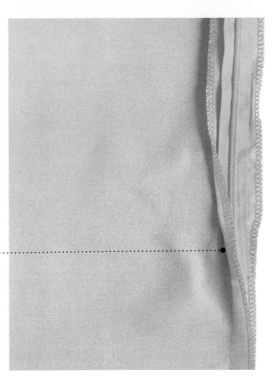

7 Sew the seam below the zipper. Use the normal machine foot for this. There will be a gap of about ⅛in (3mm) between the line for the zipper and that for the seam.

Free end of zipper tape

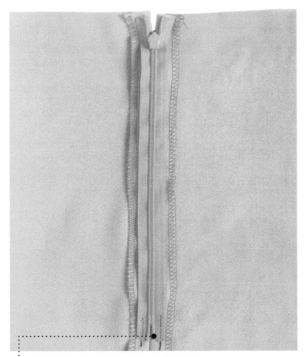

8 Sew the last 1¼in (3cm) of the zipper tape to just the seam allowances. This will stop the zipper from pulling loose.

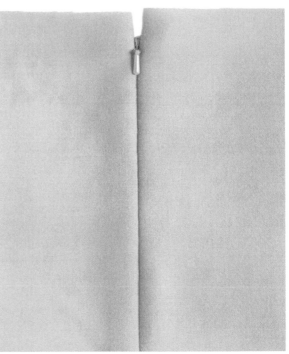

9 On the right side, the zipper is completely invisible, with just the pull visible at the top. Apply a waistband or facing and press.

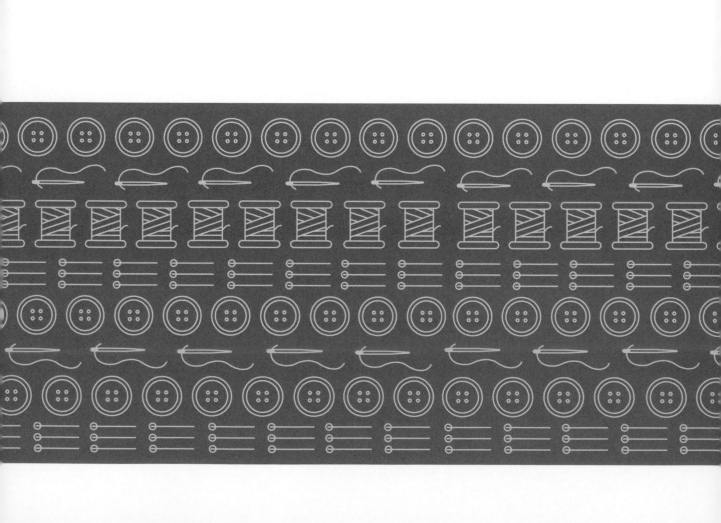

POCKETS

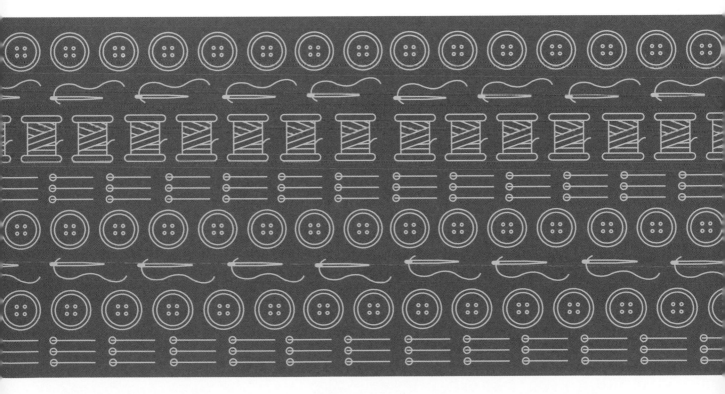

POCKETS

Pockets come in lots of shapes and formats. Some, such as patch pockets, cargo pockets, and jetted pockets with a flap, are external and can be decorative, while others, including front hip pockets, are more discreet and hidden from view. They can be made from the same fabric as the garment or from a contrasting fabric. Whether casual or tailored, all pockets are functional.

▶◀ DIRECTORY OF POCKETS

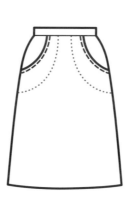

PATCH POCKET (pp.142–145)

FRONT HIP POCKET (p.148)

KANGAROO POCKET (p.149)

▶◀ UNLINED PATCH POCKET

An unlined patch pocket is one of the most popular types of pocket. It can be found on garments of all kinds and be made from a wide variety of fabrics. On lightweight fabrics, such as those used for a shirt pocket, interfacing is not required, but on medium and heavier fabrics, it is advisable to apply a fusible interfacing.

1 If needed, apply an interfacing to the pocket fabric.

2 Mark the foldlines with tailor's tacks.

Wrong side of pocket

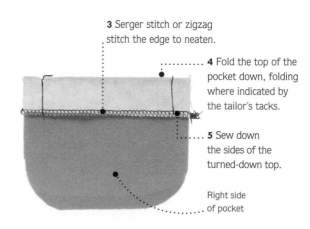

3 Serger stitch or zigzag stitch the edge to neaten.

4 Fold the top of the pocket down, folding where indicated by the tailor's tacks.

5 Sew down the sides of the turned-down top.

Right side of pocket

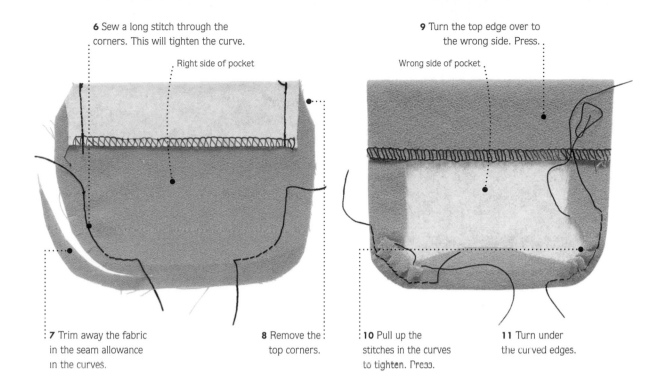

6 Sew a long stitch through the corners. This will tighten the curve.

Right side of pocket

9 Turn the top edge over to the wrong side. Press.

Wrong side of pocket

7 Trim away the fabric in the seam allowance in the curves.

8 Remove the top corners.

10 Pull up the stitches in the curves to tighten. Press.

11 Turn under the curved edges.

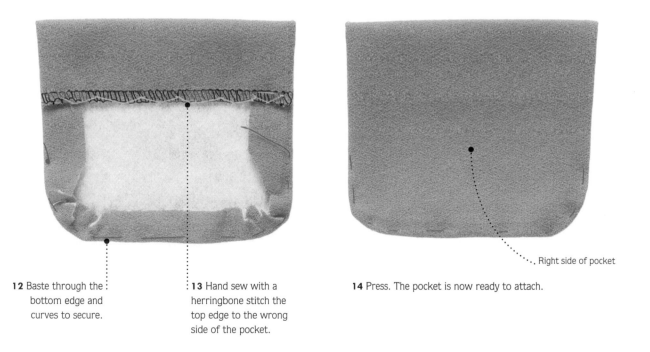

12 Baste through the bottom edge and curves to secure.

13 Hand sew with a herringbone stitch the top edge to the wrong side of the pocket.

14 Press. The pocket is now ready to attach.

Right side of pocket

▶ LINED PATCH POCKET

If a patch pocket is to be lined, it needs to be cut with the top edge of the pocket on a fold. Like an unlined pocket, if you are using a lightweight fabric, an interfacing may not be required, whereas for medium-weight fabrics, a fusible interfacing is advisable. A lined patch pocket is not suitable for heavy fabrics.

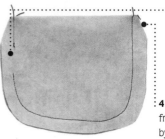

1 Cut the pocket fabric and apply a fusible interfacing, if needed.

2 Fold the pocket in half, right side to right side. Pin to secure.

3 Sew around the three open sides of the pocket. Leave a gap of 1in (3cm) for turning through.

4 Remove bulk from the corners by trimming.

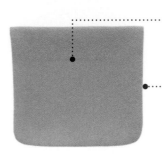

5 Trim one side of the seam allowance down to half its width.

6 Use pinking shears to trim the corners.

7 Turn the pocket through the gap to the right side. Press.

8 Hand stitch the gap (using a flat fell or blind hem stitch) in the seam. The pocket is now ready to be attached.

▶ SQUARE PATCH POCKET

It is possible to have a patch pocket with square corners. This requires mitering the corners to reduce the bulk. Use a fusible interfacing on medium-weight fabrics.

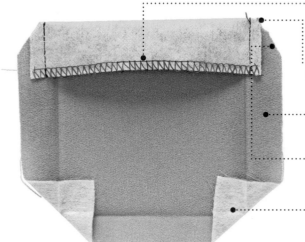

1 Cut the pocket and apply interfacing, if needed. Neaten the upper edge of the pocket with serger or zigzag stitching.

2 Fold over the upper edge and stitch down the sides.

3 Fold in the other three edges and press to crease.

4 Remove the top corners.

5 Fold in the bottom corners, then fold across these to give creases for the miters.

6 Sew the crease lines together in each bottom corner to miter it. ......

Wrong side of fabric

Flat mitered corners

7 Cut off the surplus fabric, then press the corner seam open with the toe of the iron.

8 Turn the edges of the pocket to the wrong side.

9 The finished pocket is now ready to be attached.

◤ ATTACHING A PATCH POCKET

To attach a pocket well, accurate pattern marking is essential. It is best to do this by means of tailor's tacks or even trace basting. If you are using a check or striped fabric, the pocket fabric must align with the checks or stripes on the garment.

1 Mark the pocket placement lines on the garment with tailor's tacks. ....

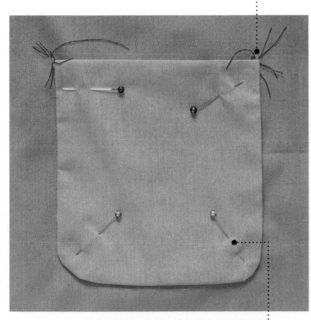

2 Take the completed pocket and place it to the fabric, matching the corners with the tailor's tacks. Pin in position.

3 To make sure the pocket remains in the correct position, baste around the edge along the sides and bottom. Keep the basting stitches close to the finished edge of the pocket.

4 Sew approximately ½2in (1mm) from the edge of the pocket.

5 Remove the basting stitches. Press.

6 Alternatively, the pocket can be hand sewn in place using a slip hem stitch into the underside of the pocket seam. Do not pull on the thread too tightly or the pocket will wrinkle.

⋊ REINFORCING POCKET CORNERS

On any patch pocket, it is essential to reinforce the upper corners, as these take all the strain when the pocket is being used. There are several ways to do this, some of which are quite decorative.

REVERSE STITCH

1 Reinforce the corner with a reverse stitch. Make sure the stitches lie on top of one another. ....

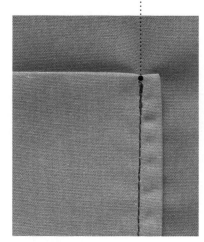

2 Pull the threads to the reverse to tie off.

DIAGONAL STITCH

1 This technique is used primarily on shirts. When sewing the pocket in place, sew along horizontally for four stitches. .

2 Turn and sew diagonally back to the side to create a triangular shape in the corner.

ZIGZAG STITCH

1 Using a small zigzag stitch, width 1.0 and length 1.0, sew diagonally across the corner.

2 Make a feature of this stitch by using a thread in a contrasting color.

PARALLEL ZIGZAG STITCH

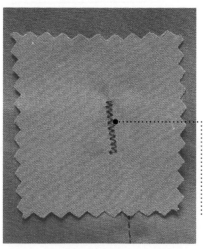

1 Place a patch on the wrong side of the garment, behind the pocket corner, to sew into for strength.

2 Using a small zigzag stitch, width 1.0 and length 1.0, sew a short vertical line next to the straight stitches.

◀ MAKING A POCKET FLAP

On some styles of garment, there is no pocket—just a flap for decorative purposes. The flap is sewn where the pocket would be, but there is no opening under the flap. This is to reduce the bulk that would arise from having the rest of the pocket.

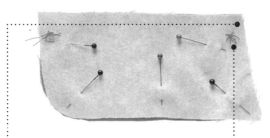

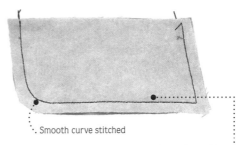

. Smooth curve stitched

1 The flap consists of two pieces—a piece of lining and a piece of interfaced fabric. Place the two pieces together, right side to right side.

2 Match the tailor's tacks, then pin to secure.

3 Sew the pocket flap together along three sides, using a ⅜in (1cm) seam allowance. Sew through the tailor's tacks. Leave the upper edge open.

4 Layer the seam allowance, trimming away the lining side.

7 Turn the flap through to the right side. Push out the point.

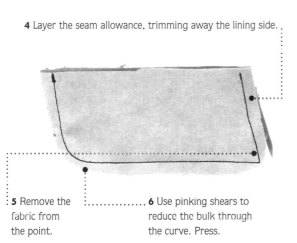

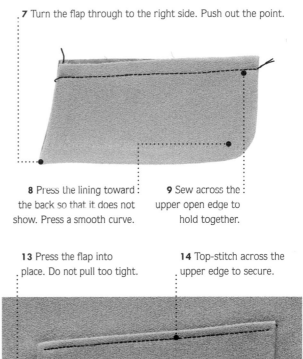

5 Remove the fabric from the point.

6 Use pinking shears to reduce the bulk through the curve. Press.

8 Press the lining toward the back so that it does not show. Press a smooth curve.

9 Sew across the upper open edge to hold together.

10 Place the flap to the garment, right side to right side. Match the edges of the flaps to the tailor's tacks on the garment.

13 Press the flap into place. Do not pull too tight.

14 Top-stitch across the upper edge to secure.

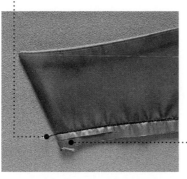

11 Sew in place over the sewn line, holding the gap at the upper edge together.

12 Reduce the seam allowance by half. Press.

◄ FRONT HIP POCKET

On many pants and casual skirts, the pocket is placed on the hipline. It can be low on the hipline or cut quite high as on jeans. The construction is the same for all types of hip pockets. When inserted at an angle, hip pockets can slim the figure.

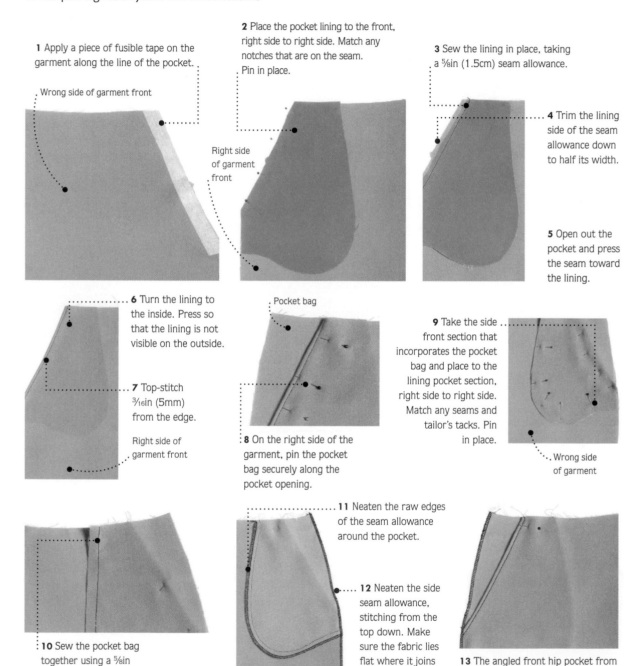

1 Apply a piece of fusible tape on the garment along the line of the pocket.

Wrong side of garment front

2 Place the pocket lining to the front, right side to right side. Match any notches that are on the seam. Pin in place.

Right side of garment front

3 Sew the lining in place, taking a ⅝in (1.5cm) seam allowance.

4 Trim the lining side of the seam allowance down to half its width.

5 Open out the pocket and press the seam toward the lining.

6 Turn the lining to the inside. Press so that the lining is not visible on the outside.

7 Top-stitch ³⁄₁₆in (5mm) from the edge.

Right side of garment front

Pocket bag

8 On the right side of the garment, pin the pocket bag securely along the pocket opening.

9 Take the side front section that incorporates the pocket bag and place to the lining pocket section, right side to right side. Match any seams and tailor's tacks. Pin in place.

Wrong side of garment

10 Sew the pocket bag together using a ⅝in (1.5cm) seam allowance. Press.

11 Neaten the raw edges of the seam allowance around the pocket.

12 Neaten the side seam allowance, stitching from the top down. Make sure the fabric lies flat where it joins the side seam.

13 The angled front hip pocket from the right side.

◄ KANGAROO POCKET

This is a variation on a patch pocket. It is a large pocket that is often found on aprons and the front of hooded sweatshirts. A half version of this pocket also features on casual jackets.

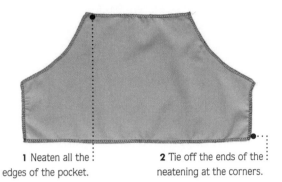

1 Neaten all the edges of the pocket.

2 Tie off the ends of the neatening at the corners.

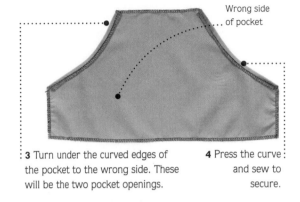

Wrong side of pocket

3 Turn under the curved edges of the pocket to the wrong side. These will be the two pocket openings.

4 Press the curve and sew to secure.

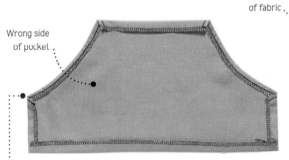

Wrong side of pocket

Right side of fabric

5 Turn under all the remaining edges of the pocket to the wrong side. If the fabric is bulky, miter the corners. Press in place.

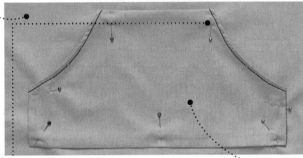

6 Place the pocket to the garment, wrong side of the pocket to right side of the garment. Make sure the pocket is sitting flat and straight. Pin in place.

Right side of pocket

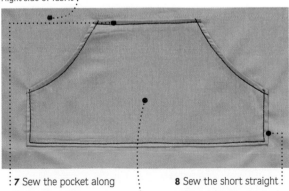

Right side of fabric

7 Sew the pocket along the upper edge.

8 Sew the short straight sides and lower edge of the pocket. Press.

Right side of pocket

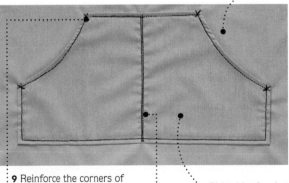

Right side of fabric

9 Reinforce the corners of the pocket with a diagonal zigzag stitch.

Right side of pocket

10 If required, stitch one or two vertical lines down the center of the pocket to divide into two pockets. Press.

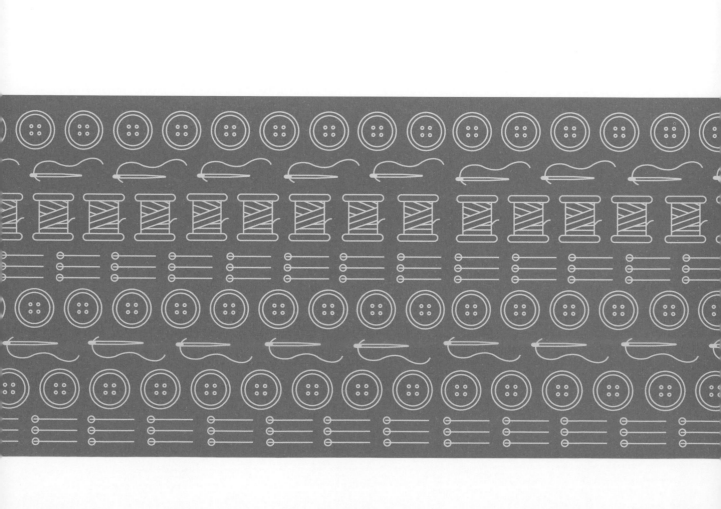

WAISTLINES, BELTS, AND TIE-BACKS

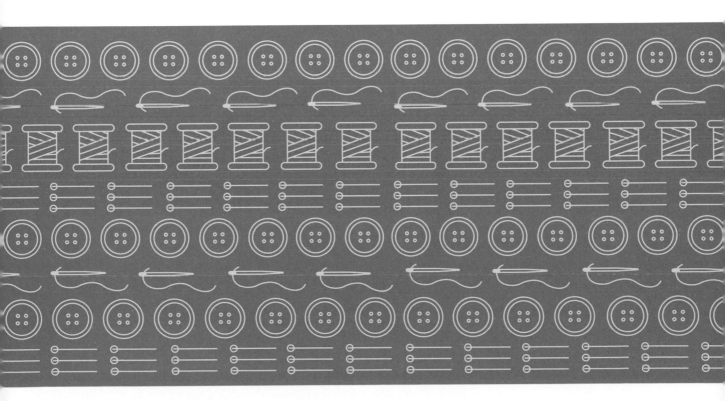

WAISTLINES

Waistlines can be formed where a bodice and skirt join together or at the waist edge of a skirt or pair of pants. Some waistlines are attached to the garment to create a feature and others are more discreet. They may be shaped to follow the contours of the body.

▶ DIRECTORY OF WAISTLINES

FITTED WAISTLINE
(p.153)

GATHERED WAISTLINE (p.153)

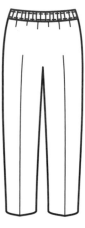

WAISTLINE WITH A CASING
(pp.154–155)

APPLIED CASING
(p.156)

MOCK CASING USING
ELASTIC (p.157)

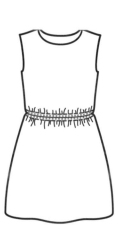

ALTERNATIVE CASING
USING A SEAM ALLOWANCE
(p.158)

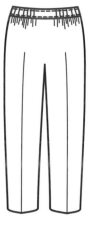

PARTIAL CASING
(p.159)

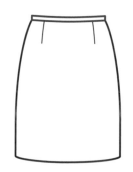

STRAIGHT
WAISTBAND (p.160)

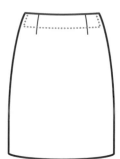

WAISTLINE WITH
A FACING (p.161)

✂ JOINING A FITTED SKIRT TO A BODICE

Many dresses feature a straight fitted skirt attached to a fitted dress bodice. When joining them together, it is important that the darts or seamlines on the bodice match up with those on the skirt.

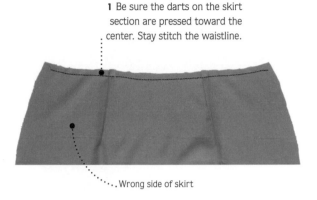

1 Be sure the darts on the skirt section are pressed toward the center. Stay stitch the waistline.

Wrong side of skirt

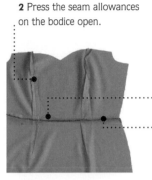

2 Press the seam allowances on the bodice open.

3 Place the skirt to the bodice, matching up the darts and the bodice seams. Pin the bodice and skirt together.

4 Sew the bodice to the skirt using a ⅝in (1.5cm) seam allowance and press.

5 Neaten the skirt/bodice seam using either a 3-thread serger stitch or a zigzag stitch.

6 Press the seam up toward the bodice.

Wrong side of garment

7 On the right side, the seams and darts match at the waist.

Right side of garment

✂ JOINING A GATHERED SKIRT TO A BODICE

When attaching a gathered skirt to a fitted bodice, the gathers must be distributed evenly around the waist. If there are seams on the gathered skirt, these must be matched to the bodice seams and darts.

1 Sew a double row of gather stitches around the waistline of a half circle skirt.

2 Pull up the gathers to fit the bodice waist.

3 Pin the gathered skirt to the bodice, making sure the bodice darts face toward the center.

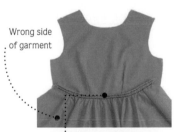

Wrong side of garment

4 Sew the gathered skirt to the bodice using a ⅝in (1.5cm) seam allowance. Neaten the seam using either a 3-thread serger stitch or a zigzag stitch.

5 Press the seam up toward the bodice. On the right side, the skirt seam is gathered into a smooth bodice seam.

Right side of garment

⋈ MAKING A CASING AT THE WAIST EDGE

An elastic waist can be featured on both skirts and pants and also at the waist on casual jackets.

A casing can be made by using a deep waist seam or by attaching a facing.

USING A DEEP WAIST SEAM AS A CASING

1 Turn under a ⅝in (1.5cm) seam allowance to the wrong side and press.

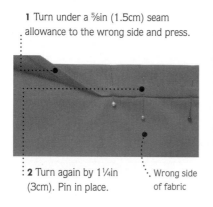

2 Turn again by 1¼in (3cm). Pin in place.

Wrong side of fabric

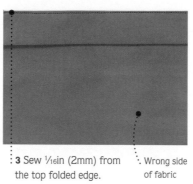

3 Sew ¹⁄₁₆in (2mm) from the top folded edge.

Wrong side of fabric

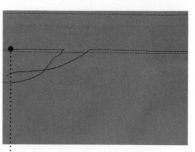

4 Sew the lower edge of the fold ¹⁄₁₆in (2mm) from the edge. Leave a 1in (3cm) gap to insert the elastic through.

5 Cut a piece of nonroll elastic the length required to go around the waist comfortably.

6 Pin one end of the elastic to the fabric just below the opening.

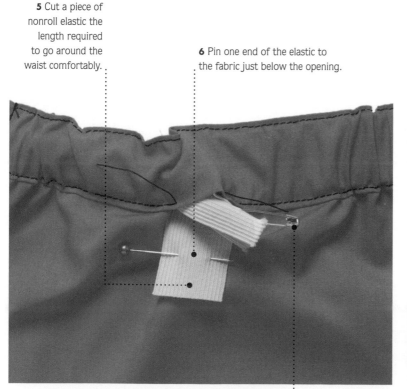

7 Pin a safety pin to the other end and thread through the casing.

8 Pull the two ends of the elastic together and machine sew to join in a square shape with an X for strength.

9 Push the elastic into the casing and sew across the gap.

USING A FACING AS A CASING

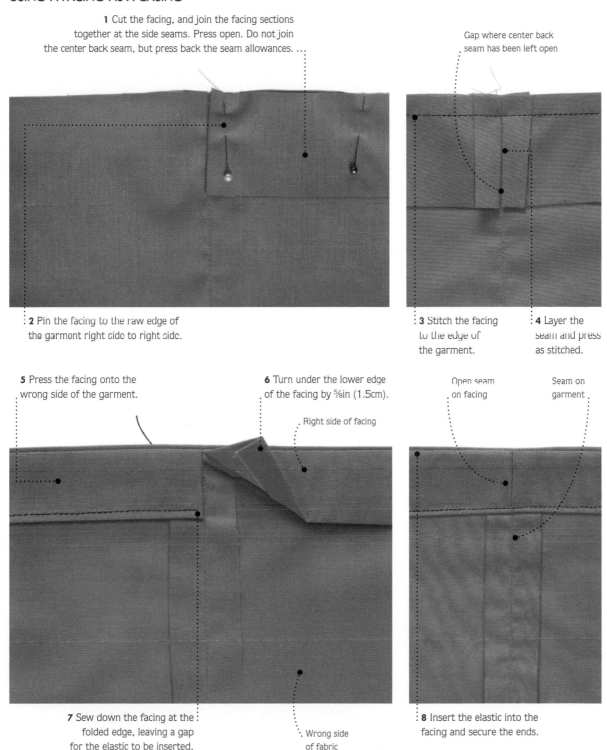

1 Cut the facing, and join the facing sections together at the side seams. Press open. Do not join the center back seam, but press back the seam allowances. ...

Gap where center back seam has been left open

2 Pin the facing to the raw edge of the garment right side to right side.

3 Stitch the facing to the edge of the garment.

4 Layer the seam and press as stitched.

5 Press the facing onto the wrong side of the garment.

6 Turn under the lower edge of the facing by ⅝in (1.5cm).

Right side of facing

Open seam on facing

Seam on garment

7 Sew down the facing at the folded edge, leaving a gap for the elastic to be inserted.

Wrong side of fabric

8 Insert the elastic into the facing and secure the ends.

▶< APPLIED CASINGS

Some elastic waists will require the application of extra fabric to make a casing into which the elastic can be inserted. The casing may be applied to the inside or the outside of the garment. A quick way is to make the casing with bias binding. The casing can also be made from the same fabric as the garment or from a facing.

INTERNAL CASING

1 This type of casing is often used on a shirt-waisted dress or on a blouson-style jacket. Cut a strip of fabric on the straight of grain wide enough to accommodate your elastic and turnings.

2 Turn under the edge at one end by ⅝in (1.5cm) and then the same along the sides. Press.

3 Mark the waist with a row of bastes.

4 Place the casing over the bastes with the finished short end toward the center front. Pin in place.

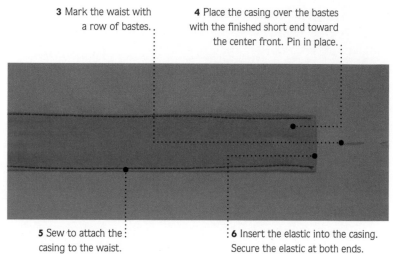

5 Sew to attach the casing to the waist.

6 Insert the elastic into the casing. Secure the elastic at both ends.

INTERNAL CASING USING BIAS BINDING

1 Be sure to use bias binding that will be wide enough to insert an elastic through after it has been sewn down. Apply the bias to the waistline and sew at ¹⁄₁₆in (2mm) from either edge.

¾in (2cm) wide bias binding

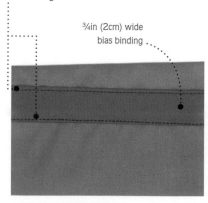

2 Insert the elastic and knot the ends.

EXTERNAL CASING

1 Cut a strip of straight grain fabric 1⅜in (3.5cm) wide x the waist measurement on the garment. Turn under all raw edges by ³⁄₁₆in (5mm) and press.

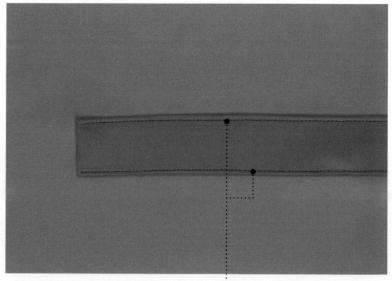

2 Place this casing over the garment waistline, with the short ends to the center front.

3 Sew in place along the long edges. Insert elastic to fit the waist.

▶ MOCK CASINGS

There are several ways to construct mock casings. The simplest is to sew on elastic at the waist. An alternative, if a bodice and skirt have a waist seam joining them together, is to insert elastic between the seam allowances. On many garments, there is elastic at the back only, in a partial casing, and a waistband interfacing at the front.

STITCHING ON ELASTIC TO MAKE A WAISTLINE

1 Cut a piece of elastic to the required length. Mark the waistline on the garment with a row of basting stitches.

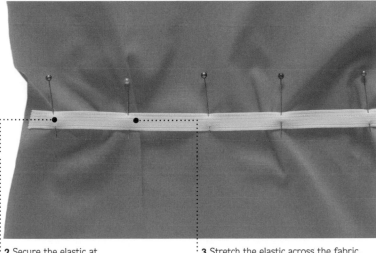

2 Secure the elastic at one end with a pin.

3 Stretch the elastic across the fabric, pinning at regular intervals. The fabric will be loose under the elastic.

4 Secure the elastic at one end with a few machine stitches.

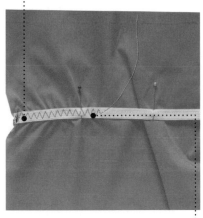

5 Place under the sewing machine and join the elastic to the fabric using a 3-step zigzag stitch, stretching the fabric and elastic together as you do so.

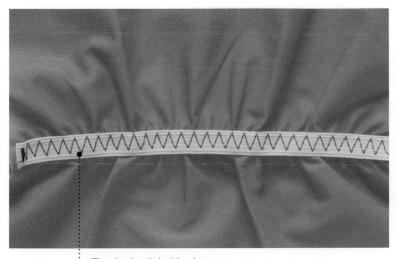

6 The elastic stitched in place.

7 On the right side, there is a neat elasticated waistline.

CASING IN A WAIST SEAM ALLOWANCE

1 Join the fabric together using a ¾in (2cm) seam allowance.

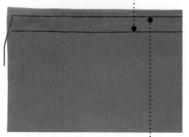

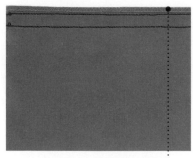

2 Sew again ⅝in (1.5cm) from this line, ³⁄₁₆in (5mm) from the raw edge.

3 Neaten the edge of the seam using a 3-thread serger stitch or a zigzag stitch.

4 Insert elastic into the casing that you have made with the help of a safety pin.

ALTERNATIVE CASING USING A SEAM ALLOWANCE

Wrong side of garment

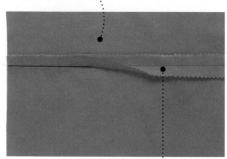

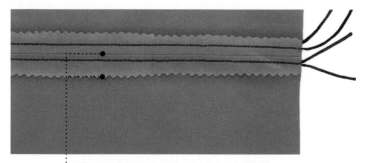

1 Press the waist seam allowances open.

2 Top-stitch the seam allowances open, stitching ⅜in (1cm) from the seam, to make a channel on either side of the seam.

Right side of garment

Wrong side of garment

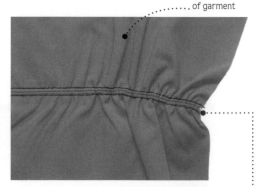

3 Using a cord elastic and a bodkin, insert a length of elastic through each channel.

4 Knot the elastic together, then gather the fabric along the elastic to the required measurement.

5 Knot the elastic together at the other end and cut off any excess.

PARTIAL CASING

1 The front waist is made by using an extended waistband. This means the waistband has been cut in one piece together with garment front. Apply a fusible interfacing to the front waistband allowance.

4 On the back of the skirt, fold down the waist allowance.

Back piece of garment

5 Top-stitch close to the fold at the upper edge.

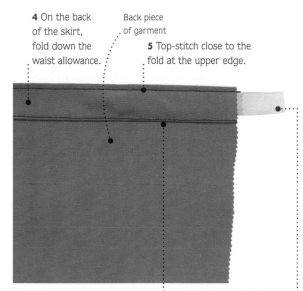

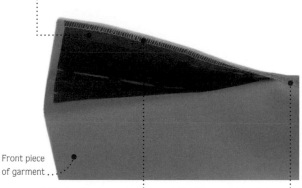

Front piece of garment

2 Neaten the raw edge with the serger or a zigzag stitch.

3 Fold the waistband down onto the skirt and sew at the lower edge to secure.

6 Turn under the lower edge and sew to make a casing.

7 Insert the elastic with a safety pin. Pull up the elastic to the required length and secure by sewing it down.

Gathered back

Front waist with waist stiffening

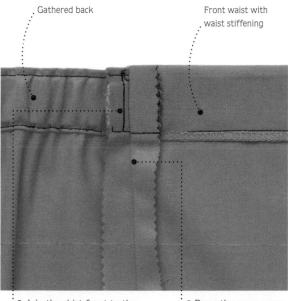

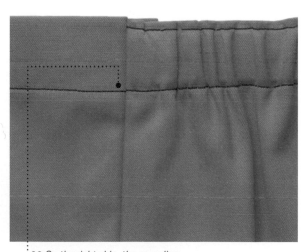

8 Join the skirt front to the back, right side to right side, at the side seams.

9 Press the seam open.

10 On the right side, the sewn line securing the front waist should be in line with the back elastic casing.

◄ ATTACHING A STRAIGHT WAISTBAND

A waistband is designed to fit snugly but not tight to the waist. Whether it is shaped or straight or slightly curved, it will be constructed and attached in a similar way. Every waistband will require a fusible interfacing to give it structure and support. Special waistband interfacings are available, usually featuring slot lines that will guide you where to fold the fabric. Make sure the slots on the outer edge correspond to a ⅝in (1.5cm) seam allowance. If waistband fusible interfacing is not available, you can use a medium-weight fusible interfacing.

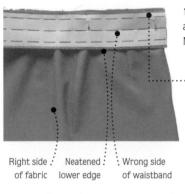

1 Cut the waistband and apply the interfacing. Neaten one long edge.

2 Pin the waistband to the skirt waist edge, right side to right side. Match the notches.

Right side of fabric · Neatened lower edge · Wrong side of waistband

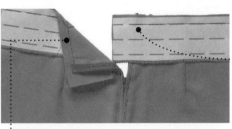

Waistband extension to be finished

3 Stitch the waistband to the waist edge using a ⅝in (1.5cm) seam allowance. The waistband will extend beyond the zipper by ⅝in (1.5cm) on the left and 2in (5cm) on the right.

4 Press the waistband away from the skirt.

Neatened lower edge · Center slot line on interfacing

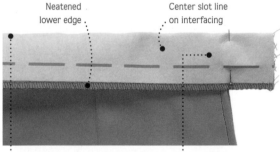

5 Fold the waistband along the center slot line on the interfacing, right side to right side. The neatened edge of the waistband should extend ⅝in (1.5cm) below the stitching line.

6 Pin the left-hand end of the waistband in line with the center back seam. Machine stitch together.

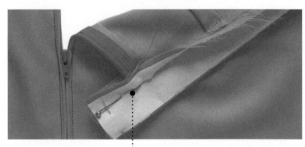

7 On the right-hand end of the waistband, extend the waist-to-skirt stitching line into the waistband and along the short end.

8 Clip the corners and turn the ends of the waistband to the right side. The extension on the waistband should be on the right-hand back.

9 Add your chosen fasteners.

10 To complete the waistband, sew through the band to the skirt seam. This is known as stitching in the ditch.

11 The finished straight waistband.

⋈ A WAIST WITH A FACING

Many waistlines on skirts and pants are finished with a facing, which will follow the contours of the waist but will have had the dart shaping removed to make it smooth. A faced waistline always sits comfortably to the body. The facing is attached after all the main sections of the skirt or pants have been constructed.

1 Apply a fusible interfacing to the facing. Neaten the lower edge of the facing with bias binding or a zigzag stitch.

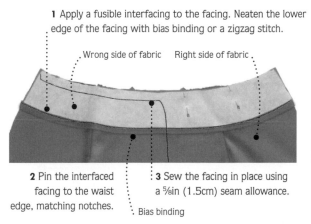

Wrong side of fabric   Right side of fabric

2 Pin the interfaced facing to the waist edge, matching notches.

3 Sew the facing in place using a ⅝in (1.5cm) seam allowance.

Bias binding

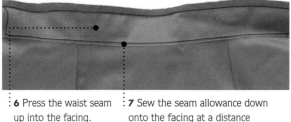

6 Press the waist seam up into the facing.

7 Sew the seam allowance down onto the facing at a distance of about ⅛in (3mm) from the original seam. (This is called understitching.)

4 Layer the seam allowance on the facing side of the seam to reduce it by half.

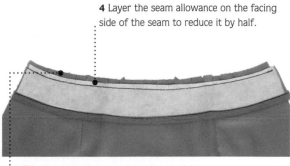

5 Clip the seam allowance by using straight cuts at 90 degrees to the stitching line.

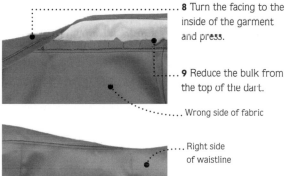

8 Turn the facing to the inside of the garment and press.

9 Reduce the bulk from the top of the dart.

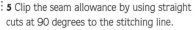

Wrong side of fabric

Right side of waistline

⋈ FINISHING THE EDGE OF A WAISTBAND

One long edge of the waistband will be sewn to the garment waist. The other edge will need to be finished to prevent fraying and reduce bulk inside.

TURNING UNDER

This method is suitable for fine fabrics only. Turn under ⅝in (1.5cm) along the edge of the waistband and press in place. After the waistband has been attached to the garment, hand sew the pressed-under edge in place.

BIAS BINDING

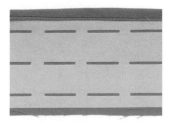

This method is ideal for fabrics that fray badly and can add a feature inside the garment. It is left flat inside the garment after construction. Apply a ¾in (2cm) bias binding to one long edge of the waistband.

BELTS AND TIE-BACKS

A belt in a fabric that matches the garment can add the perfect finishing touch. Whether it be a soft tie belt or a stiff structured belt, it will be best if it has an interfacing of some kind—the firmer and more structured the belt, the firmer the interfacing should be. A belt will also need belt loops to support it and prevent it from drooping.

▶◁ DIRECTORY OF BELTS AND TIE-BACKS

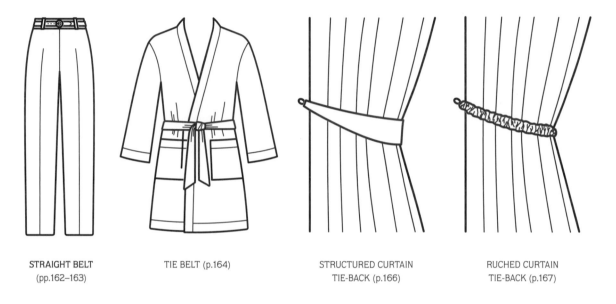

STRAIGHT BELT
(pp.162–163)

TIE BELT (p.164)

STRUCTURED CURTAIN
TIE-BACK (p.166)

RUCHED CURTAIN
TIE-BACK (p.167)

▶◁ REINFORCED STRAIGHT BELT

This is a straightforward way to make a belt to match a garment. It can be of any width, as it is reinforced with a very firm fusible interfacing, such as a craft interfacing. If one layer of interfacing is not firm enough, try adding another layer. The interfacing should be cut along its length to avoid joins. To ensure that it is cut straight, use a rotary cutter on a self-healing mat.

1 Cut the interfacing to the dimensions of the finished belt. Cut the fabric to twice the width of the interfacing plus seam allowances.

2 Fold the fabric in half lengthwise and press to mark the center line. Place the interfacing along the crease, leaving the fabric longer at the pointed end of the interfacing.

3 Fuse the cut interfacing to the fabric.

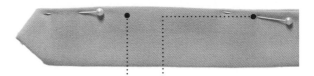

4 At the center line on the pointed end, cut through to the side of the interfacing point.

5 Press the fabric edges over the interfacing. Press the point carefully.

6 Fold one long, raw edge of the belt under and press.

7 Press under the remaining edge to match and pin in place.

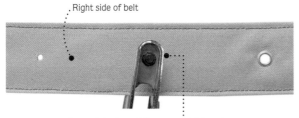

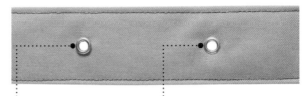

8 Baste along the pressed-under edges to sew them together.

9 Use short basting stitches around the point.

10 Sew along both long sides of the belt, sewing on the right side of the fabric. Keep the sewing line close to the edge—1/16in (2mm) from it. Make sure the sewn line is accurate through the point.

Right side of belt

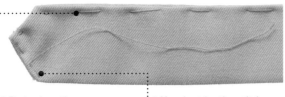

11 Measure the positioning of the grommets toward the pointed end of the belt.

12 Punch the hole for each grommet with pliers.

13 Insert a 3/16in (4mm) grommet into the hole, working from the right side of the belt.

14 Change the heads in the pliers and squeeze the grommet around the hole.

Wrong side of belt

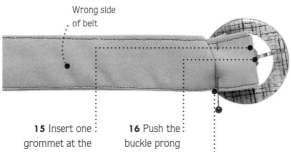

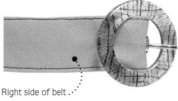

18 Sew the surplus on the wrong side with a machine or by hand, then turn the belt over.

Right side of belt

15 Insert one grommet at the other end of the belt about 2in (5cm) from the end, placing it centrally on the right side of the belt.

16 Push the buckle prong through the grommet.

17 Fold the surplus fabric over on itself under the buckle and pin.

19 When the belt is placed around the waist, check that the fit is correct. Add extra grommets if required.

⋈ TIE BELT

A tie belt is the easiest of all the belts to make. It can be any width and made of most fabrics, from cottons for summer dresses to satin and silks for bridal wear. Most tie belts will require a light- to medium-weight interfacing for support. A fusible interfacing is the best choice, as it will stay in place when tied repeatedly. If a very long tie belt is required, the belt can be joined at the center back.

1 Cut fabric for the belt, with a point at each end. Cut a fusible interfacing the same length but half the width.

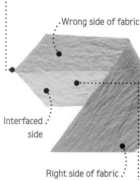

Wrong side of fabric

Interfaced side

Right side of fabric

2 Place the interfacing on one half of the fabric on the wrong side and press to fuse.

3 Fold the belt in half, right side to right side, so the fusible is showing. Pin.

4 Sew along all the raw edges using a ⅝in (1.5cm) seam allowance. Remember to leave a gap of about 3in (8cm) at the center back to turn the belt through.

5 Layer the seam by removing half of the seam allowance on the fused side.

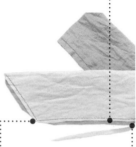

6 Remove the bulk from the corners.

7 Press the seam as stitched, then turn through while the fabric is still warm.

8 Once the belt has been turned to the right side, press the seam carefully so that it is on the very edge.

9 Press the points carefully.

10 Hand stitch the gap at the center back with a flat fell or blind hem stitch to close.

⋈ BELT CARRIERS

Belt carriers can be made from fabric strips and machine sewed to the garment, or they can be made more simply from thread loops fashioned by hand stitching. Fabric carriers are designed to support a heavier belt.

HAND-STITCHED BELT LOOPS

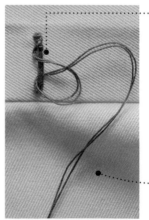

Right side of garment

1 Work the belt loop prior to the waistband being finished on the inside. Using double bold machine thread, work several strands of thread long enough to slot a belt through.

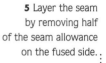

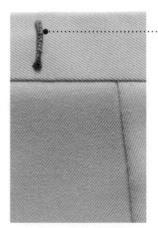

2 Use a buttonhole stitch and work the stitches across the loops.

3 When the loops are covered with buttonhole stitches, take the thread to the reverse and finish securely.

MACHINE-STITCHED BELT CARRIERS

1 Cut the fabric strips 1¼in (3cm) wide and long enough to allow for the depth of the belt plus turnings of ⅝in (1.5cm) at each end.

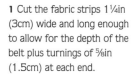

3 Press the carriers in half lengthwise.

4 Machine sew along the open edge of each carrier to secure the fold.

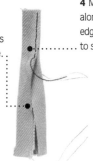

2 Press the long edges of the fabric carriers to the center, wrong side to wrong side.

5 Press again to be sure the stitch line runs down the side edge of the carrier.

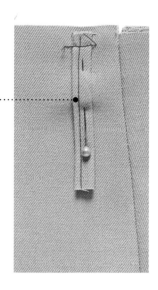

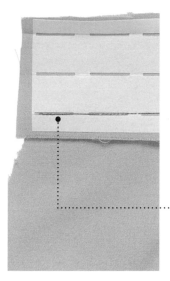

6 Starting at each side seam and then at regular intervals between, place the carriers to the waist of the garment, on the right side. Stitch to secure at the waist inside the seam allowance.

7 Apply the waistband to the garment, stitching across the carriers as you do so.

8 Press the waistband in half lengthwise to give a center crease.

9 Bring the carriers up onto the waistband.

11 When the waistband is completed, the carrier will sit on it with no visible stitching.

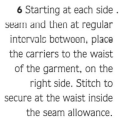

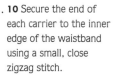

10 Secure the end of each carrier to the inner edge of the waistband using a small, close zigzag stitch.

▶◀ CURTAIN TIE-BACKS

Tie-backs are used to hold the drape of a curtain in position. Some are structured, with an interfacing, and follow a predetermined shape, while others are softer and more decorative. The construction of a tie-back is similar to that of a tie belt.

STRUCTURED TIE-BACK

1 Cut out two pieces of fabric for the tie-back. Use a heavy fusible interfacing and cut it to the same size as the fabric, minus the seam allowances of ⅝in (1.5cm) on all sides.

3 Pin the noninterfaced piece of fabric to the interfaced piece, right side to right side.

4 Sew around the two pieces, taking a ⅝in (1.5cm) seam allowance. Leave a gap of about 3¼in (8cm) at the lower edge to turn through.

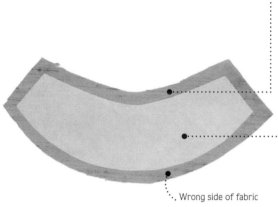

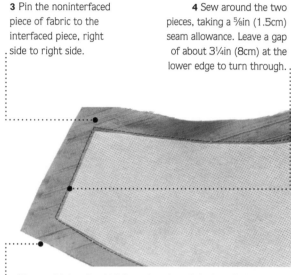

Wrong side of fabric

2 Fuse the interfacing to the wrong side of one piece of fabric.

5 The machining should follow the edge of the interfacing but not go through it.

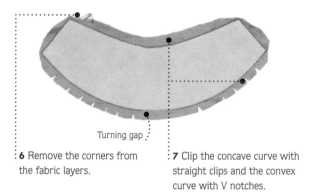

Turning gap

6 Remove the corners from the fabric layers.

7 Clip the concave curve with straight clips and the convex curve with V notches.

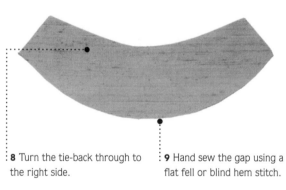

8 Turn the tie-back through to the right side.

9 Hand sew the gap using a flat fell or blind hem stitch.

10 On the two short ends of the tie-back, sew on a curtain ring using polyester all-purpose thread. Use a buttonhole stitch to secure it.

DECORATIVE RUCHED TIE-BACK

1 Cut a piece of batting 10in (25cm) wide and to the required tie-back length.

2 Roll up the batting like a sausage, but not too tight, and pin in place.

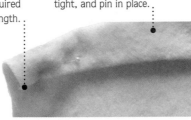

3 Using a bold-colored thread, herringbone stitch the raw edge down to hold it in position. Make sure the rolled batting is the same thickness throughout.

4 For the outer decorative layer, cut a piece of fabric 5in (12cm) wide and three times the required length.

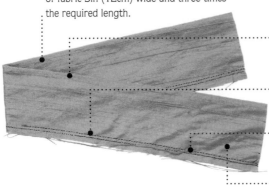

5 Fold lengthwise in half, right side to right side.

6 Sew the long raw edges together using a ⅜in (1cm) seam allowance.

7 Stitch again, between the stitching line and the raw edge. The double stitching is for strength.

8 Turn the decorative top layer fabric through to the right side and press.

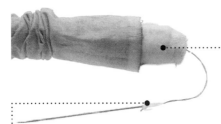

9 Tie the thread ends from the herringbone stitch on the batting to a loop turner.

10 Using the loop turner, pull the batting sausage through the decorative layer. This is difficult, as it will stick. Work the decorative fabric gently down the batting.

11 Ruche the decorative fabric up around the batting, spreading out the fabric with your fingers. Remove the loop turner.

12 Hand sew about every 1¼in (3cm) to secure the ruching on the tie-back.

13 Sew on a curtain ring at each end, using a buttonhole stitch to secure the rings.

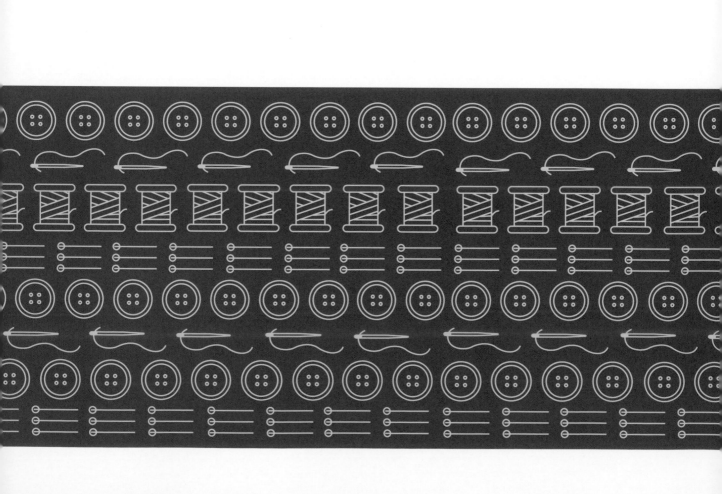

FACINGS AND NECKLINES

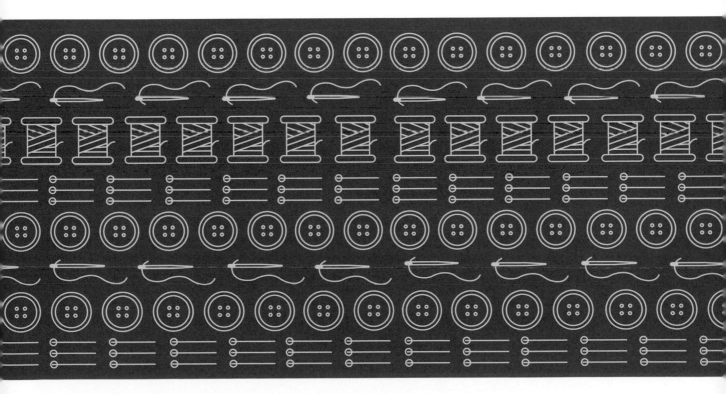

FACINGS AND NECKLINES

The simplest way to finish the neck or armhole of a garment is to apply a facing. The neckline can be any shape to have a facing applied, from a curve to a square to a V, and many more. Some facings and necklines can add interest to the center back or center front of a garment.

◤ DIRECTORY OF NECKLINES

ROUND NECKLINE (p.175)

SQUARE NECKLINE (p.175)

V-NECKLINE (p.175)

SWEETHEART NECKLINE (p.175)

SLASHED NECKLINE (p.176)

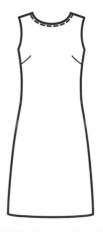

BOUND NECK EDGE (pp.177, 178)

⋈ APPLYING INTERFACING TO A FACING

All facings require interfacing. The interfacing is to give structure to the facing and to hold it in shape. A fusible interfacing is the best choice, and it should be cut on the same grain as the facing. Choose an interfacing that is lighter in weight than the main fabric.

INTERFACING FOR HEAVY FABRIC

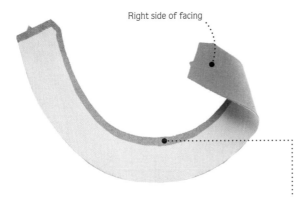

Right side of facing

For a heavy-weight fabric, use a medium-weight fusible interfacing. Remove the seam allowance on the interfacing on the inner curve to reduce bulk.

INTERFACING FOR LIGHT FABRIC

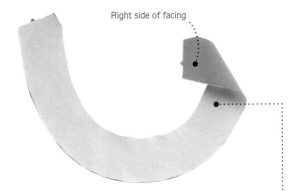

Right side of facing

For a light to medium-weight fabric, choose a lightweight interfacing and fuse it over the complete facing.

⋈ CONSTRUCTION OF A FACING

The facing may be in two or three pieces in order to fit around a neck or armhole edge. The facing sections need to be joined together prior to being attached.

The photographs here show an interfaced neck facing in three pieces.

1 Baste together the pieces of the facing at the shoulder seams.

2 Sew the shoulder seams and press open.

3 Stay stitch around the edge of the inner curve to prevent stretch.

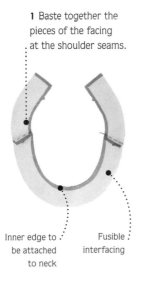

Inner edge to be attached to neck

Fusible interfacing

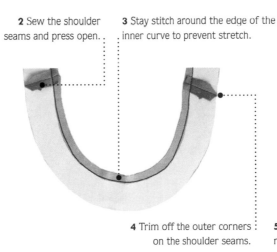

4 Trim off the outer corners on the shoulder seams.

5 The right side of the facing, ready to attach to the neckline.

▶◀ NEATENING THE EDGE OF A FACING

The outer edge of a facing will require neatening to prevent it from fraying, and there are several ways to do this. Binding the lower edge of a facing with a bias strip makes the garment a little more luxurious and can add a designer touch inside the garment. Alternatively, the edge can be sewn or pinked (see opposite page).

HOW TO CUT BIAS STRIPS

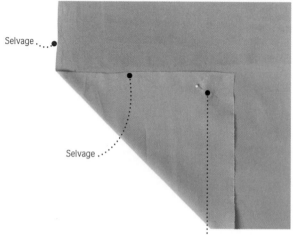

Selvage

Selvage

1 Fold the fabric onto itself at 45 degrees so the selvage edges are at right angles to each other. Pin in place.

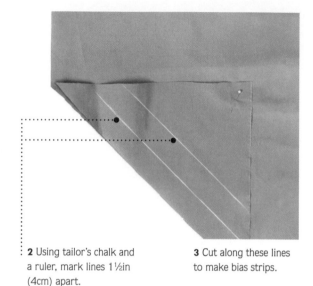

2 Using tailor's chalk and a ruler, mark lines 1½in (4cm) apart.

3 Cut along these lines to make bias strips.

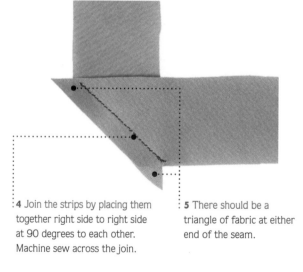

4 Join the strips by placing them together right side to right side at 90 degrees to each other. Machine sew across the join.

5 There should be a triangle of fabric at either end of the seam.

6 Press the seam open.

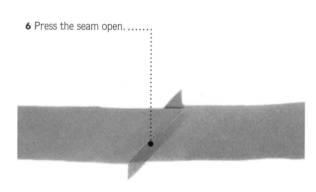

7 Press under the edges of the bias strip with the iron by running the bias strip through a 1in (25mm) tape maker.

NEATENING AN EDGE WITH A BIAS STRIP

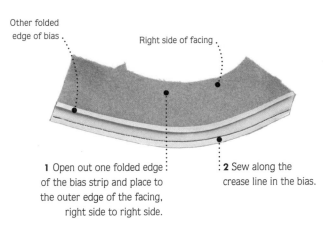

Other folded edge of bias

Right side of facing

1 Open out one folded edge of the bias strip and place to the outer edge of the facing, right side to right side.

2 Sew along the crease line in the bias.

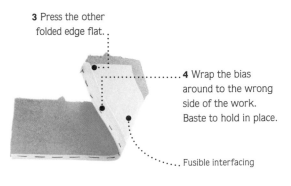

3 Press the other folded edge flat.

4 Wrap the bias around to the wrong side of the work. Baste to hold in place.

Fusible interfacing

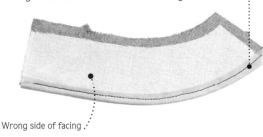

5 Working from the right side of the facing, stitch in the ditch made by sewing the bias to the facing. This attaches the bias to the wrong side.

Wrong side of facing

6 On the right side of the facing, the bias-bound edge has a neat, professional finish.

✕ OTHER NEATENING METHODS

The following techniques are alternative popular ways to neaten the edge of a facing. The one you choose depends on the garment being made and the fabric used.

SERGED

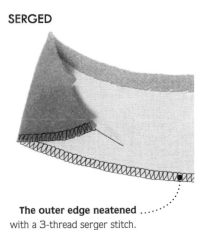

The outer edge neatened with a 3-thread serger stitch.

PINKED

Machine stitch ⅜in (1cm) from the edge and the raw edge trimmed with pinking shears.

ZIGZAG

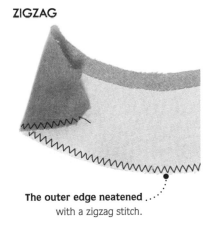

The outer edge neatened with a zigzag stitch.

⫸ ARMHOLE FACING

On sleeveless garments, a facing is an excellent way of neatening an armhole because it is not bulky. Also, as the facing is made in the same fabric as the garment, it does not show.

1 Construct the armhole facing (see p.171) and neaten outer edge by preferred method.

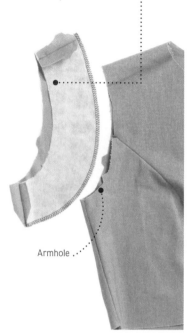

Armhole

2 Place the facing to the armhole, right side to right side. Match at the shoulder seams and at the underarm seam.

3 Match the notches, one at the front and two at the back. Pin the facing in place.

4 Sew around the armhole to attach the facing, taking a ⅝in (1.5cm) seam allowance.

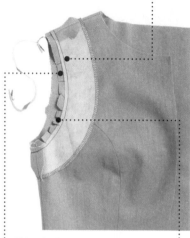

5 Trim the facing side of the seam allowance down to half.

6 Clip out some V shapes in the seam allowance to reduce bulk.

7 Turn the facing into position on the wrong side. Understitch by pressing the seam allowance onto the facing and sewing down.

8 On the underarm and shoulder seams, secure the facing to the seam allowance with cross stitches.

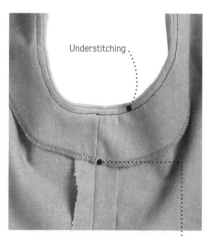

Understitching

9 Press the edge. On the right side, the armhole will have a neat finish.

◤ ATTACHING A NECK FACING

This technique applies to all shapes of neckline, whether round, square, V neck, or sweetheart.

1 Apply a fusible interfacing to the facing (see p.171).

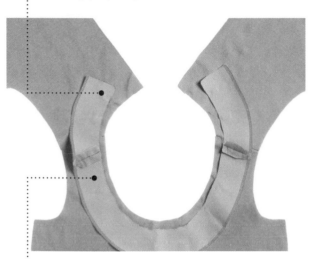

2 Lay the garment neckline flat, right side up. Place the facing on top, right side to right side.

3 Pin the facing in place, matching around the neck edge.

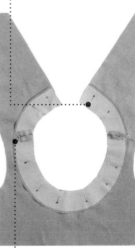

4 Match the shoulder seams on the facing and the bodice.

5 Machine sew in place using a ⅝in (1.5cm) seam allowance.

Facing and garment match at center back

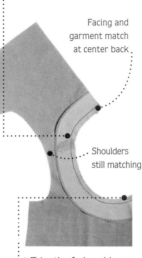

Shoulders still matching

6 Trim the facing side of the seam down to half its width.

7 Clip V shapes around the neck edge.

9 Press the seam allowance toward the facing.

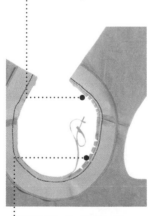

8 Clip into the facing side of the seam as well.

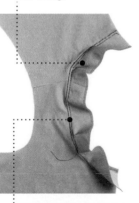

10 Understitch by sewing the seam allowance down onto the facing about ³⁄₁₆in (5mm) from the sewn line.

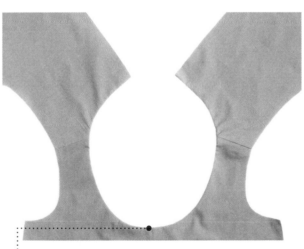

11 Turn the facing toward the wrong side and press the finished neck edge.

►◄ FACING A SLASHED NECKLINE

A slashed V-neckline occurs at either the center front or the center back neck edge. It enables a close-fitting neckline to open sufficiently to go over the head.

1 Apply a fusible interfacing to the facing (see p.171). Place the facing right side to right side on the garment, to the right side of the neckline.

3 Stitch the facing at the neck edge, pivoting to stitch along both sides of the slash between the tailor's tacks. Take one stitch horizontally at the bottom edge of the slash line.

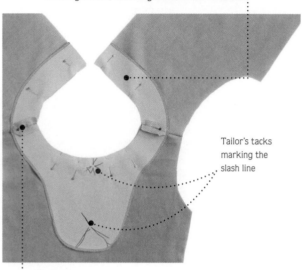

Tailor's tacks marking the slash line

2 Match the shoulder seams, then pin in place.

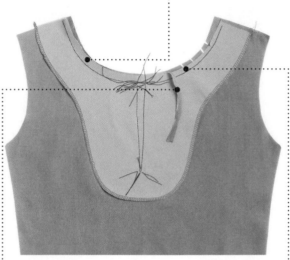

4 Trim the facing side of the seam down to half.

5 Clip V shapes at the neck edge to reduce the bulk.

6 Cut straight down the slash line between the stitching lines.

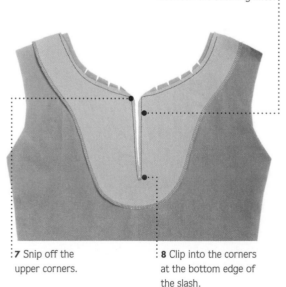

7 Snip off the upper corners.

8 Clip into the corners at the bottom edge of the slash.

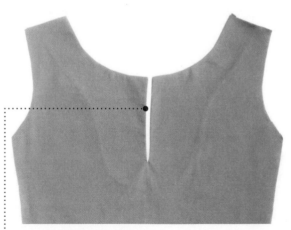

9 Turn the facing to the inside of the neckline and press.

► BOUND NECK EDGE

Binding is an excellent way to finish a raw neck edge. It has the added advantage of being a method that can be used if you are short on fabric or you would like a contrast or decorative finish. You can use bought bias tape or a bias strip cut from the same or a contrasting fabric (see p.172). A double bias strip is used on fine fabrics.

BIAS-BOUND NECK EDGE VERSION 1

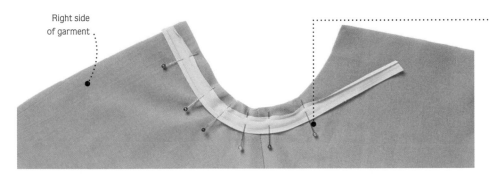

Right side of garment

1 Open out one edge of the bias strip and place the crease line on the ⅝in (1.5cm) stitching line. Pin in place.

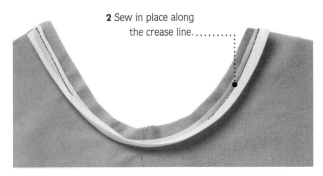

2 Sew in place along the crease line.

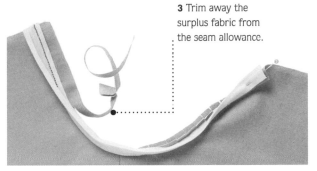

3 Trim away the surplus fabric from the seam allowance.

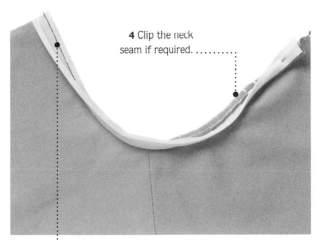

4 Clip the neck seam if required.

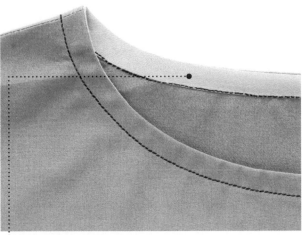

5 Wrap the bias strip over the neck to the wrong side of the garment.

6 Sew the bias strip on the inside of the garment. Press.

BIAS-BOUND NECK EDGE VERSION 2

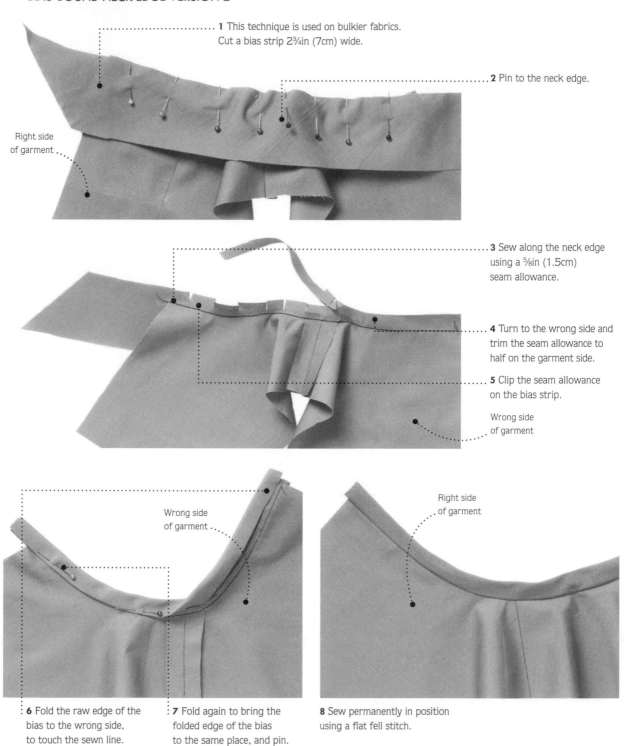

1 This technique is used on bulkier fabrics. Cut a bias strip 2¾in (7cm) wide.

2 Pin to the neck edge.

Right side of garment

3 Sew along the neck edge using a ⅝in (1.5cm) seam allowance.

4 Turn to the wrong side and trim the seam allowance to half on the garment side.

5 Clip the seam allowance on the bias strip.

Wrong side of garment

Wrong side of garment

6 Fold the raw edge of the bias to the wrong side, to touch the sewn line.

7 Fold again to bring the folded edge of the bias to the same place, and pin.

Right side of garment

8 Sew permanently in position using a flat fell stitch.

▶◀ EXTENDED FACING

A facing is not always a separate unit. Many garments, especially blouses, feature what is known as an extended facing, which is where the facing is an extension of the front of the garment, cut out at the same time.

1 Mark the foldline that divides off the facing area and crease by pressing.

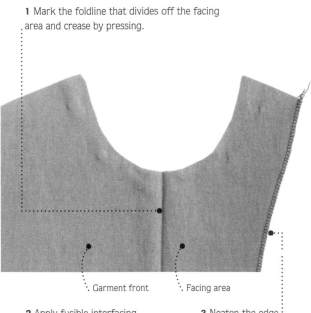

Garment front ⋯   ⋯ Facing area

2 Apply fusible interfacing to the facing area as far as the foldline.

3 Neaten the edge of the facing.

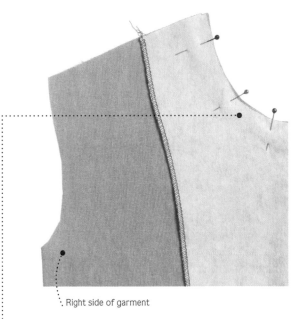

⋯ Right side of garment

4 Fold the facing back, right side to right side. Match around the neck and pin.

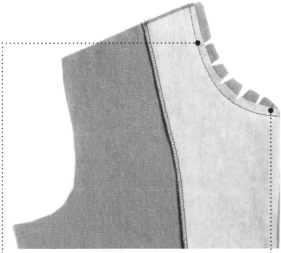

5 Sew around the neck edge to join the facing to the garment.

6 Trim the facing side of the seam and clip the seam allowance.

7 Turn through to the right side and press.

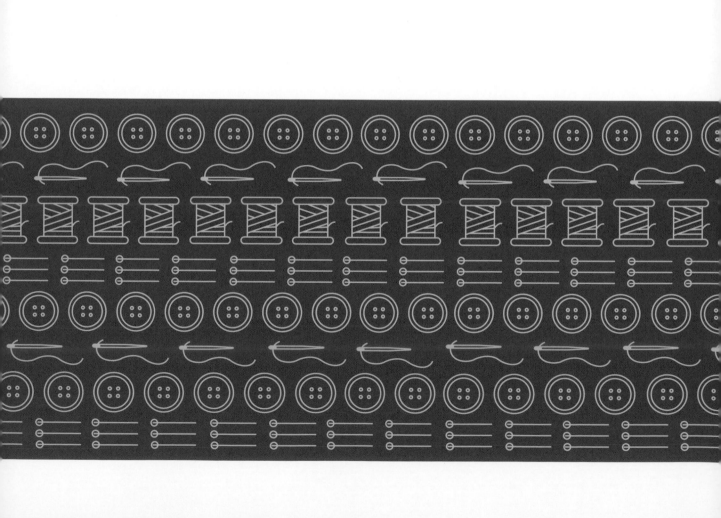

COLLARS

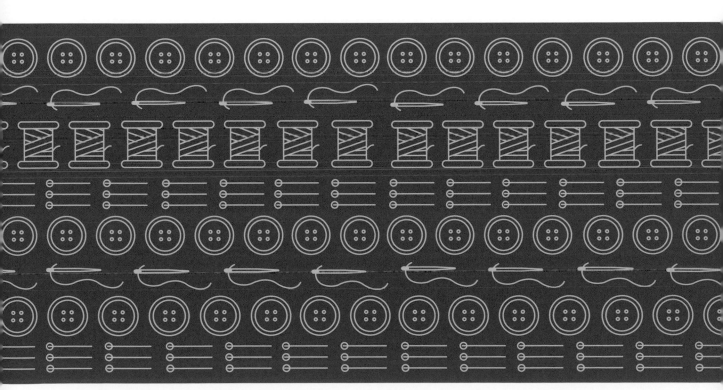

COLLARS

All collars consist of a minimum of two pieces: the upper collar (which will be on the outside) and the under collar. Interfacing, which is required to give the collar shape and structure, is often applied to the upper collar to give a smoother appearance to the fabric.

◤ DIRECTORY OF COLLARS

FLAT COLLAR (pp.183–185)

MANDARIN COLLAR (p.186)

SHAWL COLLAR (p.187)

◄ FLAT COLLAR

A flat collar is the easiest of all the collars to construct, and the techniques used are the same for most other shapes of flat collar and facings.

1 Cut out the fabric for the collar accurately. Make sure the two halves match.

2 Cut out a fusible interfacing, being sure to cut on the same grain as the collar. Apply the interfacing to the upper collar.

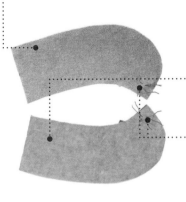

3 Insert tailor's tacks at the center front point of the collar where indicated by a dot on the pattern piece.

4 Pin the upper collar and under collar together, right side to right side. Match any notches and make sure the cut edges match.

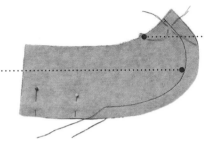

5 Sew ⅝in (1.5cm) along the raw outer curved edge to the lower edge of the collar. Make sure the stitches at the center front go through the tailor's tack. If you have problems sewing a curve, mark the fabric first with chalk.

6 Trim the under collar seam allowance to half of its width, which will reduce the bulk.

7 Trim around the curve with pinking shears, reducing both layers. This will allow the fabric to turn.

8 Press the seam allowance of the upper collar onto the collar.

9 While the collar is still warm from the steam iron, turn to the right side.

10 Working from the inside of the collar, push all the seam allowance toward the under collar.

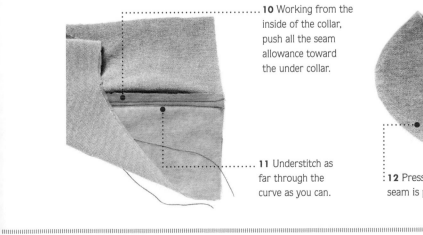

11 Understitch as far through the curve as you can.

12 Press the curved edge flat, making sure the seam is pushed out completely on the right side.

▶ ATTACHING A FLAT COLLAR

A flat collar can be attached to the neckline by means of a facing. Depending on the style of the garment, the facing may go all around the neck, which is usually found on garments with center back openings, or just be at the front. The collar with no back facing has to be attached to the garment in stages.

FLAT ROUND COLLAR WITH NO BACK FACING

1 Construct the collar (see p.183).

2 Mark the center front points on the garment and the collar with tailor's tacks.

3 Place the collar to the neckline, right side to right side. Match the notches.

Grown-on front facing, interfaced to foldline

4 Pin in place, pinning just to the tailor's tacks.

5 Snip the collar at the tailor's tacks on the shoulders. The collar should be loose across the back neck.

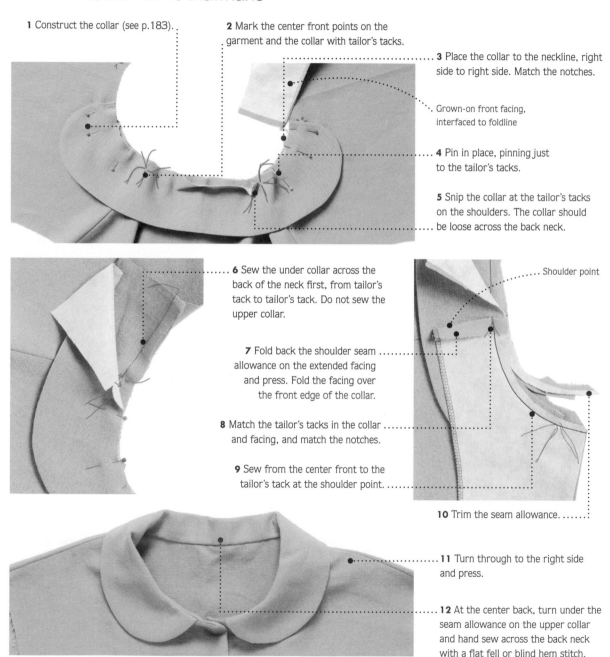

6 Sew the under collar across the back of the neck first, from tailor's tack to tailor's tack. Do not sew the upper collar.

7 Fold back the shoulder seam allowance on the extended facing and press. Fold the facing over the front edge of the collar.

8 Match the tailor's tacks in the collar and facing, and match the notches.

9 Sew from the center front to the tailor's tack at the shoulder point.

Shoulder point

10 Trim the seam allowance.

11 Turn through to the right side and press.

12 At the center back, turn under the seam allowance on the upper collar and hand sew across the back neck with a flat fell or blind hem stitch.

FLAT ROUND COLLAR WITH A FULL FACING

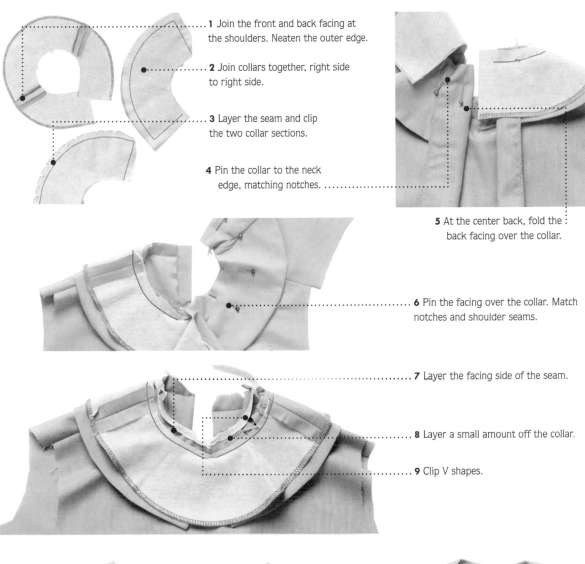

1 Join the front and back facing at the shoulders. Neaten the outer edge.

2 Join collars together, right side to right side.

3 Layer the seam and clip the two collar sections.

4 Pin the collar to the neck edge, matching notches.

5 At the center back, fold the back facing over the collar.

6 Pin the facing over the collar. Match notches and shoulder seams.

7 Layer the facing side of the seam.

8 Layer a small amount off the collar.

9 Clip V shapes.

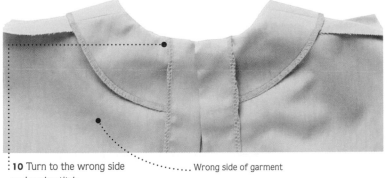

10 Turn to the wrong side and understitch.

Wrong side of garment

11 Turn to the right side and press.

◀ MANDARIN COLLAR

This collar stands upright around the neck. It is normally cut from a straight piece of fabric, with shaping at the center front edges. For a very close-fitting mandarin collar, the collar is cut with a slight curve.

1 Apply a fusible interfacing to the upper collar (see p.183). Insert any tailor's tacks as indicated on the pattern.

2 Pin the upper collar, right side to right side, to the neckline of the garment, matching any notches and tailor's tacks at the center front edge.

3 Sew the upper collar to the neckline using a ⅝in (1.5cm) seam allowance. Make sure to stop at the tailor's tack at the front edge.

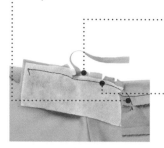

4 Reduce the seam allowance on the upper collar by half.

5 Clip through the seam allowances—this will allow the fabric to relax into shape when pressed later.

Wrong side of collar

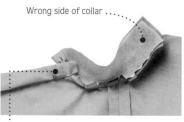

6 Working from the wrong side of the garment, turn in the center front edge as indicated by the pattern. This will leave the front edge of the collar sticking out from the garment.

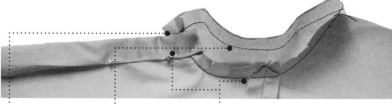

7 Pin the under collar to the upper collar, right side to right side, along the top edge.

8 Sew the two pieces together using a ⅝in (1.5cm) seam allowance.

9 At the center front, the reduced neck seam allowance needs to be pointing up into the collar so that the seamline attaching the two collar sections together goes over it. Be sure the seam is in line with the center front of the garment.

10 Reduce the seam allowance to half its width on the under collar side of the seam (the non-interfaced side).

11 Clip V shapes out of the seam allowance to reduce the bulk. Be careful not to cut through the stitches.

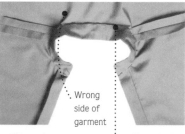

12 Press the seam as it has been sewn, and while warm, turn to the right side.

Wrong side of garment

13 Turn under the lower edge seam allowance on the under collar and tack in place around the neck edge.

14 Make sure the two leading front edges of the collar are symmetrical.

15 Use a flat fell stitch to secure the under collar at the neck edge.

✕ SHAWL COLLAR

A shawl collar, which is a deep V-neck shape that combines both collar and lapel in one, gives a flattering neckline that is often found on blouses and jackets.

Although the collar looks complicated, it is straightforward to make. The under collar is usually part of the front of the garment.

1 Join the garment fronts together at the center back and press the seam open.

2 Stay stitch the corner of the neck/shoulder at the top of the dart through the tailor's tack.

3 Slash to the tailor's tack.

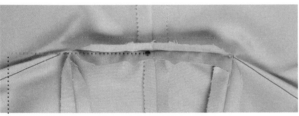

4 Make the darts in the front—these will form the roll line of the collar.

5 Join the back sections of the garment together at the center back and press the seam open.

6 Join the front to the back across the shoulder seams, stopping at the slash.

7 Join the front of the garment to the back across the back neck, working from slash line to slash line. Press open.

8 Apply a fusible interfacing to the upper collar (see p.183). Tailor tack to mark the shoulder/neck point.

9 Join the two upper collar sections together at the center back.

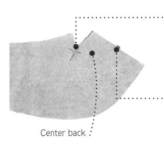

Center back

10 Pin the upper collar to the garment, matching the center back seams and any notches. Sew in place using a ⅝in (1.5cm) seam.

11 Trim the seam allowance on the under collar side (the noninterfaced side) by half. Clip V shapes into the seam to reduce the bulk.

12 Press the seam as it has been sewn and turn to the right side while still warm.

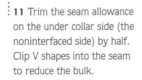

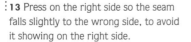

13 Press on the right side so the seam falls slightly to the wrong side, to avoid it showing on the right side.

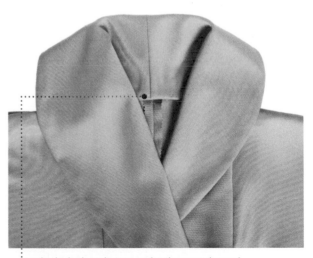

14 At the back neck, turn under the raw edge and hand sew in place with a flat fell stitch. Neaten the other raw edges of the upper collar by your preferred technique.

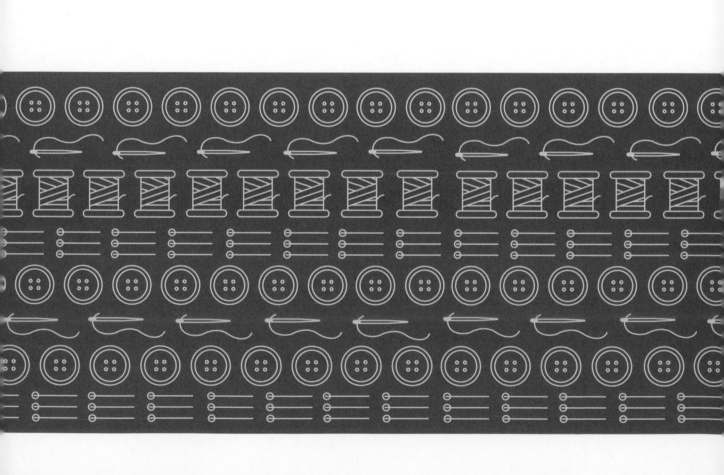

SLEEVES AND SLEEVE FINISHES

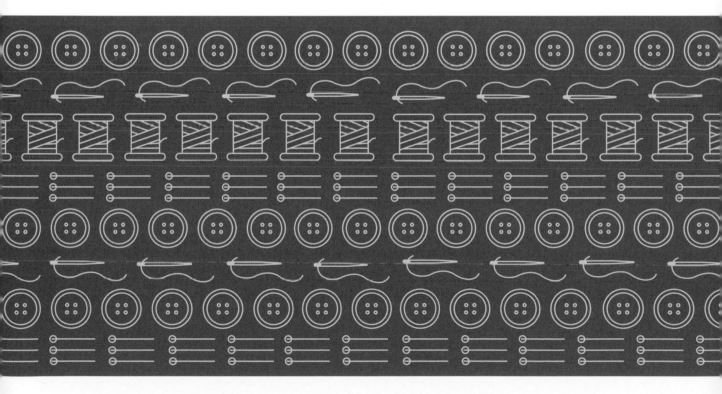

SLEEVES

A few sleeves, such as the dolman, are cut as part of the garment, but most sleeves, including set-in and raglan, are made separately and then inserted into the armhole. Whichever type of sleeve is being inserted, always place it to the armhole and not the armhole to the sleeve—in other words, always work with the sleeve facing you.

▶◀ DIRECTORY OF SLEEVES

SET-IN SLEEVE (p.191)

PUFF SLEEVE (p.193)

FLAT SLEEVE (p.192)

RAGLAN SLEEVE (p.194)

DOLMAN SLEEVE (p.194)

INSERTING A SET-IN SLEEVE

A set-in sleeve should feature a smooth sleeve head that fits on the end of your shoulder accurately. This is achieved by the use of ease stitches, which are long stitches used to tighten the fabric but not gather it.

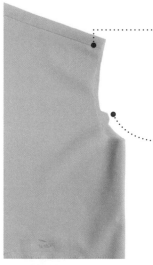

1 Sew the side seams and the shoulder seams on the garment and press them open.

Armhole with notches

2 Sew the seam of the sleeve and press open. Neaten seams. Turn the sleeve to the right side.

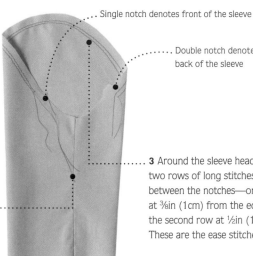

Single notch denotes front of the sleeve

Double notch denotes back of the sleeve

3 Around the sleeve head, work two rows of long stitches between the notches—one row at ⅜in (1cm) from the edge and the second row at ½in (1.3cm). These are the ease stitches.

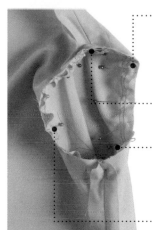

4 Place the sleeve into the armhole, right side to right side. Match the underarm seams and the notches.

5 Match the highest point of the sleeve to the shoulder.

6 Pull up the ease stitches until the sleeve fits neatly in the armhole.

7 Pin from the sleeve side.

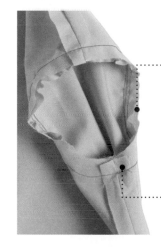

8 Sew the sleeve in, starting at the underarm seam, using a ⅝in (1.5cm) seam allowance. Sew so that the sleeve is uppermost and sew straight over the shoulder.

9 Overlap the seam at the underarm to reinforce the seam.

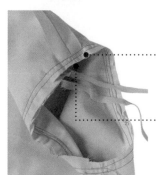

10 Sew around the sleeve again, ⅜in (1cm) inside the seam allowance.

11 Trim the raw edges of the sleeve.

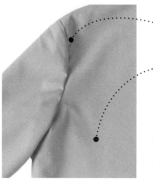

Smooth (wrinkle-free) sleeve head

Right side of the garment

12 Neaten the seam with a zigzag or serger stitch, then turn the sleeve through the armhole.

▶◀ FLAT SLEEVE CONSTRUCTION

On shirts and children's clothes, sleeves are inserted flat prior to the side seams being constructed. This technique can be difficult on firmly woven fabrics, because ease stitches are not normally used.

1 The shoulder seam on the garment should be sewn and pressed open. Place the sleeve to the armhole of the garment, right side to right side.

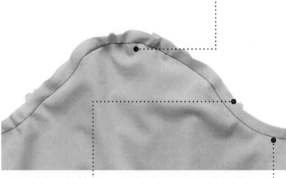

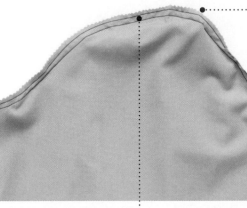

2 Match the notches and pin.

3 Sew the sleeve to the armhole at a ⅝in (1.5cm) seam allowance.

4 Sew again between the sewn line and the raw edge.

5 Neaten the seam.

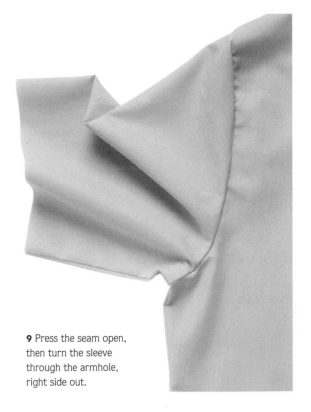

6 Press the sleeve seam toward the sleeve.

7 Fold the garment and sleeve right side to right side. Match the underarm seams.

8 Sew together with a ⅝in (1.5cm) seam allowance. Stitch up the side seam and down the sleeve.

9 Press the seam open, then turn the sleeve through the armhole, right side out.

▶◀ PUFF SLEEVE

A sleeve that has a gathered sleeve head is referred to as a puff sleeve or gathered sleeve. It is one of the easiest sleeves to insert because the gathers take up any spare fabric.

1 Sew stitch the sleeve, right side to right side, using a ⅝in (1.5cm) seam allowance. Press the seam open.

3 Place the sleeve into the armhole, right side to right side.

4 Match the notches and the underarm seams.

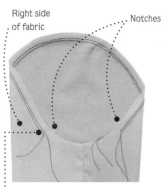

Right side of fabric

Notches

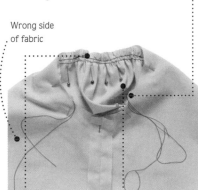

Wrong side of fabric

2 Between the sleeve notches, insert two rows of gather stitches, one row at ⅜in (1cm) from the raw edge and the second row at ½in (1.3cm).

5 Pull up the gathers to make the sleeve head fit the armhole.

6 Pin from the sleeve side.

7 Working with the sleeve uppermost, sew the sleeve to the armhole. Use a ⅝in (1.5cm) seam allowance. Overlap the seam at the underarm to reinforce.

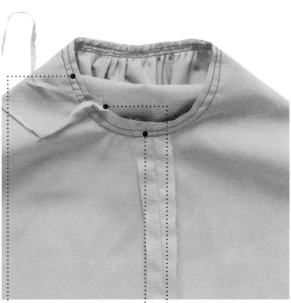

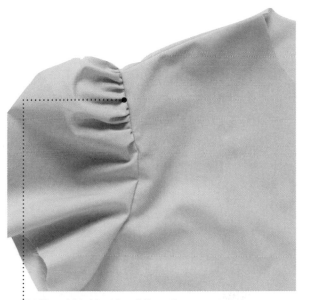

8 Sew around the sleeve seam again between the seam and the raw edge.

9 Trim away the surplus fabric by ³⁄₁₆in (5mm).

11 Turn right side out—all the gathers will be at the top of the sleeve.

10 Neaten the seam.

▶ RAGLAN SLEEVE

A raglan sleeve can be constructed as a one-piece sleeve or a two-piece sleeve. The armhole seam on a raglan sleeve runs diagonally from the armhole to the neck.

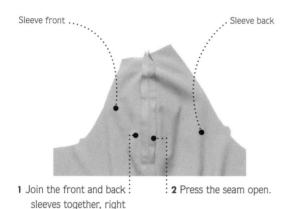

Sleeve front ……
Sleeve back ……

1 Join the front and back sleeves together, right side to right side.

2 Press the seam open.

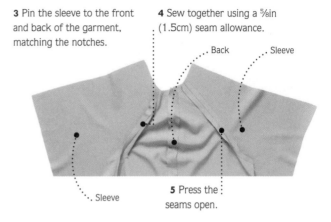

3 Pin the sleeve to the front and back of the garment, matching the notches.

4 Sew together using a ⅝in (1.5cm) seam allowance.

Back
Sleeve

Sleeve

5 Press the seams open.

6 Bring the front and the back of the garment together, right side to right side.

7 Sew the side seam of the garment and continue sewing down the sleeve.

8 Press the seam open, then turn the sleeve through the armhole to the right side.

▶ DOLMAN SLEEVE

A dolman sleeve is cut as an extension to a garment. As the armhole is very loose, it is ideal for a coat or jacket. The dolman sleeve often has a raglan shoulder pad to define the shoulder end.

1 The back and the front of the garment feature the same shape from neck to sleeve end. Sew the back and front together along the shoulder/sleeve seam.

2 Sew the underarm/ side seam.

3 Clip V shapes under the arm.

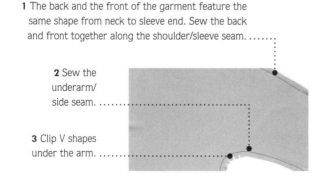

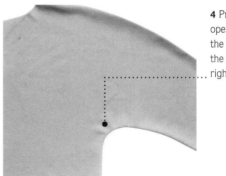

4 Press the seams open, then turn the sleeve through the armhole to the right side.

SLEEVE EDGE FINISHES

The lower edge of a sleeve has to be finished according to the style of the garment being made. Some sleeves are finished tight into the arm or wrist, while others may have a more decorative or functional finish.

◄ DIRECTORY OF SLEEVE EDGE FINISHES

SLEEVE EDGE WITH SELF HEM (p.196)

SLEEVE EDGE WITH BIAS-BOUND HEM (p.197)

ELASTICATED SLEEVE EDGE (p.198)

◤ SLEEVE HEMS

The simplest way to finish a sleeve is to make a small hem, which can be part of the sleeve or additional fabric that is attached to turn up. A self hem is where the edge of the sleeve is turned up onto itself. If there is insufficient fabric to turn up, a bias binding can be used to create the hem. You can use purchased bias binding or make your own bias strips.

SELF HEM

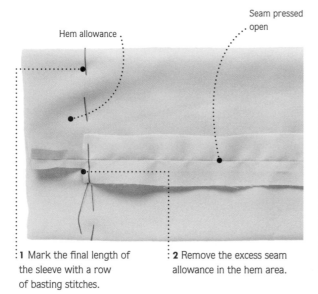

Hem allowance

Seam pressed open

1 Mark the final length of the sleeve with a row of basting stitches.

2 Remove the excess seam allowance in the hem area.

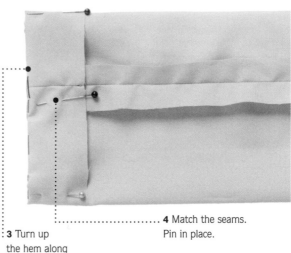

3 Turn up the hem along the basted line.

4 Match the seams. Pin in place.

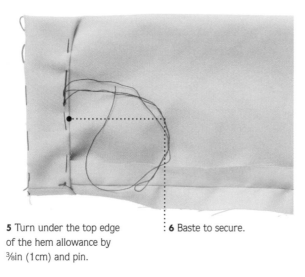

5 Turn under the top edge of the hem allowance by ⅜in (1cm) and pin.

6 Baste to secure.

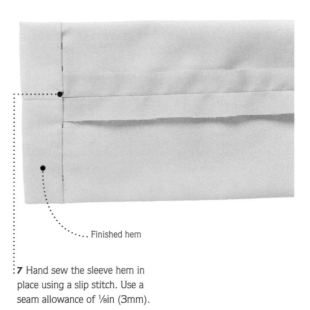

Finished hem

7 Hand sew the sleeve hem in place using a slip stitch. Use a seam allowance of ⅛in (3mm).

BIAS-BOUND HEM

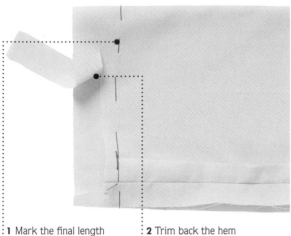

1 Mark the final length of the sleeve with a row of basting stitches.

2 Trim back the hem allowance to ³/₁₆in (5mm).

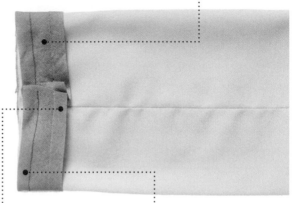

3 Cut a strip of ³/₄in (2cm) wide bias binding to the required length. Attach the bias to the sleeve, right side to right side.

4 Turn under the end of the bias, placing the fold of the bias to the sleeve seam.

5 Sew in place using a ³/₁₆in (5mm) seam allowance.

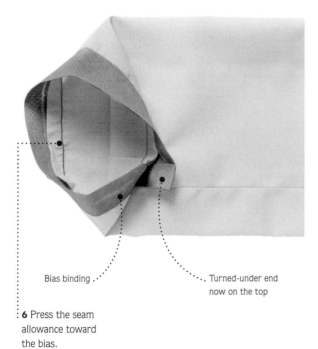

Bias binding

Turned-under end now on the top

6 Press the seam allowance toward the bias.

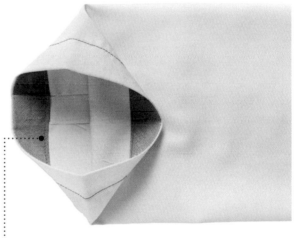

7 Turn the bias to the inside of the sleeve and sew in place, sewing along the upper edge of the bias.

◤ ELASTICATED SLEEVE EDGE

The ends of sleeves on workwear and children's clothes are often elastic to produce a neat and functional finish.

Elastic that is ½in (12mm) or 1in (25mm) wide will be most suitable.

1 Make up the sleeve and press the seam open.

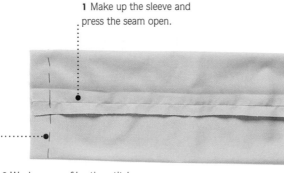

2 Work a row of basting stitches on the foldline of the hem.

3 Turn up ¼in (6mm) at the raw edge and press.

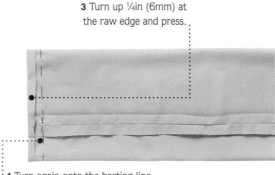

4 Turn again onto the basting line.

Gap to insert the elastic

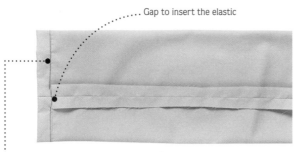

5 Sew to hold the turn-up in place, ⅟₁₆in (2mm) from the folded edge. Leave a 1in (3cm) gap next to the seam allowance through which you will insert the elastic.

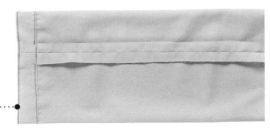

6 Sew the bottom of the sleeve ⅟₁₆in (2mm) from the edge to give a neat finish. This will also help prevent the elastic from twisting.

7 Cut a piece of elastic to fit the arm or wrist and insert it into the sleeve end between the two rows of machining.

8 Secure the ends of the elastic together, sewing an X for strength.

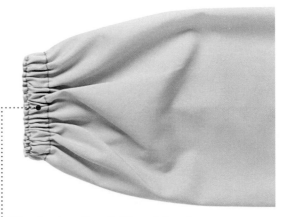

9 Turn the sleeve through the armhole and check that the elasticated edge is even.

▶ A CASING ON A SLEEVE EDGE

A casing is often used on the edge of a sleeve to insert elastic into, which will allow you to gather the sleeve in a specific place. The casing may be extended, which means it is part of the sleeve, or it may be applied separately. The photographs below show an applied casing of bias binding.

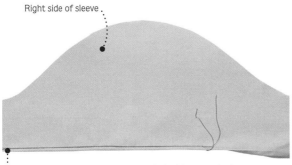

Right side of sleeve

1 Before the sleeve is constructed, double turn the lower edge, turning to the wrong side, and sew in place.

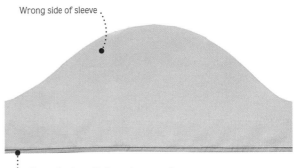

Wrong side of sleeve

2 Press the hem that you have made.

3 Apply ⅜in (10mm) bias binding, sewing along either side.

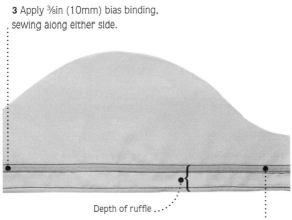

Depth of ruffle

4 Cut a length of elastic to fit your arm or wrist. Insert the elastic behind the bias binding and secure at one end by sewing through all layers.

5 Push up the bias binding along the elastic to tighten the edge of the sleeve to fit the arm or wrist. Secure at the other end by sewing.

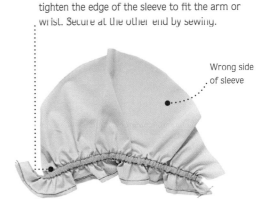

Wrong side of sleeve

6 To complete, join the sleeve seam, matching through the elastic and casing.

7 Press the seam open, then turn the sleeve through the armhole to the right side. You can adjust the ruffles if they are not evenly placed.

CUFFS AND OPENINGS

A cuff and an opening are ways of producing a sleeve finish that will fit neatly around the wrist. The opening enables the hand to fit through the end of the sleeve, and it allows the sleeve to be rolled up.

There are various types of cuffs—single or double, and with pointed or curved edges. All cuffs are interfaced, with the interfacing attached to the upper cuff. The upper cuff is sewn to the sleeve.

◤ DIRECTORY OF CUFFS AND OPENINGS

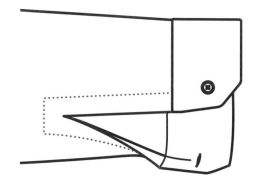

SINGLE CUFF WITH FACED OPENING (p.202)

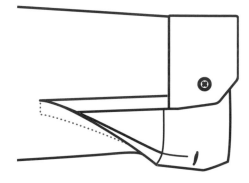

SINGLE CUFF WITH BOUND OPENING (p.203)

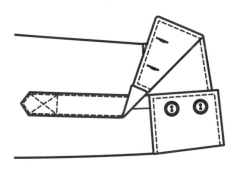

SHIRT CUFF WITH PLACKET OPENING
(pp.204–205 and p.207)

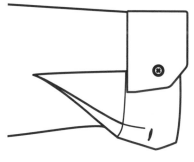

LAPPED CUFF (p.206)

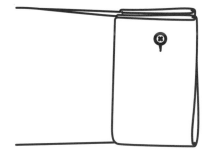

DOUBLE FRENCH CUFF (p.207)

⋈ ONE-PIECE CUFF

A one-piece cuff is cut out from the fabric in one piece, and in most cases only half of it is interfaced. The exception is the double French cuff (see p.207).

1 Apply fusible interfacing to the half of the cuff that will be the upper cuff.

4 Fold the cuff in half, right side to right side.

Seam allowance free on interfaced side of cuff

Wrong side of fabric

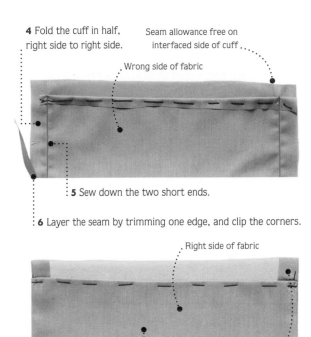

5 Sew down the two short ends.

6 Layer the seam by trimming one edge, and clip the corners.

Right side of fabric

Wrong side of fabric

3 Layer the seam by trimming the excess.

2 Turn under a seam allowance on the noninterfaced side and baste to secure.

7 Turn the cuff through to the right side and press.

Seam allowance ready to sew onto sleeve

⋈ TWO-PIECE CUFF

Some cuffs are cut in two pieces: an upper cuff and an under cuff. The upper cuff piece is interfaced.

1 Apply fusible interfacing to the upper cuff.

2 Turn under a seam allowance on the under cuff and baste in place.

5 Sew the two short ends together. Also sew together along the lower edge.

Seam allowance on upper cuff free

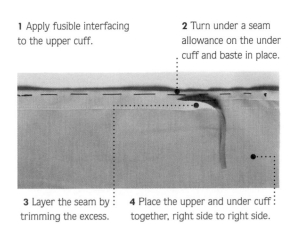

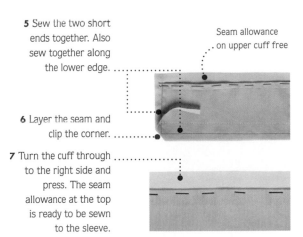

6 Layer the seam and clip the corner.

7 Turn the cuff through to the right side and press. The seam allowance at the top is ready to be sewn to the sleeve.

3 Layer the seam by trimming the excess.

4 Place the upper and under cuff together, right side to right side.

◤ FACED OPENING

Adding a facing to the area of the sleeve where the opening is to be is a neat method of finishing.

This type of opening is appropriate to use with a one-piece cuff.

1 Turn under the long edges and one short edge on the facing by about ⅛in (3mm). Sew to secure.

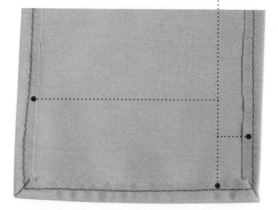

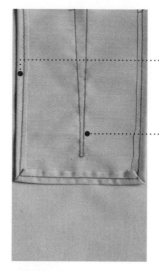

2 Place the right side of the facing to the right side of the sleeve at the appropriate sleeve markings.

3 Sew vertically up the center of the facing. Take one stitch across the top and then sew straight down the other side. Keep a distance of about ¼in (6mm) between the lines at the raw edge.

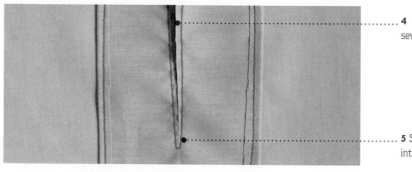

4 Snip between the sewn lines.

5 Snip with small scissors into the corners.

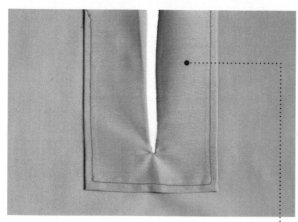

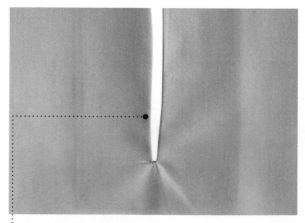

6 Turn the facing to the wrong side of the sleeve and press.

7 The finished opening on the right side.

✕ BOUND OPENING

On a fabric that frays badly or a sleeve that may get a great deal of wear, a strong bound opening is a good idea. It involves binding a slash in the sleeve with a matching bias strip.

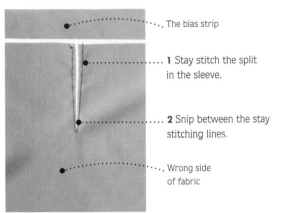

···· The bias strip

1 Stay stitch the split in the sleeve.

2 Snip between the stay stitching lines.

···· Wrong side of fabric

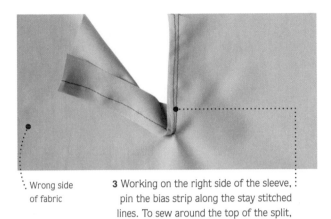

Wrong side of fabric

3 Working on the right side of the sleeve, pin the bias strip along the stay stitched lines. To sew around the top of the split, open the split out into a straight line.

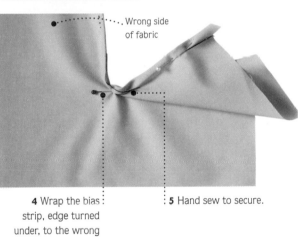

····Wrong side of fabric

4 Wrap the bias strip, edge turned under, to the wrong side and pin in place.

5 Hand sew to secure.

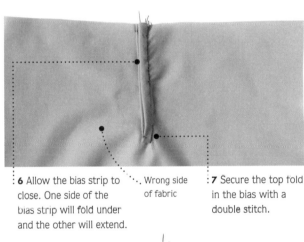

6 Allow the bias strip to close. One side of the bias strip will fold under and the other will extend.

···· Wrong side of fabric

7 Secure the top fold in the bias with a double stitch.

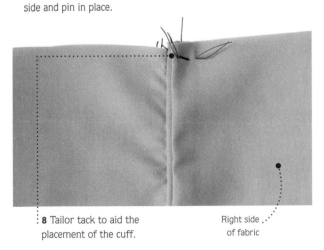

8 Tailor tack to aid the placement of the cuff.

Right side of fabric ····

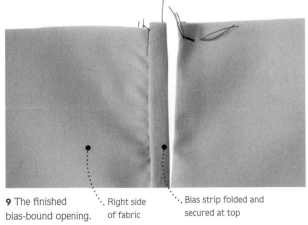

9 The finished bias-bound opening.

···· Right side of fabric

···· Bias strip folded and secured at top

▶◀ SHIRT SLEEVE PLACKET

This is the opening that is found on the sleeves of men's shirts and tailored ladies' shirts. It looks complicated but is straightforward if you take it one step at a time.

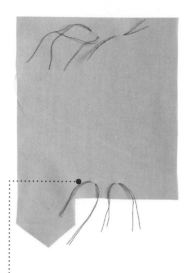

1 Cut out the placket and mark the pattern dots with tailor's tacks. Only these four tailor's tacks are required.

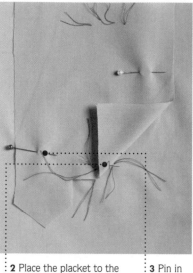

2 Place the placket to the shirt sleeve, right side of the placket to the wrong side of the sleeve, sewing the tailor's tacks.

3 Pin in place.

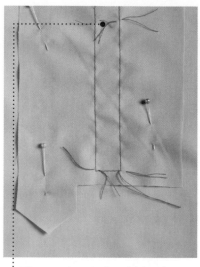

4 Sew a rectangular box, joining the tailor's tacks together. Make sure the rows of stitches are parallel. Remove tailor's tacks.

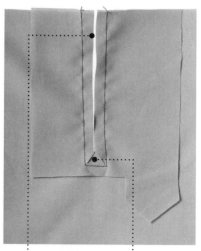

5 Snip through the placket and sleeve straight down the center, between the rows of seams.

6 Snip into the corners of the rectangle.

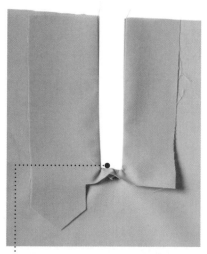

7 Open up the placket to the right side of the fabric and press. You will have a rectangular gap with sharp corners.

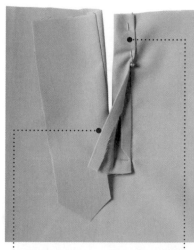

8 Fold back the long edge of the shorter side of the placket.

9 Place the folded edge on top of the sewn line and pin in place.

10 Sew the folded edge with a ⅟₁₆in (2mm) seam allowance. Stop sewing at the top of the gap.

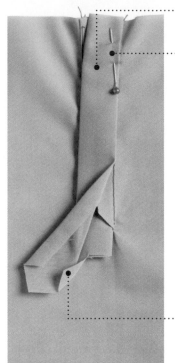

11 Fold the other side of the placket across the shorter side.

12 Press under the long edge. Fold back so that the pressed-under edge is on the sewn line. Pin in place.

13 Fold under the top pointed end, following the cut edge, and press.

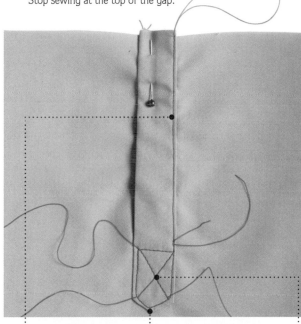

14 Sew the long folded edge in place. Make sure the underside of the placket is not caught by the stitches.

15 Continue the sewing around the point.

16 Sew an X through the point.

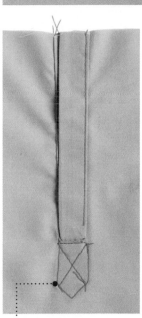

17 Pull all the ends of the threads through to the reverse and tie off.

18 On the right side, the completed placket will be neatly stitched.

⧖ ATTACHING A CUFF

There are various types of cuffs that can be attached to sleeve openings. The one-piece, overlapped cuff works well with a bound or faced opening. A two-piece barrel cuff is usually on a sleeve with a placket opening but works equally well on a bound opening. The double cuff, or French cuff, is for men's dress shirts and tailored shirts for both ladies and men and may be cut in one or two sections. It is usually found with a placket or bound opening.

LAPPED CUFF

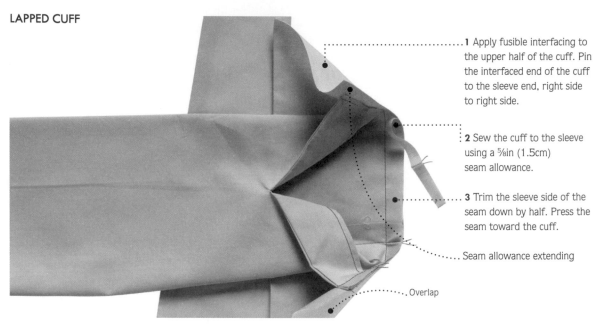

1 Apply fusible interfacing to the upper half of the cuff. Pin the interfaced end of the cuff to the sleeve end, right side to right side.

2 Sew the cuff to the sleeve using a ⅝in (1.5cm) seam allowance.

3 Trim the sleeve side of the seam down by half. Press the seam toward the cuff.

Seam allowance extending

Overlap

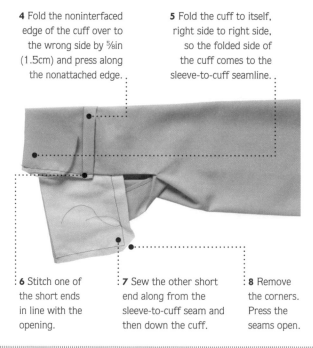

4 Fold the noninterfaced edge of the cuff over to the wrong side by ⅝in (1.5cm) and press along the nonattached edge.

5 Fold the cuff to itself, right side to right side, so the folded side of the cuff comes to the sleeve-to-cuff seamline.

6 Stitch one of the short ends in line with the opening.

7 Sew the other short end along from the sleeve-to-cuff seam and then down the cuff.

8 Remove the corners. Press the seams open.

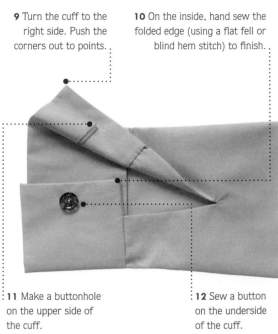

9 Turn the cuff to the right side. Push the corners out to points.

10 On the inside, hand sew the folded edge (using a flat fell or blind hem stitch) to finish.

11 Make a buttonhole on the upper side of the cuff.

12 Sew a button on the underside of the cuff.

BARREL CUFF

1 Apply fusible interfacing to the upper cuff. Place it to the sleeve end, right side to right side, with a seam allowance extending at either end. Pin in place.

Upper cuff

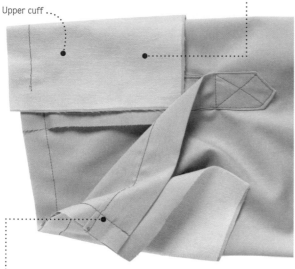

2 Sew using a ⅜in (1.5cm) seam allowance.

3 Place the right side of the under cuff to the right side of the upper cuff. Sew together around three sides, sewing in line with the sleeve opening.

4 Trim down the under cuff side of the seam.

5 Remove bulk from the corners. Press.

6 Turn the cuff to the right side and press.

7 Turn under the raw edge of the under cuff and place to the end of the sleeve. With this type of sleeve, the edge of the cuff is sewn in place.

8 Add buttonholes to the upper cuff and attach buttons to the under cuff.

DOUBLE FRENCH CUFF

1 Apply interfacing to the whole of the cuff. Attach the cuff to the sleeve end, right side to right side, using a ⅝in (1.5cm) seam allowance.

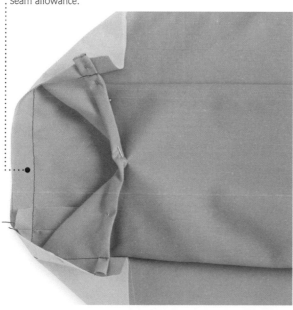

2 Fold the cuff back onto itself, right side to right side.

3 Sew the two sides in line with the sleeve opening.

4 Trim the bulk from the seams and corners.

5 Press, then turn the cuff through to the right side.

6 Fold the cuff up in half so that it is doubled. Press.

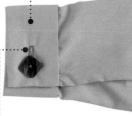

7 Hand sew inside to finish the other edge of the cuff.

8 Insert a buttonhole through the top two layers of the cuff and sew a button onto the under cuff.

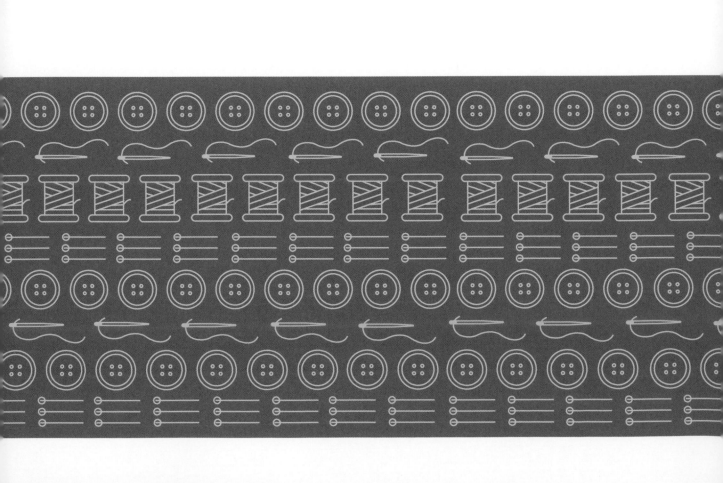

DECORATIVE TECHNIQUES

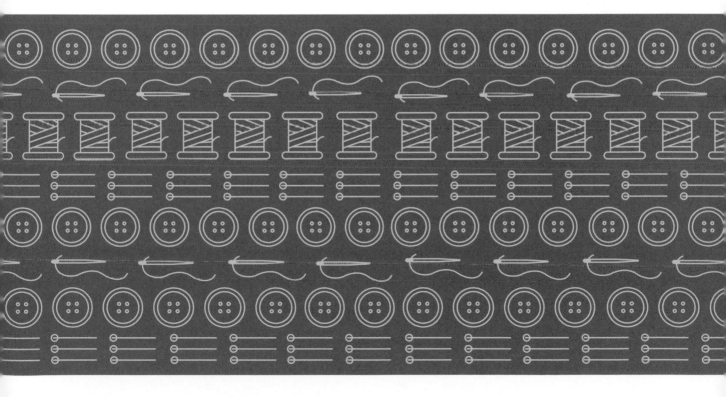

FINISHING TECHNIQUES

Simple finishing touches can be used to good effect on many items. The term appliqué applies to one fabric being sewn to another in a decorative manner. The fabric to be appliquéd must be interfaced to support the fabric that is to be attached. Appliqué can be drawn by hand, then cut and sewn down, or it can be created by a computer pattern on the embroidery machine. The embroidery machine can also be used to create quilting, or this can be done by hand or with a sewing machine.

✕ HAND-DRAWN APPLIQUÉ

This technique involves drawing the chosen design onto a piece of double-sided fusible web, after which the design is fused in place on fabric prior to being sewn.

1 Draw a decorative shape, such as a flower, onto a piece of double-sided fusible web.

2 Using the iron, fuse the web onto your chosen fabric.

3 Cut out the shape from the fabric.

4 Place the shape, fusible web side down, where it is to be positioned on fabric and fuse in place.

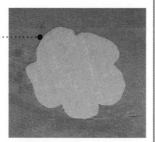

5 Using a wide, close zigzag stitch, sew around the shape.

6 For a flower, sew on top of the fabric appliqué to make petal shapes.

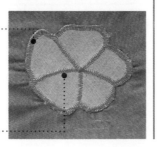

✕ MACHINE APPLIQUÉ

There are designs available for appliqué if you have an embroidery machine. You will need to use a special fusible embroidery backer on both the fabric for the appliqué and the base fabric.

1 Place the base fabric and appliqué fabric in the embroidery hoop and stitch out the first part of the design.

2 Trim the appliqué fabric back to the stitched lines.

3 Complete the computerized embroidery.

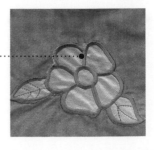

⋈ QUILTING

This is a technique that involves sewing through two layers of fabric, one of which is a batting. The sewing sinks into the batting, creating a padded effect. Quilting can be done by hand, with a sewing machine, or using computerized embroidery.

COMPONENTS OF QUILTING

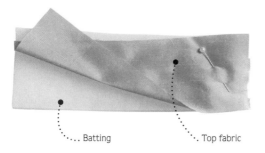

····· Batting   ·· Top fabric

HORIZONTAL QUILTING

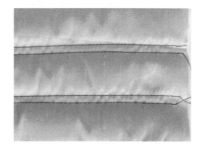

Baste the batting and top fabric together. Sew double lines with spaces between. Use a stitch length of 4.0 on your machine.

DIAMOND QUILTING

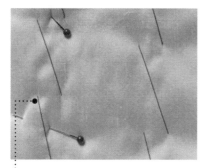

1 Diagonally baste the batting and top fabric together.

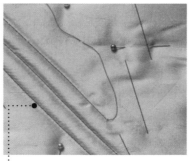

2 Set the machine to a stitch length of 4.0, with the needle on the one side of the foot. Sew rows of machining diagonally across. Use the width of the machine foot as a guide to keep the rows parallel.

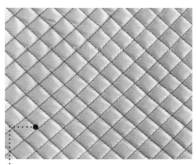

3 Sew parallel rows in the opposite diagonal directions to create diamond shapes.

FREEFORM QUILTING

Baste the batting and top fabric together. Sew at random.

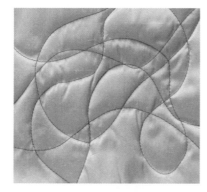

COMPUTERIZED QUILTING

Baste the batting and top fabric together, then sew on a quilted pattern with the embroidery machine.

▶◀ ROSES AND BOWS

On special-occasion wear, a rose can add a superb finishing touch. When the raw edges of a rose are exposed, as in version 2 below, it also looks great made in tweed and suiting fabrics to add a decorative finish to a tailored jacket. A bow that is permanently fixed in place is a beautiful embellishment on bridal wear.

ROSE VERSION 1

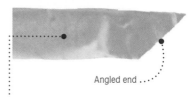

Angled end ....

1 Cut a bias strip 4in (10cm) wide. Fold in half lengthwise, wrong side to wrong side.

2 Pin the raw edges together.

3 Insert two rows of gather stitches at the raw edge— one row at ⅜in (1cm) from the edge and the other row at ½in (1.3cm).

4 Pull up the gathers, grouping them together and leaving spaces between the groups. The groups and spaces will give the impression of petals.

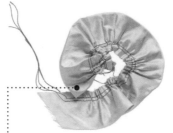

5 Hold the lower edge of one end in your left hand and loosely wrap the strip around.

6 When you have a rose shape, tuck any raw edges that show into the base.

7 Secure at the base edge with hand stitches.

ROSE VERSION 2

1 Cut a bias strip 4in (10cm) wide.

2 Insert two rows of gather stitches along the center of the strip. Leave a gap of ⅛in (3mm) between the sewn lines.

3 Pull up the gathers into groups and spaces (see step 4 above).

4 The groups and spaces will pull up to give a diagonal effect. Fold in half along the sewn lines.

5 Hold the end of the gathers in your left hand and wrap the strip around loosely.

6 Secure at the base with hand stitches. Although the edge is raw, fraying is minimal, as the strip has been bias-cut.

BOW

1 To make the loops, cut a piece of silk or other fabric that is four times the length of the loop required and twice the width plus seam allowances.

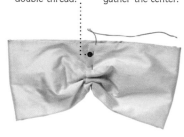

2 Interline with dress net to the wrong side. Baste the net around the raw edge.

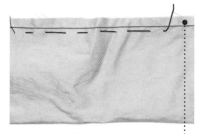

3 Fold in half, right side to right side. Sew along the raw edge, leaving a ⅝in (1.5cm) seam allowance.

4 Turn through to the right side. Fold so that the seamline is in the center.

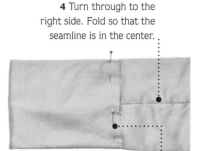

5 Bring the short end to the center. Pin in place.

6 Baste through the center using double thread.

7 Pull along the basting stitches to gather the center.

8 Next, make the two ends. Cut two pieces of fabric the required finished length and twice the required width plus seam allowances.

9 Baste dress net to the wrong side of the fabric.

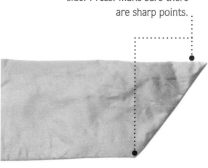

10 Fold each piece of fabric in half, right side to right side, and sew along the long raw edge and at an angle at one end.

11 Remove bulk from the corners.

12 Turn through to the right side. Press. Make sure there are sharp points.

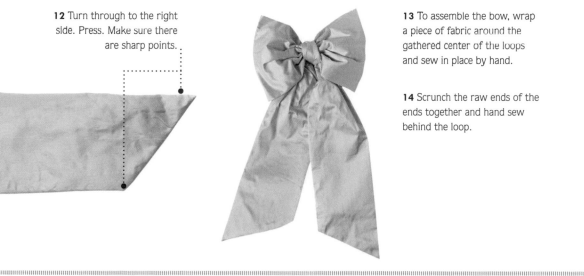

13 To assemble the bow, wrap a piece of fabric around the gathered center of the loops and sew in place by hand.

14 Scrunch the raw ends of the ends together and hand sew behind the loop.

GLOSSARY

Appliqué
One piece of fabric being stitched to another in a decorative manner.

Backstitch
A strong hand stitch with a double stitch on the wrong side used for outlining and seaming.

Basting stitch
A temporary running stitch used to hold pieces of fabric together or for transferring pattern markings to fabric.

Bias
Forty-five-degree line on fabric that falls between the lengthwise and the crosswise grain. Fabric cut on the bias drapes well. *See also* Grain.

Bias binding
Narrow strips of fabric cut on the bias. Used to give a neat finish to hems and seam allowances.

Binding
Method of finishing a raw edge by wrapping it in a strip of bias-cut fabric.

Blanket stitch
Hand stitch worked along the raw or finished edge of fabric to neaten and for decorative purposes.

Blind hem stitch
Tiny hand stitch used to attach one piece of fabric to another, mainly to secure hems. Also a machine stitch consisting of two or three straight stitches and one wide zigzag stitch.

Blind tuck
A tuck that is stitched so that it touches the adjacent tuck without machine stitches showing. *See also* Tuck.

Bodice
Upper body section of a garment.

Boning
Narrow nylon, plastic, or metal strip—available in various widths—that is used for stiffening and shaping close-fitting garments, such as bodices.

Box pleat
Pleat formed on the wrong side of the fabric that is fuller than a knife pleat. *See also* Pleat.

Button shank
Stem of a button that allows room for the buttonhole to fit under the button when joined.

Buttonhole
Opening through which a button is inserted to form a fastening. Buttonholes are usually machine stitched but may also be worked by hand or piped for reinforcement or decorative effect.

Buttonhole stitch
Hand stitch that wraps over the raw edges of a buttonhole to neaten and strengthen them. Machine-stitched buttonholes are worked with a close zigzag stitch.

Casing
Tunnel of fabric created by parallel rows of stitching through which elastic or a drawstring cord is threaded. Often used at a waist edge. Sometimes extra fabric is required to make a casing; this can be applied to the inside or outside of the garment.

Contour dart
Also known as a double-pointed dart, this is used to give shape at the waist of a garment. It is like two darts joined together. *See also* Dart.

Crease
Line formed in fabric by pressing a fold.

Cross stitch
A temporary hand stitch used to hold pleats in place and to secure linings. It can also be used for decoration.

Cross tuck
Tuck that crosses over another by being stitched in opposite directions. *See also* Tuck.

Cutting line
Solid line on a pattern piece used as a guide for cutting out fabric.

Dart
Tapered stitched fold of fabric used on a garment to give it shape so that it can fit around the contours of the body. There are different types of darts, but all are used mainly on women's clothing.

Darted tuck
A tuck that can be used to give fullness of fabric at the bust or hip. *See also* Tuck.

Double-pointed dart
See Contour dart

Double ruffle
Decorative trim made from two plain ruffles where one side is longer than the other. Also a ruffle made from doubled fabric.

Drape
The way a fabric falls into graceful folds; drape varies with each fabric.

Drop
The length of fabric required to make a curtain, the "drop" being the measurement from top to bottom of the window.

Ease
Distributing fullness in fabric when joining two seams together of slightly different lengths—for example, a sleeve to an armhole.

Ease stitch
Long machine stitch used to ease in fullness where the distance between notches is slightly greater on one seam edge than on the other.

Enclosed edge
Raw fabric edge that is concealed within a seam or binding.

Facing
Layer of fabric placed on the inside of a garment and used to finish off raw edges of an armhole or neck of a garment. Usually a separate piece of fabric, the facing can sometimes be an extension of the garment itself.

Felt
A natural wool fabric can felt when it is stimulated by friction and lubricated by moisture and the fibers bond together to form a cloth. Felting can also be done in a washing machine in a hot cycle.

Flat fell seam
See Run and fell seam.

Flat fell stitch
A strong, secure stitch used to hold two layers together permanently. Often used to secure linings and bias bindings.

French dart
Curved dart used on the front of a garment. *See also* **Dart**.

French seam
A seam traditionally used on sheer and silk fabrics. It is stitched twice, first on the right side of the work and then on the wrong side, enclosing the first seam.

Fusible tape
Straight grain tape used to stabilize edges and also replace stay stitching. The heat of the iron fuses it into position.

Galloon lace
Decorative lace trim shaped on both sides used to edge a hem.

Gathers
Bunches of fabric created by sewing two parallel rows of loose stitching, then pulling the threads up so that the fabric gathers and reduces in size to fit the required space.

Grain
Lengthwise and crosswise direction of threads in a fabric. Fabric grain affects how a fabric hangs and drapes.

Gusset
Small piece of fabric shaped to fit into a slash or seam for added ease of movement.

Hem
The edge of a piece of fabric neatened and stitched to prevent unraveling. There are several methods of doing this, both by hand and by machine.

Hem allowance
Amount of fabric allowed for turning under to make the hem.

Hemline
Crease or foldline along which a hem is marked.

Hemming tape
Fusible tape with adhesive on both sides. Iron in place to fuse and secure hems that are difficult to hand stitch.

Herringbone stitch
Hand stitch used to secure hems and interlinings. Worked from left to right.

Herringbone weave
A zigzag weave where the weft yarn goes under and over warp yarns in a staggered pattern.

Hong Kong finish
A method of neatening raw edges, particularly on wool and linen. Bias-cut strips are wrapped around the raw edge.

Interfacing
A fabric placed between garment and facing to give structure and support. Available in different thicknesses, interfacing can be fusible (bonds to the fabric by applying heat) or nonfusible (needs to be sewn to the fabric).

Interlining
Layer of fabric attached to the main fabric prior to construction to cover the inside of an entire garment to provide extra warmth or bulk. The two layers are then treated as one. Often used in jackets and coats.

Keyhole buttonhole stitch
A machine buttonhole stitch characterized by having one square end while the other end is shaped like a loop to accommodate the button's shank without distorting the fabric. Often used on jackets.

Kick pleat
Inverted pleat extending upward from the hemline of a narrow skirt to allow freedom when walking. *See also* **Pleat**.

Knife pleat
Pleat formed on the right side of the fabric where all the pleats face the same direction. *See also* **Pleat**.

Lapped seam
Used on fabrics that do not fray, such as suede and leather, the seam allowance of one edge is placed over the edge to be joined, then top-stitched close to the overlapping edge. Also called an overlaid seam.

Lining
Underlying fabric layer used to give a neat finish to an item, as well as concealing the stitching and seams of a garment.

Locking stitch
A machine stitch where the upper and lower threads in the machine "lock" together at the start or end of a row of stitching.

Miter
The diagonal line made where two edges of a piece of fabric meet at a corner, produced by folding.

Mock casing
Where there is an effect of a casing, but in fact elastic is attached to the waist or is used only at the back in a partial casing.

Multisize pattern
Paper pattern printed with cutting lines for a range of sizes on each pattern piece.

Nap
The raised pile on a fabric made during the weaving process, or a print pointing one way. When cutting out pattern pieces, make sure that the nap runs in the same direction.

Notch
V-shaped marking on a pattern piece used for aligning one piece with another. Also a V-shaped cut taken to reduce seam bulk.

Notion
An item of haberdashery, other than fabric, needed to complete a project, such as a button, zipper, or elastic. Notions are normally listed on the pattern envelope.

Overedge stitch
Machine stitch worked over the edge of a seam allowance and used for neatening the edges of fabric.

Overlaid seam
See **Lapped seam**.

Pattern markings
Symbols printed on a paper pattern to indicate the fabric grain, foldline, and construction details, such as darts, notches, and tucks. These should be transferred to the fabric using tailor's chalk or tailor's tacks.

Pencil pleat
The most common curtain heading where the fabric forms a row of parallel vertical pleats. *See also* **Pleat**.

Pile
Raised loops on the surface of a fabric—for example, velvet.

Pill
A small, fuzzy ball formed from tangled fibers that is formed on the surface of a fabric, making it look old and worn; it is often caused by friction. To remove fabric pills, stretch the fabric over a curved surface and carefully cut or shave off the pills.

Pin tuck
Narrow, regularly spaced fold or gather. *See also* **Tuck**.

Pinch pleat
Decorative curtain heading in which groups of two or three pleats are stitched together. *See also* **Pleat**.

Pinking
A method of neatening raw edges of fray-resistant fabric using pinking shears. This will leave a zigzag edge.

Piping
Trim made from bias-cut strips of fabric, usually containing a cord. Used to edge garments or home goods.

Pivoting
Technique used to machine stitch a corner. The machine is stopped at the corner with the needle in the fabric, then the foot is raised, the fabric turned following the direction of the corner, and the foot lowered for stitching to continue.

Placket
An opening in a garment that provides support for fasteners, such as buttons, snaps, or zippers.

Plain weave
The simplest of all the weaves; the weft yarn passes under one warp yarn, then over another one.

Pleat
An even fold or series of folds in fabric, often partially stitched down. Commonly found in skirts to shape the waistline, but also in soft furnishings for decoration.

Pocket flap
A piece of fabric that folds down to cover the opening of a pocket.

Raw edge
Cut edge of fabric that requires finishing—for example, using a zigzag stitch—to prevent fraying.

Rever
The turned-back front edge of a jacket or blouse to which the collar is attached.

Reverse stitch
Machine stitch that simply stitches back over a row of stitches to secure the threads.

Right side
The outer side of a fabric, or the visible part of a garment.

Rouleau loop
Button loop made from a strip of bias binding. It is used with a round ball-type button.

Round-end buttonhole stitch
Machine stitch characterized by one end of the buttonhole being square and the other being round to allow for the button shank.

Ruching
Several lines of stitching worked to form a gathered area.

Ruffle
Decorative gathered trim made from one or two layers of fabric.

Run and fell seam
Also known as a flat fell seam, this seam is made on the right side of a garment and is very strong. It uses two lines of stitching and conceals all the raw edges, reducing fraying.

Running stitch
A simple, evenly spaced straight stitch separated by equal-sized spaces used for seaming and gathering.

Seam
Stitched line where two edges of fabric are joined together.

Seam allowance
The amount of fabric allowed for on a pattern where sections are to be joined together by a seam; usually, this is ⅝in (1.5cm).

Seam edge
The cut edge of a seam allowance.

Seamline
Line on paper pattern designated for stitching a seam; usually ⅝in (1.5cm) from the seam edge.

Selvage
Finished edge on a woven fabric. This runs parallel to the warp (lengthwise) threads.

Shell tuck
Decorative fold of fabric stitched in place with a scalloped edge. *See also* **Tuck**.

Shirring
Multiple rows of gathers sewn by machine. Often worked with shirring elastic in the bobbin to allow for stretch.

Slip hem stitch
Similar to herringbone stitch but is worked from right to left. Used mainly for hems.

Straight stitch
Plain machine stitch used for most applications. The length of the stitch can be changed to suit the fabric.

Stretch stitch
Machine stitch used for stretch knits and to help control difficult fabrics. It is worked with two stitches forward and one backward so that each stitch is worked three times.

Tailor's buttonhole
A buttonhole with one square end and one keyhole-shaped end used on jackets and coats.

Tailor's tacks
Loose thread markings used to transfer symbols from a pattern to fabric.

Toile
A test or dry run of a paper pattern using calico. The toile helps you analyze the fit of the garment.

Top-stitch
Machine straight stitching worked on the right side of an item, close to the finished edge, for decorative effect. Sometimes stitched in a contrasting color.

Top-stitched seam
A seam finished with a row of top-stitching for decorative effect. This seam is often used on crafts and home goods, as well as garments.

Trace basting
A method of marking fold and placement lines on fabric. Loose stitches are sewn along the lines on the pattern to the fabric beneath, then the thread loops are cut and the pattern removed.

Tuck
Fold or pleat in fabric that is sewn in place, normally on the straight grain of the fabric. Often used to provide a decorative addition to a garment.

Underlining
Strip of fabric placed under the main fabric to strengthen it, for example, under a pleat or buttonhole.

Understitch
Machine straight stitching through facing and seam allowances that is invisible from the right side; this helps the facing to lie flat.

Waistband
Band of fabric attached to the waist edge of a garment to provide a neat finish.

Warp
Lengthwise threads or yarns of a woven fabric.

Warp knit
Made on a knitting machine, this knit is formed in a vertical and diagonal direction.

Weft
Threads or yarns that cross the warp of a woven fabric.

Weft knit
Made in the same way as hand knitting, this uses one yarn that runs horizontally.

Welt
Strip of fabric used to make the edges of a pocket.

Whip stitch
Diagonal hand stitch sewn along a raw edge to prevent fraying.

Wrong side
Reverse side of a fabric, the inside of a garment or other item.

Yoke
The top section of a dress or skirt from which the rest of the garment hangs.

Zigzag stitch
Machine stitch used to neaten and secure seam edges and for decorative purposes. The width and length of the zigzag can be altered.

INDEX

ACKNOWLEDGMENTS

Author's acknowledgments

No book would ever be written without a little help. I would like to thank the following people for their help with the techniques and projects: Jackie Boddy, Nicola Corten, Ruth Cox, Helen Culver, Yvette Emmett, Averil Wing, and especially my husband, Nigel, for his continued encouragement and support, as well as my mother, Doreen Robbins, who is responsible for my learning to sew. The following companies have also provided invaluable help by supplying the sewing machines, haberdashery, and fabrics: Janome UK Ltd., EQS, Linton, Adjustoform, Guttermann threads, the Button Company, YKK zippers, Graham Smith Fabrics, Fabulous Fabric, Simplicity Patterns, and Freudenberg Nonwovens LP.

Dorling Kindersley would like to thank:

For the first edition, DK India: Alicia Ingty, Ekta Sharma, Neha Ahuja, Divya PR, Era Chawla, Mansi Nagdev, Mini Dhawan, Glenda Fernandes, Navidita Thapa, Pankaj Sharma, Sunil Sharma, Dheeraj Arora, Jagtar Singh, Tarun Sharma, and Sourabh Challariya; DK UK: Danielle Di Michiel, Jane Ewart, Roxanne Benson-Mackey, Dawn Henderson, Marianne Markham, Nicola Powling, Ben Marcus, Alice Sykes, and Sonia Charbonnier. Thanks also to Heather Haynes and Katie Hardwicke for editorial assistance, Elaine Hewson and Victoria Charles for design assistance, Susan Van Ha for photographic assistance, Hilary Bird for indexing, Elma Aquino, Alice Chadwick-Jones, and Beki Lamb. Special thanks from all at DK to Norma MacMillan for her exceptional professionalism and patience.

For the second edition, DK would like to thank Millie Andrew for editorial assistance and Sophie State and Satish Gaur for design assistance.

Picture credits:

Additional photography: Laura Knox p.70 bl, br, 72 t, 74 tr, br, 75 b

Illustrator: Debajyoti Datta

Patterns: John Hutchinson, pp.66–67, 75

Additional artwork: Karen Cochrane p.67 r

ABOUT THE AUTHOR

Alison Smith is a trained fashion and textiles teacher who taught for many years at one of the largest schools in Birmingham, England, where she was Head of Department. In 1992, she set up the School of Sewing—the first of its kind in the UK—teaching all aspects of sewing, including dressmaking, tailoring, and corsetry. Alison has also taught at the Liberty Sewing School in London and at Janome's sewing school in Stockport. In 2004, she opened a fabric shop in Ashby de la Zouch to complement the School of Sewing. In 2013, Alison was awarded an MBE for her services to sewing and corsetry. She also teaches online for Craftsy.com and writes regularly for sewing magazines, including *Love Sewing*. Alison lives in Leicestershire with her husband and has two adult children.

www.schoolofsewing.co.uk

www.sewwardrobe.co.uk

www.etsy.com/uk/shop/SewWardrobe

DK LONDON
Senior Designer Glenda Fisher
Editor Amy Slack
Editorial Assistant Oreolu Grillo
US Editor Kayla Dugger
Jacket Designer Amy Cox
Jacket Coordinator Lucy Philpott
Pre-production Producer Tony Phipps
Producer Rebecca Parton
Managing Editor Stephanie Farrow
Managing Art Editor Christine Keilty
Art Director Maxine Pedliham
Publishing Director Mary-Clare Jerram

DK INDIA
Senior Editor Arani Sinha
Assistant Editor Ankita Gupta
Managing Editor Soma B. Chowdhury
Pre-production Manager Sunil Sharma
Senior DTP Designer Tarun Sharma
DTP Designer Umesh Singh Rawat

This American Edition, 2020
First American Edition, 2011
Published in the United States by DK Publishing
1450 Broadway, Suite 801, New York, NY 10018

A catalog record for this book
is available from the Library of Congress.
ISBN 978-1-4654-9108-4

DK books are available at special discounts when purchased in bulk for sales promotions, premiums, fund-raising, or educational use. For details, contact: DK Publishing Special Markets, 1450 Broadway, Suite 801, New York, NY 10018, or SpecialSales@dk.com.

Printed and bound in China

All images © Dorling Kindersley Limited
For further information see: www.dkimages.com

A WORLD OF IDEAS:
SEE ALL THERE IS TO KNOW

www.dk.com